Praise for *Imperfect Leadership*

This is the most perfectly brilliant book about imperfect leadership that any great leader could possibly write. There is no other book like it. Unlike most political memoirs, it is not a tedious recollection of meetings and events. Unlike corporate leadership texts, it is not a narrative of vainglorious self-congratulation either. Nor is it a self-indulgent confession of failure and wrongdoing. Instead, Steve Munby's *Imperfect Leadership* is an honest, open and articulate account of a life of leadership lived as a public servant for the public good in constantly changing times.

If you are or aspire to be a leader in the education or social sector, and if you have even an ounce of integrity, *Imperfect Leadership* is a must-read.

**Andy Hargreaves, Research Professor, Boston College,
and Visiting Professor, University of Ottawa**

Imperfect Leadership is an important book. It's important in its subject matter, in its point of focus, and most of all in its unblinking honesty.

Like Steve Munby, I've led organisations and teams with mixed results, and during the journey I've discovered one great truth: you learn far more from your failures than your successes. Through a rigorous and sometimes painful process of self-questioning, Steve offers all of us the opportunity to reflect, to improve, and to possibly even inspire those around us.

Lord David Puttnam, Chair, Atticus Education

From small groups to large countries, it's hard to overestimate the impact of leadership on the culture and effectiveness of organisations. For that reason, there's a burgeoning library of scholarly research and popular books on leadership. *Imperfect Leadership* is something different, however. Part memoir, part social history and part practical handbook, this book gives us a deeply human, close-grained account of Steve Munby's evolution as a leader as he steered a key national organisation through the white waters of educational change in England. Resoundingly honest and soul-searching, *Imperfect Leadership* is also an inspirational and practical guide to handling the complex challenges – and navigating the steep learning curves – that caring leaders face.

**Sir Ken Robinson, PhD, educator and
New York Times bestselling author**

It's rare to come across a book as wise about leadership as this one. Beginning with the title itself, this is no sentimental, misty-eyed account of a hero leader; instead, it's about authentic, resilient leadership that acknowledges our own imperfections, recognises the anxieties that gnaw away at all true leaders, and goes on to inspire others to give their best.

With an extraordinary mix of personal insights and his insider's knowledge of recent education policy – plus a range of perspectives from various international experts – Steve Munby deepens our thinking, nudges us to be more ambitious in our aspirations, and inspires us to understand and then enact all that great leadership can achieve.

Imperfect Leadership is a book of breathtaking wisdom. I can't recommend it highly enough.

**Geoff Barton, General Secretary,
Association of School and College Leaders**

As the world changed around us, Steve's integrity was always a fixed point, to be relied on completely – and in *Imperfect Leadership* he provides deep insights into two decades of education reform and improvement in England. The book is a guide to personal leadership in education and how it can make a difference, and Steve brings to its pages – as he brings to everything – wisdom, self-knowledge and wit.

Anyone interested in learning what it takes to bring about a school system that delivers both equity and high standards will benefit from reading *Imperfect Leadership*.

**Sir Michael Barber, author of *How to Run a Government*
and founder of Delivery Associates**

Imperfect Leadership is an extraordinary book. It is a story of highly successful adaptive leadership, of a quest for personal and professional growth and the exercise of principled influence – both with and through others – and above all it communicates the power of imperfect leadership.

At once disarmingly honest and penetratingly insightful, it will inspire all educators, particularly school and system leaders.

**Anthony Mackay, President and CEO,
National Center on Education and the Economy**

Imperfect Leadership is an inspiring, globally resonant leadership tour de force that outlines the experiences and challenges that Steve Munby has faced as a leader over more than three decades.

It is a self-reflective study of the qualities needed to be a successful leader in the education sector, and is a revealing and fascinating look behind the scenes of the contexts and structures where Steve has been a leader – tracing the humanity and humility that he has brought to every organisation he has led.

The structure of the book enables us to remind ourselves of the passionate and thoughtful speeches Steve has made throughout his career. Each provides a different building block to help him construct a leadership framework that we can all follow and can become part of his legacy for system-wide improvement. The opening chapter shows us that asking for help is a strength, not a weakness – and the chapter on power and love is drawn from a speech I remember well, having been in the audience on the day he presented it. In this Steve speaks about the morality of leadership: describing the need to go beyond having good intentions and wanting the best for children, to having the single-minded determination to make a real difference. As an MAT CEO at the time, I needed to hear that message, and I drew on it on multiple occasions to reassure myself that the changes I was leading were changes that would have long-term benefits for the children I was accountable for.

We live in an era where the understanding of leadership is expanding quicker than at any time I can remember. If there is one book that describes how we lead in complex times, that reveals the development of an education system over 30 years, and that reminds us about the heart and soul of leadership, then this is it. *Imperfect Leadership* is the story of our lives as school leaders.

Steve Munby is a man of his word who set out to make a difference. He delivered!

**Sir David Carter, Executive Director of
System Leadership, Ambition Institute**

Steve Munby's *Imperfect Leadership* is a fitting tribute to his leadership journey, his moral compass, his fierce devotion to sustainable principles, and his adherence to values-informed leadership. It transports us to the pinnacle of what world-class leadership looks like, and, delivered in Steve's own inimitable way, provides honest, soul-searching insights into what leading-edge leadership looks like.

Guided by his core, sustaining values, Steve deftly untangles the complexities of leadership and illuminates various leadership types, styles and possibilities. He dispels myths and false dichotomies, identifies his own highs and lows and moments of exhilaration, and subtly flexes his muscles by deconstructing leadership and its potential impact.

At a time in our history when leaders must address issues such as rising nationalism and generational shifts in visions, values, mandates and expectations, the takeaway for me from *Imperfect Leadership* is the need to pay attention to the 'sleeping', 'newspaper', 'mirror' and 'teenager' leadership tests that he discusses: to focus on the inner voice and to exercise moral purpose as a tribute to the moral compass that Steve himself has exercised over a lifetime of exemplary leadership in education. For all the hurdles we face as leaders across the globe, we all want to share his humility, quiet confidence, fidelity to moral purpose, and the legacy of his ability to influence the educational outcomes and life chances of the students he has advocated for throughout his illustrious career. I offer rapturous applause to Steve, who we have grown to rely on to take us to places that we would not have gone without him.

Offering oases of hope, tranquillity and optimism, *Imperfect Leadership* provides both challenges and validation for those who aspire to or are currently wearing the mantle of leadership that Steve so aptly constructs and articulates for us.

**Dr Avis Glaze, international education adviser
and former Ontario education commissioner**

Are good leaders born or made? In *Imperfect Leadership* Steve Munby argues that good leaders recognise they are imperfect, and that it's through this recognition and consequent openness to learning that good leadership is built. Steve is reflective and honest throughout, providing a compendium of tried-and-tested ideas and tips on how to maintain clear-headed, context-aware, ethical leadership. And as he shares eye-opening stories and incisive analysis of education policy, we are treated to a wealth of long-developed expertise and a robust evaluation of the English school system.

Ultimately, Steve exemplifies and charts how to accomplish what we all want – to thrive as successful, judicious leaders, while remaining decent people.

Imperfect Leadership is a book for those considering, or already involved in, the hard and challenging task of leading organisations. Emerging leaders will gain wisdom, advice, encouragement; more experienced leaders will find sustenance and reinvigoration.

Professor Becky Francis, Director, UCL Institute of Education

Steve Munby won't thank me for saying this, but he is a hero to many of us who have worked with him. In my time as a head teacher, he was always there with gentle advice, a challenge or an insight.

Steve's humility, humanity and intellect – and ability to make the complex simple – shine through in this remarkable and deeply insightful book. *Imperfect Leadership* is perhaps the most honest and, ironically, perfectly formed text on leadership I have ever read.

Richard Gerver, educator, speaker and author

Imperfect Leadership is full of wisdom on how to lead educational organisations with passion and integrity in the face of relentless challenge and political pressure. Its compelling cases and reflections will inspire school and system leaders to pursue their vision and ideals through the toughest of times.

Viviane Robinson, Distinguished Professor Emeritus, University of Auckland

In compiling this honest, authentic and remarkable account of his own leadership journey, Steve Munby has written a book which I found just impossible to put down. As well as giving a fascinating insight into the inner workings of government and large organisations, he weaves into the narrative powerful leadership messages that will both inspire and challenge the leaders of today.

In his characteristically optimistic, pragmatic and thought-provoking way, Steve takes the reader on a roller-coaster ride that's full of ups and downs – and reminds us that leadership is, in the end, about our passion and belief in what we do and why it matters.

I challenge any reader not to be absolutely enthralled by this tour de force of a book.

Andy Buck, CEO, Leadership Matters

Steve Munby's *Imperfect Leadership* is a heartfelt account of what it means to be at the helm of a national organisation and of what it takes to make a difference to both people and outcomes. Moral purpose, networks, capacity for decision-making, care and – above all – tenacity and attention to detail are the key messages that flow from this book, which also offers a frank and insightful set of reflections that get to the crux of educational leadership.

A must-read for anyone who seeks to better understand the art of successful leadership.

**Professor Christopher Chapman, Director,
Policy Scotland, University of Glasgow**

Imperfect Leadership is Steve's reflection on his professional life and work, and it contains the insights of someone who has experienced the thick and thin of the changes in the education sector – offering not only a glimpse into his inner world in leading change, but also a commentary on the shifts that have taken place in the English education system over a period spanning 2004–2017. From the book, one can sense the joys and frustrations of leaders in education, as well as their dedication and sacrifice. Readers will also gain much from the episodes that Steve shares about his leadership journey, as he eloquently argues that the best leaders are those who are aware of their strengths and weaknesses – and who do not try to be perfect at everything, but rather look for people who will make a complete team.

This book could be the perfect gift to encourage those who are humbly striving to improve their leadership – not for perfection, but rather for their service to education.

**Dr Pak Tee Ng, Associate Professor, National Institute of Education,
Nanyang Technological University, Singapore**

Steve Munby

Imperfect
Leadership

A book for leaders who
know they don't know it all

Foreword by Michael Fullan

Crown House Publishing
www.crownhouse.co.uk

First published by

Crown House Publishing Ltd
Crown Buildings, Bancyfelin, Carmarthen, Wales, SA33 5ND, UK
www.crownhouse.co.uk

and

Crown House Publishing Company LLC
PO Box 2223, Williston, VT 05495, USA
www.crownhousepublishing.com

British Library of Cataloguing-in-Publication Data
A catalogue entry for this book is available from the British Library.

Print ISBN 978-178583411-0
Mobi ISBN 978-178583427-1
ePub ISBN 978-178583428-8
ePDF ISBN 978-178583429-5

LCCN 2019935636

Printed and bound in the UK by TJ International, Padstow, Cornwall

To my wife, Jacqui, whose love and wise counsel have helped me
to be a better leader and a better person.

Foreword
by Michael Fullan

My colleagues and I have a fantastic conclusion about educational change. Whether we are considering the school, the local authority or the system as a whole, one change fact stands out: about 80% of the best ideas come from leading practitioners. Steve Munby has embodied this truth over three decades of being the CEO of three complex organisations, operating in volatile, sometimes roller-coaster, circumstances. Fortunately for us, he kept track of what was happening, reflected on it in real time, made corrections, and made himself vulnerable to his own inner self and to those he led. At the end of this chapter of his life, at age 61, he is still an imperfect leader, but he now knows what this means and he shares the lessons with us.

The core of these lessons in some ways centres on the eight years he spent as CEO of England's National College for School Leadership. Each year in June he gave an inspirational speech at an event entitled Seizing Success. Each year the crowds got bigger, from 400 in year one to a door-busting 2,000 leaders in the final years. They did not come just to see Steve, although that was part of it. They came because this was *the* place to be with colleagues if you wanted to know about and be at the forefront of leading ideas for changing England's schools and your own, whatever country you lived in.

By 2012, Steve had left the college to become CEO of CfBT, a trust organisation doing international work in developing countries. The annual event, Seizing Success, became Inspiring Leadership and Steve continued to give his annual speeches.

The themes of his 12 annual speeches reflect the roiling and rolling circumstances he contended with and helped to improve. Whether they represented gut-wrenching setbacks – like having to cut 40% of the college's budget or seeing his beloved National College whittled into extinction by an unfriendly government – or soaring success – like when schools across the country achieved better and better student results because of improved school leadership – Steve epitomised the meaning of a lead learner.

The evolution of the titles of his speeches capture the essence of the imperfect leader in action: 'Enthusiastic and Invitational Leadership' (2005), 'Authentic System Leadership' (2006), 'Imperfect and Courageous Leadership' (2007), 'Power and Love in Leadership' (2012), 'Grown-up and Restless Leadership' (2016) and 'Principled Leadership in Challenging Times' (2017).

Because I was attuned to learning from lead practitioners, I found Steve early – just after he took his first CEO job in 2000, as director of education in Knowsley, a small local authority in north-west England which had scored second-last in GCSE performance in the country. After one year of Steve's leadership, Knowsley had become the worst performer in England! Imperfect became one step backward, before Steve and his team led a remarkable turnaround at Knowsley. The so-called worst local authority became a success story – one of the first in the country to demonstrate that you can turn around an entire education authority from terrible to great.

Like many other what I call 'nuance leaders', Steve combines empathy, closeness and toughness, mobilising the commitment of scores of people to do what seems impossible. The National College was founded in 2000. Its first few years were characterised by a diffuse agenda and it was hard to locate its centre of gravity. Steve took over in 2005 and one of the first things he did was to take a cue from the leadership of his mentor, Tim Brighouse, the former Birmingham chief education officer. He decided to personally call every leader of every local leadership group and association. There were about 500 of them across the country. He said publicly in his first speech that this was exactly what he was going to do. And he did it, asking each one how the college was serving their needs and how it might change for the better. He launched a new era for the National College.

In my book, *Nuance*, I delved into how some leaders are effective, while others using many of the same strategies fail. Now that I review my extended definition, I see much of Steve in it:

> Nuance leaders have a curiosity about what is possible, openness to other people, sensitivity to context, and loyalty to a better future. They see below the surface enabling them to detect patterns and their consequences for the system. They connect people to their own and each other's humanity. They don't lead, they teach. They change people's emotions, not just their minds. They have an instinct for orchestration. They foster sinews of success. They are humble in the face of challenges, determined for the group to be successful, and proud to celebrate success. They end up developing incredibly accountable organizations because the accountability gets built into the culture. Above all they are courageously and relentlessly committed to changing the system for the better of humanity.[1]

Read *Imperfect Leadership* to see how Steve fits the definition of nuance. He has written an honest, fascinating and engrossing book. Afterwards, ask yourself what a perfect leader would do in this or that situation. The answer will almost always be that there is no such thing because the world is imperfect and always will be. We need people like Steve to take the job anyway.

Acknowledgements

There are a great number of people I would like to thank for their help not only in the production of this book but also in helping to shape my leadership over many years.

Sir Tim Brighouse, Sir Michael Barber and Baroness Estelle Morris have had a profoundly positive impact on me and on my leadership and I am hugely grateful to them for that. I have tried to follow in their footsteps.

Michael Fullan, more than anyone else, has helped me – through his writings – to articulate the leadership that I have attempted to demonstrate. Andy Hargreaves, Tony Mackay, David Albury and Vanni Treves have shared their wisdom, their support and their friendship with me in equal measure, for which I am deeply grateful. In my early career, Kevyn Smith, Mark Pattison and Steve Gallagher, in their own individual ways, showed me what leadership could be and modelled it for me. I will never forget what they did for me.

I am greatly in the debt of Maggie Farrar and Geoff Southworth, not only for their significant contribution to improving the manuscript for this book but also for demonstrating on a daily basis the power of leadership that is principled and full of integrity.

I would like to publicly acknowledge the fantastic support (and challenge) provided by my senior colleagues at the National College (especially Toby Salt and Caroline Maley) and at CfBT/Education Development Trust (especially Patrick Brazier, Tony McAleavy, Bob Miles, Chris

Tweedale and Philip Graf). I would also like to acknowledge my fabulous executive assistants over the years – Lynn Morley, Chloe Smith and Alison Millar.

I am greatly indebted to the people who have helped me to craft the speeches in this book, especially Michael Pain, Tony McAleavy and Matt Davis, but also Patrick Scott, Christine Gilbert, John Dunford, Marie-Claire Bretherton, Jane Creasy and Lucy Crehan.

I would like to extend a huge thank you to the exceptional Laura McInerney for her wise advice on the manuscript and also to Toby Greany for giving me such expert, helpful and constructive feedback.

Finally, I would like to thank my dear friends, Peter Batty and John Turner, not only for reading and commenting on the manuscript but also for helping to influence my leadership for the better over many years.

Contents

Introduction

Many's the time I've been mistaken.

And many times confused.

Paul Simon, 'American Tune'

I am in a meeting of my leadership team and we are about to receive the financial figures for our annual budget. I am very nervous. The figures show yet another huge deficit of more than £4 million – putting the organisation under great strain and my leadership under considerable pressure. I have been in the CEO role for 18 months and there is still no turnaround as far as the bottom line is concerned. Should I resign? Will the board still have confidence in me? How much time will I be given? Have I got the strategy wrong?

This was not the first time I had experienced these feelings of self-doubt and potential failure. In 2000, I had taken up the role of director of education in Knowsley Council. Knowsley was a small local education authority (LEA) with about 80 schools, including 11 secondary schools. When I was appointed in October, we had the second worst GCSE results out of all the secondary schools in the country. After nearly a year of my leadership, we had the worst GCSE results in the country. I went live on Radio Merseyside on results day and the broadcaster said to me, 'With respect, why don't you just give up? It's hopeless.' Later that week I received a telephone call from the *Daily Mail* saying that they wanted to do a story on the worst LEA in the country and asking would I do an interview. Within a few days, there was a call for my resignation in the *Liverpool Echo*, suggesting I had brought disgrace to the borough of Knowsley. If it hadn't been for a wise mentor at that time, who helped me to see that I was doing the right things but just needed more time for them to make an impact, I might have walked away and given up.

Five years later, in 2005, after some success in Knowsley, I took up a national role as CEO of the National College for School Leadership, feeling well out of my depth. By 2010, having made some progress, the context changed completely and we had a new right-of-centre coalition government with a radical secretary of state for education – Michael Gove. I wondered whether I should continue to try to lead the National College under these completely new circumstances. Should I resign, or should I try to make it work positively for school leaders? And if the latter, what should my new strategy be? Much later, in 2014, I found myself – as chair of the CST multi-academy trust (MAT) – being challenged by a minister of the Crown and by a board member of the Department for Education, who were pushing for my resignation.

As this book outlines, there have been many times in my leadership when I have doubted whether I was the right person for the role. Many leaders will have been in situations in which they have asked themselves similar questions. There have been several mistakes and some pretty fundamental errors in my leadership, but there has also been some success and, overall, a legacy of which I am proud.

This is, I hope, an honest book about leadership. It is about my leadership journey – some of the highs and lows, and, most of all, how I learned to improve my leadership. It is about messy leadership, trial and error leadership and butterflies in the stomach leadership. It is also about thoughtful leadership, invitational leadership and, most of all, imperfect leadership.

'Imperfect leadership' is one of the best terms I can think of to describe my own leadership. This is not something I am ashamed about; imperfect leadership should be celebrated. Too often we are given examples of leaders who are put on some kind of pedestal – superhero leaders, leaders who have it all worked out, who are hugely successful and so good at what they do that nobody else can come close. This book is, I hope, the antidote to that concept. I have yet to meet a perfect leader, even if they might be portrayed by others as such. The notion that a leader needs to be good at all aspects of leadership is not only unrealistic, it is also bad for the mental and physical health of leaders and will do nothing to attract new people into leadership.

As you read this book I hope that the value of imperfect leadership and the positive impact it can make will shine through. For those reading it who have yet to step up into leadership, my sincere hope is that it will encourage and empower you rather than put you off.

What also makes this book different is the fact that between 2005 and 2017 I made an annual keynote speech to a large audience of school leaders. These speeches are at the heart of the book. In them I attempted to map the educational landscape for school leaders in England at the time – to help them understand their own shifting context and their role as leaders within it. The speeches attempted to describe, to analyse, to challenge and to inspire. In some cases, the speeches became very personal and, on several occasions, I was speaking to myself as a leader as much as I was speaking to the audience. They are, in part, a commentary on the changes in the education system in England over a 12-year period; but they are more than that, and I hope also that they will be of interest to those who are not familiar with the English system. In these speeches, I increasingly tried to describe for school leaders the kind of leadership that I believed was necessary at that moment in time. This is a question that every leader, in whatever context and in whatever country, should be asking of themselves on a fairly regular basis.

This book begins with my appointment as CEO of the National College, so it might be helpful for readers to know a little bit about my career background. After completing a degree in philosophy and a postgraduate certificate in education, I started work as a secondary school history teacher in Birmingham and, later, in Gateshead. After seven years, I became an advisory teacher in Sunderland, working for the Technical and Vocational Education Initiative. This was followed by a short period as a lecturer at Sunderland Polytechnic and two years employed by the North East Local Education Authorities as an expert consultant on assessment and records of achievement for students. I spent eight years at Oldham LEA as a school adviser and inspector, and then I made a big step up to become assistant director for school improvement and lifelong learning in the new unitary LEA of Blackburn with Darwen. After quite a bit of success, including the local authority being awarded Beacon

Status for school improvement, I was appointed as director of education and lifelong learning in Knowsley in 2000.

One of the overall messages in this book is that context matters. What works well in one context may be unsuccessful in another. As Dylan Wiliam has written, 'In education, "what works?" is not the right question because everything works somewhere and nothing works everywhere, so what's interesting, what's important in education is: "Under what circumstances does this work?"[2] We should never think that a leadership approach or strategy which was a great success in our previous organisation can just be transplanted into our new organisation. As Michael Fullan argues, if strategies are to travel well, we need to show nuance in our leadership.[3]

Context is subtle; it doesn't just apply when we change roles or move schools, and there is no place for standing still. What worked for us as leaders last year, even within the same organisation, won't necessarily work for us this year. Moreover, a tough year can be followed by another tough year, or by a year of success, and sometimes these things are not entirely within our control. At times, the context changes and requires a new approach from us as leaders, but we can be so close to things that we don't see it until it is too late. That has certainly happened to me on more than one occasion.

Leaders need to develop their own leadership style based on their beliefs and values, their expertise and skills, their personality and their context. Much of this is fixed but some of it changes, so we need to change with it.

This book describes some fundamental changes in the English education system over a 12-year period and how school leaders altered their leadership as this context changed. It also describes how my own leadership developed as my personal context changed.

But there are also some fundamental aspects of leadership that never change, in spite of the context: the need for us to be self-aware, to be learners, to be enthusiastic, to be authentic, to be invitational and to be principled.

In the final chapter, I try to bring all this together – summarising my views on the current educational landscape in England and the lessons I have learned about leadership, including the power of imperfect leadership.

Chapter One
Asking for Help

I'm on my way,

I don't know where I'm going.

Paul Simon, 'Me and Julio Down by the Schoolyard'

In December 2004, I was interviewed for the role of CEO of the National College for School Leadership. I was excited about the role and did my very best at the interview, preparing thoroughly, but I didn't really expect to be offered the job. Surely others with more experience of working at the national level than I had would apply and be appointed? Anyway, why would they appoint someone who had never been a head teacher to be the CEO of the National College – wouldn't that be like appointing someone who had never been a police superintendent to lead the College of Policing or someone who had never been an officer in the army to lead Sandhurst?

And yet I did get the job. I found out later that this was only after the interview panel (who had recommended me for appointment) had been asked by the Prime Minister's Office to reconsider because I had not been a head teacher. They did reconsider and they still recommended me for the role. So, several weeks after I had been interviewed, the then secretary of state for education, Charles Clarke, signed off my appointment and I suddenly found myself thrust into the public eye as a national figure in the education world.

The National College for School Leadership was set up in 2000. The first CEO, Heather Du Quesnay, oversaw the creation of the college – its brand, its staffing and, of course, its new building: a residential conference centre with a high-class restaurant, 100 en-suite bedrooms, a moat and a lake. It was very plush – it even had Molton Brown shampoo and soap in the bedrooms.

I started the new role in March 2005 and I immediately felt out of my depth. I had moved from being director of education in Knowsley (a deprived and challenging part of Merseyside), where the view from my office window had been a car park and a McDonald's, to an office in Nottingham where the view was of a lake with swans and the occasional heron. When I arrived for the first time late one afternoon – to have a briefing with the outgoing CEO – the head waiter asked me if I would like a glass of wine. It was a completely new world to me.

The National College had been set up as a body that was at arm's length from government, with its own board, but the chair of the board and the CEO were both appointed by the education secretary. Each year a 'remit letter' was sent to the National College by the education secretary, allocating a budget and outlining what the government expected to be delivered in return for that budget. The CEO of the National College also had a formal role to advise the education secretary on matters relating to school leadership. I had never worked with a board before. I had never even met a secretary of state, let alone had responsibility for advising one (by this time the education secretary was Ruth Kelly) and I had no real idea how the national political process worked.

The National College had got off to a good start under its previous leadership. The impressive building had been put up and several high-quality leadership programmes had been developed, but certain things were beginning to go wrong. Overall, the government was not happy and had commissioned an end-to-end review of the organisation, led by David Albury.[4] The review praised the innovation and energy of the college but also expressed a number of concerns. It was criticised for taking on too many initiatives (usually at the request of government!) which were not always directly about school leadership, and, as a result, the college had begun to lose its focus and identity. Moreover, many of the most highly regarded and high-profile school principals had formed the view that it had nothing to offer them and was not listening to their views. In addition, there was a feeling that too much of the content and design of the various leadership programmes was being done by a small number of experts at the centre and that the organisation was not making enough use of the widespread expertise that was out there. It said that the college needed to become a commissioner instead of designing its own programmes. In short, the government was starting to wonder if the National College was becoming a problem. In the wake of the report, the chair of the board had resigned and a new chair, Vanni Treves, was appointed. Soon after that, Heather Du Quesnay left to take up a role in Hong Kong and, as the new CEO, it was my remit to implement the recommendations of the review.

After speaking with the author of the review, as well as with officials at the Department for Education and Skills (DfES), I soon realised that the National College was actually in trouble – more trouble than I had realised when applying for the job.

My first decision, before I even started in the role, was to seek out some mentors. Imperfect leaders know that they don't have all the answers – they ask for help. It has always slightly bewildered me that so many people take up leadership roles without thinking that they need a mentor. I find it equally bewildering that others seem to understand the need to have a mentor but then agree to have one allocated who doesn't have the expertise they need. Others seem to think that there is a kind of rule that you are only supposed to have one mentor. I knew that I needed people to help me who had the expertise that I lacked.

I chose four mentors and, to my delight, each one of them said yes.

Estelle Morris was a former secretary of state for education and now sat in the House of Lords. She was herself a former teacher and someone I admired greatly, though I had never met her. I emailed her and we met for coffee at Waterstones in Charing Cross. She agreed to be one of my mentors, and immediately I had access to someone who understood how the national system worked in Whitehall, who could advise me on how to get things done, who to talk to and how to conduct myself. This proved to be a huge help to me over the next few years.

My second mentor was Tim Brighouse. Tim had been an informal mentor to me when I had been director of education in Knowsley. He was already one of my heroes. I remember the honour I felt when he agreed to speak at our first Visioning Conference in Knowsley. I introduced him by saying: 'I have five heroes: Leonard Cohen, Bob Dylan, Mark Knopfler, Kevin Keegan and Tim Brighouse – and Tim isn't even at the bottom of that list!' I needed Tim to help me focus on my moral purpose and to make sure that I did the right things for children and for schools. I also needed him to help me connect with school leaders. Tim gave me two pieces of advice straight away:

1. Go and see Ted Wragg and get him onside – then he won't write negative things about the National College in the back of the *Times Educational Supplement* (a national weekly publication about education issues).

2. Find a way of writing personal cards to head teachers. Even though there are 22,000 schools in England, you can get a lot of powerful messages across through personal contact and it will mean a great deal to them.

I took Tim's advice. I went to see Ted Wragg and asked for his advice on what to do. He was delightful and helpful, though he tragically died less than a year later. With regard to the personal cards, this was already something I had been doing a lot of in Knowsley, but Tim gave me the confidence that it would work at a national level, in spite of the numbers. He could not have been more right about this. Over the next eight years, I wrote personal handwritten cards to hundreds of school leaders – probably more than a thousand – and even today, many years later, I meet people who tell me how much it meant to them. Being a school principal can be such a lonely job, so being thanked or congratulated in a personal way really matters. Tim is not only an authentic leader, he is also a genius.

My third mentor was Tony Mackay. Tony actually had a home in Australia but appeared to spend most of his time on an aeroplane travelling the world. He never seemed to get jet lag because he rarely stayed long enough in one place for his body to know what time it was supposed to be. Tony is the best networker I have ever met and also a world-class facilitator. He was doing lots of work at the time for the DfES and he was also a member of the governing council of the National College. Tony helped me to get in touch with the right people and made sure that I never neglected the importance of forming positive relationships with the key influencers in the system – those who could help me and those who could potentially do me harm.

My final mentor was David Albury. I chose David because he was the author of the fairly critical end-to-end review of the college. I figured that if he knew what was wrong with the place then he could help me to fix it too. This proved to be an excellent move, especially in my first couple of years as CEO.

In my interview for the role, Sir Michael Barber had asked me if I was up to organising a national conference that would inspire and motivate school leaders. I replied that if appointed I had every intention of doing so. Fortunately for me the National College, with support from Sir Iain Hall, who was then on the governing body, had already begun to organise its first ever national conference. It was called Seizing Success and it took place in Birmingham at the International Convention Centre in early March 2005, a few weeks before I commenced my role as CEO. Geoff Southworth was acting CEO and we agreed that he would do the first half of the speech and then hand over to me as 'CEO designate'. This was my first ever Seizing Success speech. To be honest, I still didn't know that much about the National College, and I hadn't spent very long thinking about leadership, for that matter. My theme was how the emerging new challenges of school leadership were mirrored by my new challenges as CEO of the National College.

This theme of talking 'leader to leader' proved to be a very powerful one for me over the next 12 years, as I began to develop my own views on leadership at a school level and at a national level. I have always had the utmost respect for school leaders and could never understand the mentality of some of my colleagues in LEAs who were disparaging or dismissive. For me, school leaders have an extraordinarily demanding job, and I can honestly say that I never thought that my job as a director of education in an LEA or as CEO of the National College was harder or easier than theirs – just different. Having a wife who was a secondary head teacher probably helped!

In this speech I made a very important public commitment: I declared that I would personally telephone the chair of each secondary head teachers' group, each primary head teachers' group and each special head teachers' group in each LEA, along with other key stakeholders, and that

I would invite them all to attend one of nine regional conferences to discuss the future of the National College. As there were 150 LEAs, I was publicly committing myself to making about 500 telephone calls to school principals within the first few months of being in the role.

This notion of making public commitments and then implementing that commitment became part of my leadership style.

Imperfect leaders make public promises because they are acutely aware of their own weaknesses, and they know that without making public promises they might fail to deliver on something that is really important. It was my way of making sure that I made myself do things that were hard but extremely important. In fact, I had a very tough time trying to make those 500 phone calls. I needed to do them in the space of 10 weeks, which meant that on average I needed to make 10 phone calls per day for 50 consecutive working days. If I hadn't made a public commitment to do this, I probably would have given up. I had no idea how hard it was going to be.

As the director of education in Knowsley, if I telephoned a school in Knowsley then the school principal invariably took the call. But now that I was telephoning schools from all over the country, often the school office thought that I was trying to sell something and refused to put me through. I often had to call back two or three times to actually get to speak to the principal. But I made all those calls myself – every single one – without going through my PA, and it turned out to be one of the most effective things I did as CEO of the National College. Some principals never forgot that I had called them personally to listen to their views, and the message soon spread in every LEA that the new CEO of the National College wanted to listen to the voice of school leaders.

It also meant that after conducting 500 phone calls with head teachers, and asking them what advice they would give me to improve the National College, I knew more than anyone else in the country what school leaders wanted from the college, which gave me a strong hand when discussing the way forward for the National College with ministers and officials. I learned from this, and from my experiences later, that making public commitments can sometimes be risky, but it can also keep you on track and help to make sure that you do the right thing when you are under pressure.

The speech reproduced below was written at a time when the Every Child Matters agenda was really beginning to take off. This was partly as a result of the tragic death of Victoria Climbié, which could have been prevented if various agencies had shared the information they knew about the child. The Children Act 2004 was passed and schools were now encouraged – and, indeed, required – to work jointly with other agencies in the interests of children. The idea of 'extended schools' was also being promoted by the government, with more and more multi-agency services located on school sites and with school buildings open for much longer than the school day.

At the same time, the Building Schools for the Future initiative – led by Schools Minister David Miliband – had started to pour significant additional capital resources for new schools into the system, but only in certain areas. Also, the Tomlinson Report had led to the publication of a white paper on 14–19 education.[5] This proposed creating a single unified qualification for academic and vocational studies for students aged 14–19 and, at the time of my speech, this seemed likely to happen. In the end, Prime Minister Tony Blair backed away from the idea, concerned that the 'gold standard' of A levels would be damaged. Incidentally, this resulted in the education secretary getting heckled at the annual conference of the Secondary Heads Association (SHA) later that year.

In 2005, the government was also pushing what David Miliband called 'a new relationship with schools' which was less 'top-down' and suggested that school leaders should be trusted more to get on with things and to make a difference.[6] Sir Michael Barber was at this time suggesting that strategies that will take a system from awful to adequate are different from strategies that will move a system from good to great.[7] As part of this reduced top-down approach, schools would receive support and challenge not from an inspector or adviser from an LEA, but instead from something new called a school improvement partner (SIP). A SIP would likely be a successful serving head teacher. Now it was all going to be about head teachers helping each other – lateral leadership rather than top-down leadership; school leaders themselves leading the system.

Finally, this speech was delivered at a time when the government was pushing workforce reform. A workforce agreement had been signed with all the teacher and head teacher unions. The agreement stated that teacher workload would be addressed by limiting the number of hours they could be required to work and by adding a greater number of teaching assistants and support staff to the school workforce, thus enabling teachers to focus less on administration and more on actual teaching.

It was against this policy background that, in February 2005, I rather nervously got onto the stage, shook Geoff Southworth's hand and, looking out at the 400 or so school leaders huddled in the centre of the large and mainly empty auditorium, made the following speech.

Enthusiastic and Invitational Leadership

Seizing Success Conference 2005

I am proud and honoured to be taking up the role as chief executive of the National College. My mum and dad are proud too – not because they understand much about the National College or even because there was an article about me in the *Times Educational Supplement*, but because I made it into a small column in the *Newcastle Evening Chronicle*. My dad says that if I ever make it into the *North Shields Gazette* then I will really have made it.

It is, I believe, a very challenging time to be a school leader. And I say 'school leader' rather than 'head teacher' because I believe in leadership teams and distributive leadership. There is no evidence of an improving work–life balance for school leaders – if anything it is getting worse. Vacancies for head teachers are up 50 per cent since 2000, throwing up challenges about how we develop and attract future school leaders. I say 'challenges' but these are also opportunities to think again about succession planning and how we grow tomorrow's school leaders – research that I know the National College has commenced. The workforce reform agenda is challenging, especially with limited funds, but it also provides great opportunities to rethink the way we do things in schools and how we maximise the expertise of staff.

There also is the need to respond to the demands of the Children Act and the Every Child Matters agenda, with its focus on the extended school, multi-agency working, children's centres and schools at the heart of their local communities. This poses real issues regarding the changing role of leadership and governance – especially if, in some cases, there is a campus approach, with more than just learning going on. In addition, there are the changes being introduced through the 'new relationships with schools', a different Ofsted framework and inspection system, Building Schools for the Future and the white paper on 14–19 education. In fact, we are in a time of more radical change than we have been, in my view, for many years. This is a time of change and uncertainty.

During this time of change, what should leaders be doing?

Clarifying the focus and joining the dots

It is tough as a leader in a school. You want to be ahead of the game and make the right decisions for your school and for the children and young people, but there are so many initiatives that you constantly have to make decisions about how you are going to respond. On the one hand, you don't want to overload your staff; on the other, you don't want the school to be left behind. Your job is relentless and exhausting and multifaceted.

How should a school respond to all of the initiatives – national and local?

Well, the weak school leader either lets them all in or lets none of them in. Some schools are what Michael Fullan calls 'Christmas tree schools'.[8] They always join new initiatives. They look good from a distance, with lots of awards and coordinators, but in some cases there is not enough implementation. They never go past the initiative stage into the real implementation phase. Other leaders think they are protecting their staff and their workload by keeping all new initiatives out, but in the end most of these schools become too insular and start to coast or go backwards.

The effective leader is the one who decides which initiatives are right for the school and which ones should be given less of an emphasis. Effective heads are good at connecting the dots to create a coherent whole – they know what is best for their own school community, they know the direction they want to go with their school and they use the appropriate initiatives in the right way in order to get there. You need to be an effective gatekeeper of what is right for your school. Obviously, you will take great care if there are statutory requirements, but for most of these initiatives that is not the case.

I don't care who is making demands or requests of you – the local education authority, the Department for Education and Skills, the National College for School Leadership – you know best what is right for your school and for your community. If you let everything in you would lose focus. It is not that the initiatives are wrong – they are very often good – it is about timing and about coherence. I think extended schools, the primary strategy, children's centres, specialist schools status, 14–19 collaboration, school self-evaluation and so on are all good things in themselves, but you can't do everything.

So, my first question is: are you really clear about the direction and focus that you want for your school? Are you then joining the dots in a coherent way to help you achieve that goal? Are things coherent or incoherent for your staff and your school community?

The same question needs to be asked of myself and the governing council and leadership team of the National College. Are we joining the dots about the college? Is it a coherent, united and focused organisation that knows what it stands for and where it is going? Is it clear about its core business and about which initiatives it should be picking up and which ones it should be saying no to? Does it help you, as school leaders, to make sense of the agenda in schools? I think the college may have tried to do too much, to develop too many initiatives, to say 'yes' to too many things. In my view, the time is right for the college to take a step back, to be really clear about what its core business is and then to communicate its role effectively so that everyone understands what it is about. It will then also be in a position to advise ministers effectively on leadership issues. Like you in schools, the National College needs to be clear about its focus, take some clear decisions and join the dots.

Looking outward as well as inward – listening to the community

The children's services agenda and the emphasis on extended schools throws up new challenges for us. There is a greater understanding that schools can't transform communities on their own, but that they can play a part by working with others. In his book, *Bowling Alone*, Robert Putnam explains that interconnected communities – communities that talk to each other and engage in activities together – have lower crime, better education results and better care of the vulnerable.[9] And as Professor Charles Desforges from Exeter University has demonstrated, the impact on attainment by good parenting is stronger than the impact of the school. He concludes that in terms of attainment at school, if a child had a choice between moving from having a bottom quartile parent to having a top quartile parent or moving from a bottom quartile school to a top quartile school, the child should change the parent every time.[10] That is why we have to engage with our parents as well as with our children in this grand endeavour, in whatever way we can, even though that can be tough. We need to be outward facing, connecting with parents and the community.

It is also why we need to ensure that we listen to the voice of young people. Not what we think they are saying and feeling, but what they are actually saying and feeling.

The challenge for us is connecting with the individual young person – at their level and with their issues. Sometimes it works and sometimes it doesn't, but we should take their views seriously. We recently carried out a local survey in Knowsley of young people's views about what they wanted from school. In the top 12 were, of course, things like doing well in exams, developing skills for a future job or career, but also things like feeling valued and having decent toilets. As a former head teacher friend of mine says, 'School improvement should always start with the toilets.'

We have come a long way on listening to the voices of young people, and I am pleased to see that school councils are flourishing all over the country. But I think what is still not as common as it should be is young people genuinely involved in their own self-assessment and giving structured feedback on the effectiveness of the school's policies.

The same challenges apply to the National College. Just as your key clients are children and their parents, our key clients are school leaders and future school leaders. Many of you know about the National College, but how many of you or your colleagues around the country think of it as *your* college? To what extent is the National College listening to its key clients – leaders in schools?

I like the quote from Heifetz and Linsky which says that effective leaders spend time on the balcony as well as on the dance floor.[11] That's where the National College comes in. The role of the college is to help you spend quality time on the balcony. The National College – your college – therefore needs to ensure that it is flexible and responsive to your development needs. It needs to ensure that schools have a strong voice in its development and ownership of its programmes.

We will be running nine regional conferences in June and July to hear directly from heads and from other key stakeholders on how we can move the college forward together. In the next few months, I will personally be telephoning the chairs of the secondary head teachers, primary head teachers and, where they exist, special head teacher groups in each local authority to invite them to come along to the regional conferences with another primary and secondary head teacher colleague. I will also be telephoning directors of children's services to ask them to attend too. We need to listen to your voice.

The college also needs to be building on the best national and international research and applying it to its development programmes so that you know that when you participate in a college programme it will be up to date and leading edge.

Being a self-evaluating learning organisation and working collaboratively with others

Healthy organisations welcome external challenge – provided they know the criteria and trust the people carrying out that challenge. I support strongly the new Ofsted inspection model with its greater involvement of Her Majesty's Inspectors (HMIs) and its greater emphasis on self-assessment, and I like the concept of a school improvement partner to support and challenge schools, especially if that person has real credibility with head teachers. It is encouraging that there is going to be a new relationship with schools where the focus is on delivering outcomes, not on the external monitoring of individual funding streams. If we can get the delivery right – and if we put the right people in those posts as school improvement partners, with the right training, development and accreditation – this can be a very important step forward. I also think that the role of school improvement partners will be a vital development opportunity for our best leaders – a chance, you might say, to spend some time on the balcony by supporting and challenging other schools.

Schools need an external perspective. Frankly, even the best leaders can become used to the existing environment and begin to take things for granted as the way things have to be.

Many years ago, a colleague inspected a primary school and found that they all did art on a Wednesday afternoon. This struck him as not a very good use of resources so he asked the teachers why they all did art at the same time. They said that the caretaker insisted on it, so that he could manage the cleaning of the school effectively. He went to see the caretaker and asked, 'Is it true that you insist all classes do art on a Wednesday afternoon?' He said he didn't mind what day they did art. 'But,' my colleague said, 'the teachers have told me that it is because of the caretaker.' He replied, 'That was the last caretaker – he retired a few years ago!' So, the school's curriculum was being controlled by the caretaker who had retired a few years ago, yet the school carried on anyway because it hadn't occurred to anyone to change it.

As leaders we have to be prepared to look at things differently and to ask ourselves some hard questions. It doesn't have to be the way it has always been.

We also access support through partnership working and collaboration. I know that there are probably too many networks for head teachers and too many meetings, but I really believe that collaboration, when managed properly, can be a real strength. Where I currently work – in Knowsley – the collaboration between schools is of the highest quality. Schools are taking responsibility for supporting each other and they also carry out peer review in a focused and challenging way. They are lending staff to each other and providing real ongoing mentoring and coaching for each other. Head teachers meet to focus on the outcomes of action research in their schools and across their schools, and the learning from that is very powerful.

If we are going to have system-wide reform we need to develop capacity and we do that through collaboration and partnerships. My experience is that collaboration and partnership working take more time but give you higher quality outcomes in the long run.

In the same way, at the National College we will be seeking to work in collaboration with other organisations to act together in the interests of schools and school leaders.

Demonstrating unfailing optimism – developing the culture

If you do not seriously believe that the children in your school can improve their learning significantly, then frankly you are in the wrong job. Just as there is no place in our schools for staff who are sarcastic and demeaning towards young people, so there is no place in our schools for leaders who don't believe that pupils' learning can and will improve. And if you do have very high expectations of the young people in your school – and I'm sure you do – but all around you there is a different culture, then you have a major challenge. The culture of the organisation will align itself to the strongest voice. As leaders, you have to become the strongest voice and establish a new norm at a higher level. That is our job as leaders – to help our staff see what can be achieved and to go for it. That is why we need to exhibit unfailing optimism. If we don't believe it can be done, how can we expect our staff to do so?

In 2001, a few weeks after secondary schools in Knowsley had achieved the worst examination results in the country, I brought all the head teachers together and told them that in three years' time people would be coming from all over the country to find out how we had been so successful. That was a risk but I believed it to be true. What was needed at that time was optimistic leadership.

Demonstrating integrity

I am an enthusiast for enthusiasm. But we need to combine that enthusiasm and unfailing optimism with integrity, otherwise it will become hollow. What we do and how we behave is far more important than what we say. We cannot talk our way out of situations that we have behaved our way into. Integrity and optimism go a long way when it comes to managing change and getting people to come along with you. That need for optimism, high expectations and integrity applies to all leadership positions, whether in a school or, indeed, in the National College.

What do I mean by integrity? I mean being consistent, being driven by a strong set of values and principles, and if you get things wrong – and we all do sometimes – apologising and trying to put it right.

I believe that the National College is already a good college and is already making a difference to leadership in this country. I absolutely believe that it can make a profound impact on you and on the school leaders that come after you, and, through you, directly improve the quality of learning for our young people. I am more excited – and more scared – about this job than any job I've ever had.

If your school is going to be successful, and if the National College is going to be successful, then we need to hold on to these principles. And they challenge us all:

- Clarify the focus and join the dots.

- Look outward and listen to the community.

- Be a self-evaluating organisation.

- Collaborate and learn.

- Demonstrate optimism and integrity.

This conference is rightly entitled 'Seizing Success'. It requires us to be pro-active in taking control of our own situations and making it work for us and for the children and young people that we serve. You in your role in schools and we in our role as leaders in the college.

There is a story about a wise man who always seemed to know the answer to everything. One day a young man tried to catch him out. He decided to catch a butterfly and put it behind his back and then say to the wise man, 'If you are so wise, is the butterfly behind my back alive or dead?' If the wise man said alive then he would crush it quickly and bring it forward dead, and if the wise man said dead he would bring it forward alive. Either way the wise man would, for once, be wrong. So, he caught a butterfly and put it behind his back. He went to the wise man and said, 'If you are so wise, tell me whether the butterfly behind my back is alive or dead'? And the wise man said: 'It is in your hands.'

The future is in our hands – let's seize it.

This speech set the tone for all my future speeches. It started the process of me talking 'leader to leader' at these conferences – emphasising the importance of trying to model in the leadership at the National College what I hoped school leaders would do in their schools. Already some of the themes of imperfect leadership are coming through, including my early struggles as director of education in Knowsley and my public promise as the incoming CEO of the National College to listen to the voice of school leaders.

Chapter Two
How Radical Do I Need to Be?

I can see clearly now the rain has gone.

I can see all obstacles in my way.

Johnny Nash, 'I Can See Clearly Now'

Imperfect leaders invite others to help to shape the vision

One of the key things I needed to do in 2005 was to develop a vision for the National College. The trouble with creating a vision is that the people in your organisation expect you, as the leader, to have a compelling vision. They don't expect you to turn up on the first day and say, 'I have no idea where we should be heading.' That isn't good leadership. But, on the other hand, they don't want something imposed completely from on high and top down. They don't want a vision that shows no understanding of their real context – they want to help to shape the vision.

Just before I started my role as CEO of the National College, I was invited to speak, as CEO designate, at a conference for all the staff. I told them the story of how my wife and I had heard that the view in Santorini, looking over the blue Aegean Sea and the caldera, was supposed to be one of the most beautiful in the whole world. We organised a holiday there, flew in and rushed to the clifftop to see this wonderful view. But the mist had come down and we couldn't see anything. We knew it was a fantastic view, we knew that the sea would be a deep blue and the caldera would be magnificent, but we just couldn't see it, so we couldn't yet say precisely what it looked like. In the same way, I said to the staff, 'I have a great vision for the National College. I know it is going to be fantastic. But it is still a misty vision. I want you to work with me to clear the mist away, to firm up this vision and turn it into a reality.'

It is one thing to begin to develop ownership of a vision amongst 200 staff at the National College but quite another to develop ownership of a vision for the National College amongst school leaders in more than 22,000 schools across England. That is partly why I made the 500 phone calls. During each call, I asked the head teacher what the National College needed to be and what advice they would give me as the new CEO. The calls helped to clarify and focus my vision – to clear the mist. Having worked internally with staff at the college, and having had lengthy discussions with the board about vision and strategy, I was then ready for the nine regional 'visioning conferences' in June and July 2005.

I was absolutely determined that the National College would become 'our college' as far as school leaders were concerned. We achieved good attendance at these events so that, overall, I was able to engage with more than 1,000 school leaders. Jane Creasy – who was at the time a senior member of staff at the National College – facilitated each of these events. This was her first experience of facilitating national, high-profile events, and she turned out to be superb at it – cool, calm, professional and humorous. She later went on to be a highly successful national and international facilitator.

At each of these conferences I made two speeches – one about the issues and challenges facing school leadership and one about my analysis of the strengths and weaknesses of the National College and my vision for the future. The school leaders worked in groups to critique the speeches and we used technology to record what each group was saying directly onto a screen, in real time. We then chose some of the most controversial and challenging comments to highlight in the plenary session, with Jane putting me on the spot to answer questions and respond to comments. The fact that everyone could see their own groups' comments up on the big screen, and the fact that Jane deliberately chose some of the most challenging issues to raise with me, helped to build a sense of ownership, authenticity and transparency.

At the end of each event, everyone in the room had an electronic button to press to vote on whether or not they supported the vision. I remember even now how it felt when they all pressed their buttons to reveal their collective votes on the screen behind me, showing the extent to which the proposed vision for the National College was supported. In the end, the support from delegates all over the country was overwhelmingly positive and gave me a platform for moving forward.

The vision that we agreed through this process was summed up in the following diagram. It served us well for two or three years, but then, like all vision statements, it needed to be refreshed and amended.

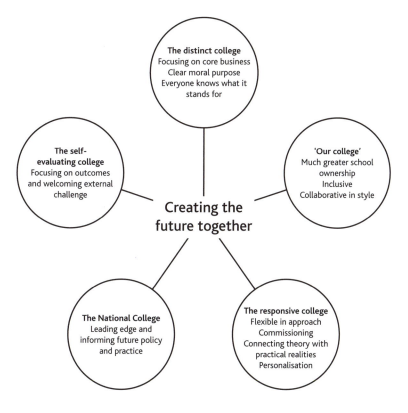

Much later, I reflected to myself that the process of visioning I had used was based on a style of leadership that might be called 'invitational'. What do I mean by invitational leadership? I mean asking for help and advice, inviting challenge, looking for support externally, listening to the views of others and then trying to shape that into something that worked for our context. Invitational leadership proved to be one of my main leadership styles in my first few years at the National College.

Imperfect leaders ask for help

In the first few months in the role, I asked advice from anyone I could. Peter Housden, the director general at the DfES, said to me: 'Spend time in London and talk to people. Tell the story of what you are going to do. Keep telling the story and then deliver on the story.' This proved to be one of the best pieces of advice I received and I followed it enthusiastically. I had meeting after meeting, lunch after lunch, dinner after dinner with the key influencers in the education system – senior officials, CEOs of agencies, influential head teachers, general secretaries of unions and professional associations, leaders of think tanks and so on. I asked each of them for their advice about what I should do.

This had two significant benefits. The first was that I got access to advice and expertise to help to inform my thinking about how to lead the National College and to help me understand the new political and national context in which I was now working. But there was a second very significant benefit: the people I approached and asked for advice were more willing to help me as a result. I realised (and I understand this much more now than I did at the time) that asking for help is a really positive way of getting people onside. It shows that you respect their expertise and value what they have to say. In many cases they agreed to speak at events or at a meeting of our governing council or to write something for our journal that went out to schools. I knew that if things got tough for the college politically – and I expected that they would at some point in the future – these individuals would, as result, be more likely to speak up in our favour. I found out later – during 2009–2011, and a period of change in government – that this strategy had largely worked (with a few exceptions!).

The theme of how radical leadership needs to be at any given time is one that I returned to in several of my speeches over the next 12 years. It is what I wrestled with in my first year as CEO at the National College. It is always hard to get this right. If you are too radical or too transformational, the organisation can implode and you can damage things irreparably. I have seen this happen in schools, especially in the early days of the academy movement – too much innovation and not enough focus on systems and on doing the basic things well, and a failure to understand context or to get under the skin of an organisation.

Alternatively, you can decide to play it safe and just try to do the current things better and more effectively. Many new head teachers choose this option. But too often, in spite of their best efforts, the organisational culture is stuck and the best they can achieve is only marginal gains – and at worst the school can go backwards. Once you have decided not to be radical in your first year or two, it is much harder to be so in year three or four. It is interesting that in their second headship most head teachers decide to challenge things more than they do in their first.

It was clear to me (and to DfES officials) that more of the same was not an option at the National College and that transformation and radical change were needed. To achieve this there would need to be significant changes at the top of the organisation, not just a change in CEO. We needed a structure and a senior team that was appropriate for the new vision and the new strategy. I decided early on, with the encouragement and support of the chair of the board, Vanni Treves, that I needed to appoint a deputy, and I chose Geoff Southworth, who had been the acting CEO after Heather Du Quesnay left.

I could not have made a better choice. Geoff proved to be wise, kind, good at relationships, loyal, strategic and very astute. He was my deputy for the first four years of my time at the National College and was absolutely exceptional in that role. Together, in the autumn of 2005, we drew up plans for a fundamental restructure of the organisation to create a leaner senior team (there were at that time 30 people in the senior management group). We also needed to bring in expertise from outside, including expertise in commissioning and expertise from serving school leaders.

After overcoming the initial concerns from Vanni about the danger of changing things so much that 'the wheels might come off', we moved ahead with our fundamental restructure of the leadership team. Apart from the posts of CEO and deputy CEO, 28 roles were deleted and 18 new roles were created. Everyone who wanted to stay had to apply for a new job and go through the interviewing process. This was tough on senior staff and not something I entered into lightly, but Geoff and I knew that change was needed and it was needed fast. In the end, only eight members of staff retained their roles, and we then went on to appoint 10 new senior members of staff externally.

Dealing with that process, including making so many senior staff redundant, was one of the very toughest things I did as CEO – losing a lot of sleep in the process and, of course, going through self-doubt that maybe I was introducing too much change too quickly and that it would backfire. I am certainly not proud of the way that some colleagues were treated at this time and, on reflection, I could have done things a little differently – perhaps been slightly less distant and inscrutable. During the period of the restructure, Geoff was the only person within the organisation who I could talk to and for a few months the two of us virtually had to lead the organisation on our own. It is at times like these that having superb mentors, a great chair and an excellent deputy proved so important to me. Leadership can be very lonely at times, especially during organisational restructuring.

Early in the summer term of 2005, I received my first remit letter from the education secretary which outlined what the government expected of the National College in the coming year and allocated our budget for the financial year. The remit letter asked me to provide advice on what should be done about leadership in poor and struggling schools.

I regarded this request as a golden opportunity to demonstrate our usefulness to the government and to help to change the perception that had been articulated in the end-to-end review that the National College was more of the problem than the solution. I therefore treated this with the utmost seriousness and set about commissioning some research into what might be done – in particular, to look at the various emerging models of executive headship piloted by people like David Triggs in Essex and Dexter Hutt in Birmingham.

At the time, the prevailing models to improve schools that were rated by Ofsted as inadequate and in need of special measures were:

1. Close the school down and reopen it as a new school or academy under new leadership.

2. Send in LEA inspectors to monitor progress and provide advice and challenge.

3. Get rid of the head teacher and try to persuade a really talented and experienced head from another school to apply for the role.

All of these models had some positive aspects, but option 1 is very expensive and time-consuming and option 2 can sometimes lead to lots of monitoring but insufficient actual improvement. Option 3 has two problems with it:

1. Rationale and motivation – why would highly successful head teachers leave the school they are in and take on the headship of a failing school, knowing that if it all goes wrong they will soon lose their job and, with it, the reputation and credibility they've built up over many years?

2. Sustainability – there aren't enough outstanding heads wanting to do this kind of 'turnaround' work. We just end up moving a small number of heads around the system to deal with the next crisis and picking up the pieces in the schools they leave behind.

Incidentally, in our research we asked heads who had moved to take on a school in special measures why they had done it. The three most popular responses (in order) were: 'Someone asked me to do so' (usually the LEA), 'I needed a new challenge' and 'These children were being let down and something needed to be done.'

As a result of our research, we recommended that we identify school leaders who would be willing to remain principal of their existing school but, in addition, provide leadership support to struggling schools, thus making the most of their leadership expertise without the risk of 'career suicide' and avoiding simply moving good heads around the system. This, of course, was building on the concept of 'consultant leaders' that had begun to be so effective in the London Challenge.

The idea was given a green light by officials and I was asked to work it up into a strategy. I decided to set up an advisory group which included a formidable collection of educationalists including, amongst others, Tim Brighouse (schools commissioner for London), David Woods (director of school improvement for the London Challenge), David Hopkins (adviser to the education secretary on school standards), the general secretaries of the two professional associations for head teachers (the Secondary Heads Association (SHA) and the National Association of Head Teachers (NAHT)) and several outstanding and well-known head teachers. Chairing this group of powerful and influential educators proved to be a huge challenge, but I learned so much about good chairing during those meetings, especially the skill of summarising the views that I had heard as succinctly as I could and then pushing hard to find a way of encapsulating the majority view in the meeting and turning it into something that I could legitimately take forward to officials and ministers.

In the end – as a direct result of the advice from this group – we turned what might have been a 'hero head' model into an initiative that was not just about great head teachers (who were accredited as national leaders of education (NLEs)) but also their whole school team (the school became a national support school (NSS)). An important by-product was that I had formed good relationships with the key players in the advisory group and, in doing so, had enhanced the credibility of the National College.

The education secretary (who by then was Alan Johnson) supported those proposals and asked the National College to go ahead and set it up. I wrote to all the schools in the country asking if they would consider applying to become NLEs/NSSs. I didn't have any idea what the response would be. We set the bar high for applications. Amongst other things, schools had to have been identified as outstanding in their last Ofsted inspection report and there had to be evidence of capacity at senior and middle leadership in the school, not just an exceptional head teacher.

We weren't offering any more money to heads – just one-off payments to each NSS (£60,000 to secondary schools and £30,000 to primary schools) to support capacity building. In return for being able to put the title on their business cards and a plaque in the school's reception area, we were asking NLEs and NSSs to be willing to take responsibility for helping schools in trouble. I was appealing to the moral purpose of head teachers and also to their sense of personal pride. I argued that we needed our most talented school leaders to help to make a difference in our most challenging schools. At that time, this was a relatively new concept and I didn't know how well it would be supported. I received hundreds of enthusiastic replies and we appointed our first 68 NLEs.

By the time of the second annual Seizing Success conference, I had made the 500 phone calls, held the regional visioning conferences and agreed the vision, carried out the leadership restructure and appointed most of the new and very talented senior leaders, chaired the NLE advisory group and was about to write to all schools to invite applications to become an NLE/NSS. It had been a tough year but I really did feel that we were making progress. I had learned the importance of asking for advice from others and genuinely listening to what they had to say. I had also been reminded of how tough and lonely leadership can get at times and why leaders need mentors and support. Asking for help is a key aspect of imperfect leadership.

At this time, there was great suspicion about executive head teachers as empire builders, driven by their own ego (this is still a concern as I write this book in 2019!). I was determined in my speech that we should portray NLEs not as hero heads or empire builders but as leaders who lead because they care about children. I was already learning that most people in school leadership roles respond well to the concept of moral purpose and values, rather than empire building and competition. My speech also addresses the challenge of succession planning. We had identified from our own research that the demographics showed worrying signs of an ageing profession and a potential shortage of school leaders over the coming years and, as a response, the education secretary had asked me in his remit letter for 2006–2007 to provide advice on what to do about succession planning.

We also knew that the National Professional Qualification for Headship (NPQH) needed revising. Too many people were gaining the qualification who weren't ready for headship and it was too top down, not connecting well enough with people's own leadership context. We announced a review and I was keen to get over the key thinking behind it.

My first speech, in March 2005, had been about who I was and what I hoped to do in leading the National College – it tried to set the tone. In my second speech, I wanted to demonstrate that we knew about and understood the issues in school leadership and that we were determined to have a positive influence on the system. So, in May 2006, I walked onto the stage at the second Seizing Success conference in Birmingham, in front of about 800 school leaders, and made this speech.

Authentic System Leadership

Seizing Success Conference 2006

As the media have been quick to point out, I am an educationalist but I have never been a head teacher. Because I have never done the job, it is even more important that I listen to what school leaders are saying, understand their issues and find out where there is good practice so that, as a college, we can support its dissemination and identify what might be done to help school leadership to be even more effective.

The National College for School Leadership is engaging with school leaders more than ever before: I estimate that I have talked to or with leaders from about a quarter of all schools in England over the past 12 months. That's about 6,000 schools. Our aim is to be the college for all school leaders and, through its work, help to transform the lives and life chances of the children and young people in this country.

Our four corporate goals are:

1. Develop excellent school leadership to transform children's achievement and well-being.

2. Develop leadership within and beyond the school (system leadership).

3. Identify and grow tomorrow's leaders (succession planning).

4. Be a fit for purpose National College.

I want to focus on two of those goals: the first is about school leaders leading the system across schools and the second is about succession planning.

They are closely linked — and if we get it right, we can address the two aspects together in a win-win for the profession and for children and young people.

System leadership

It has been great in recent years to see a new kind of leader who wants to work beyond their school, and with more than one school at a time, to benefit the whole system. They have a strong sense of moral purpose which says that every child matters, irrespective of which school they attend.

System leaders — or at least the system leaders that the National College would like to see — are not fundamentally empire builders, driven by their own egos. This is not about the Gordon Gekko approach — the guy with the braces played by Michael Douglas in the film *Wall Street*. His motto was invade the new territory, defeat it and rebrand it. He set out to take over and extend his control and empire. In contrast, these system leaders lead by careful relationship building.

The model of system leadership that the National College is propounding is more the Sir Ernest Shackleton approach. Shackleton took 27 men on an expedition to the Antarctic. After his ship was wrecked in the ice, he and his men were stranded for two years, 1,200 miles from civilisation and with no means of communication and no hope of rescue. Under his extraordinary leadership every man survived, not only in good health but in good spirits.

It is the Shackleton kind of leadership that we are starting to see in today's school leaders who are system leaders. Here is what Shackleton had to say about his own leadership:

> Some people say it is wrong to regard life as a game; I don't think so. Life to me means the greatest of all games. The danger lies in treating it as a trivial game, a game to be taken lightly, and a game in which rules don't matter much. The rules matter a great deal. The game has to be played fairly, or it is no game at all. And even to win the game is not the chief end. The chief end is to win honourably and splendidly. To this end, several things are necessary. Loyalty is one. Discipline is another. Unselfishness is another. Courage is another. Optimism is another. And Chivalry is another.[12]

This new group of genuine system leaders are not about empire building and commercial interest, they are trying to create something more akin to a commonwealth or a cooperative — a mutually supportive environment in which every child can be a powerful learner. Of course, tough decisions are made, poor performance is challenged, risks are assessed, behavioural standards are reinforced, pace and a sense of urgency is expected, there is a tight focus on learning and achievement, monitoring systems are rigorous and the direction is clear. But what runs through everything is the focus on the ultimate goal – the well-being of the child. Relationships are powerful and empowering. Teamwork and mutual respect are at the very heart of how things function. These leaders and the organisations they lead have soul.

There are more head teachers operating in system leader roles than many people realise, and they are not being properly acknowledged by parents, the media or the wider profession. Often they do not self-promote as they are too focused on the job in hand. As Jim Collins, in his book *Good to Great,* explains, the really outstanding leaders are often quite humble and self-effacing – not looking for personal glory.[13] As a college, we want to celebrate what these school leaders are achieving.

What kind of system leaders already exist? There are already hundreds of consultant leaders who are providing focused support to other schools – for example, through the London Leadership Strategy led by the National College. Another example is the work of school leaders under the auspices of the Specialist Schools and Academies Trust through initiatives such as the Raising Achievement Transforming Learning programme. Many school leaders are demonstrating system leadership through their involvement with the National Strategies as consultants or school improvement partners. Many of these system leaders are also working with their local authority to take responsibility for leading a school in difficulty or leading a federation or a collaborative or a network.

National leaders of education are not hero heads who are into themselves and their own glory. They are outstanding leaders (in primary, secondary or special schools) who currently lead high capacity schools and who, with their school, can provide leadership and capacity to enable a school to come out of special measures.

Success for our most vulnerable children and for our most challenging schools will only come when all of us in an educational leadership role regard it as our fundamental moral purpose to ensure that all children and young people experience the very best learning and well-being opportunities, no matter which school they attend. Schools in special measures usually need outstanding leadership and some external support to address the issues in the school and to build capacity. My hope for this initiative is that it will attract our most successful school leaders to demonstrate their leadership in our toughest schools.

Succession planning

The second issue that I want to talk about is succession planning.

We face a major challenge of sustainability and succession planning. If we want to leave a collective legacy for the future of schools and learning in this country then we have to do something about it. We have to think ahead – and think strategically – and take some tough decisions. And this strategy needs to be coherent and joined up rather than a list of unconnected initiatives. As Hargreaves and Fink say, 'Sustainability is a meal, not a menu' and 'you have to eat all your "greens"'.[14] We have some hard stuff to do.

The problem is partly the demographics. There is a large peak of older teachers who will retire in the next few years, leaving a gap of experienced teachers. But there is also a problem about the perception of the role of head teacher. Why do some people not want to become heads or school leaders, and how can we increase the number who do?

When other senior managers in schools are asked why they don't want to become head teachers they tend to give seven main reasons:

1. Work–life balance/stress.

2. Personal commitments.

3. Less pupil contact.

4. Less teaching involvement.

5. Not an ambition.

6. Admin demands.

7. Accountability/inspection.

When we ask deputy heads and middle leaders, they often say that the job of head teacher is unattractive.

However, when we ask head teachers what they think of the role, this is what we get: the majority of head teachers are positive about their leadership role – 9 in 10 say they feel confident in what they do and enjoy it (91 per cent) (on a good day!).[15] When we ask heads if they would rather go back to being a deputy, most say they prefer being a head teacher. They say that no other role can have as much impact on the overall lives of children and young people. They are right. For good or ill, the person in charge has the most influence on the organisation.

I went on a rail journey recently to the south coast and found myself in one of those old-fashioned railway carriages with a number of strangers. At first everyone tried to ignore one another. Gradually we relaxed and, after a while, began to copy each other's behaviour. One person had a sweet, so I got out a mint and then someone else had one too. One person went to the buffet car and, when he came back, someone else went and then someone else. Novels were picked up at roughly the same time. By the time the journey came to an end, I swear we were all starting to sit in the same way. If that is what happens in a railway carriage over the course of a few hours, what happens in a school over months and years? Learned and copied behaviour – that's what happens.

If you are the leader then multiply the effect 10 times. They will be watching what you say, how you conduct yourself and even the type of clothes you wear. As a leader you cast a shadow. You shape that culture. For most heads this is a privilege, and is why they chose to be a head – the opportunity to make a difference on a large scale.

What, then, are the solutions to the challenges of succession planning?

Review the role of school leader

We need a thorough and wholesale review of school leadership. We need to consider whether we do, in fact, need a strategic leader in each school or whether we need more executive head teachers who can perform the strategic leadership role in more than one school to enable leaders within the school to focus on the day job. Can federations and collaboratives help to perform that strategic leadership role to make the job more manageable at an individual school level? We need to have models of school leadership that are appropriate for our future, not just our past.

We need to have more realistic expectations of what an individual can do. We need to consider how we can develop more distributed leadership strategies in schools so that senior leaders can take a more strategic role and so there is less expectation by parents, governors, staff and others that they must always see and have dealings with the head teacher.

We also need to see the development of business and premises managers, bursars and a range of other support staff. We need to regard the best of these senior admin staff as full members of the leadership team who have as much to contribute – albeit different – as the senior leaders who are qualified teachers.

School leaders are at the front line of school improvement. Most are doing an excellent job. But they need to have a role that is fundamentally manageable and fit for purpose.

Identify leadership talent at local level in a systematic way

We must avoid national solutions to local problems.

Many years ago when I was working in the north-east of England, an ex-teacher told me the story of when he was teaching in Newcastle at a time when they had student counsellors in the school. One of his students came up to him and said, 'I won't be in your lesson today, sir.' The teacher said, 'That's a shame, why not?' The student replied, 'I've got to go and see the Problems Woman.' 'Oh, I see,' said the teacher, 'but I didn't know you had a problem – what's your problem?' To which the student replied, 'I don't know, sir. I haven't been to see her yet!' The existence of an initiative was helping to create problems that the student didn't even know he had.

In the same way, national top-down initiatives can sometimes appear to be providing solutions to issues that you don't even have in your school or in your locality. Every region and locality is different. The data confirm that. Rural schools have their own challenges regarding recruitment and succession planning, as do small schools, aided schools, schools in areas of expensive housing and schools in areas of high deprivation. What we need is not top-down single solutions but local solutions.

We need to become much better at identifying potential leadership talent and doing something about it at a local level. On average, it takes about 20 years of cumulative development to become a head teacher in this country. That will have to be speeded up if we are going to successfully replace those who will leave in the next few years. We need to consider, together, what more we can do to identify early our potential school leaders and find ways to fast-track their development. If 'Education England' was a business, potential leaders would be identified in their first year in teaching and given managed opportunities to experience a range of different contexts – urban, rural, multi-ethnic, large, small and so on – to fast-track them towards senior leadership. That does not happen in our education system.

Most school leaders tell me that the quality of teachers coming into the profession over the past five years is considerably better, on the whole, than it was for the 10 years before that. This means there is a strong chance that you have greater potential talent at less senior positions in your school than you have at senior positions. They have the potential to become senior leaders but not the opportunity. That is why we need to work together across schools.

This local solution requires genuine collaboration – identifying potential leadership talent on the understanding that the ultimate gains may not be in your own school. The local solution requires us all to take responsibility for mentoring, job swaps and learning challenges for the potential leadership talent in our local area or network. This is a hard one to get right because your own school still needs to be led and you are still accountable, but school leaders who only focus on their own school will not solve the nation's succession planning problem. One of the school leadership team's strategic goals should be to increase the number of their staff who gain promotions to other schools and subsequently reach senior leadership positions. This is a new kind of system leadership, and it has a clear moral purpose.

Stepping up and moving on

The problem is often one of perception. Most of those who say that they don't want to be heads have never been acting heads. They perceive the negatives more than the positives. Those who have tried headship in an acting capacity are more likely to believe that they can do it and want to do it – they become more confident. Senior leaders need to consider how they might create more opportunities for staff to act up and experience a more senior role. Hopefully, as more and more heads become involved in system leadership through the role of school improvement partners, executive headships, national leaders of education, the consultant leader role and leaders of federations and collaborations, this may happen more. In other words, system leadership and succession planning go hand in hand as a way forward. This is the potential win-win I mentioned earlier.

After many years in the role, effective school leaders can become increasingly worn out. Some of this is just about adapting your leadership style. Newcastle United's Alan Shearer was still one of the leading goal scorers in the country well into his thirties. In his early to mid-twenties he outpaced defenders, using the flanks and taking the ball over the top. In his late twenties and thirties he adjusted his game. He knew that defenders were faster than him and that he couldn't outpace them, so he used his knowledge of positional play better. He concentrated on holding up the play for others to break forward and he focused on scoring more goals from inside the penalty area. He used the skills and talents of his teammates more effectively.

Many school leaders are not as young as they used to be. Maybe you can't work at the pace you were able to when you were younger. It is the same for me. So, like Alan Shearer, we have to adjust our game. We don't have to be a superhero leader, working all hours. Our experience brings with it wisdom, knowledge and expertise which is hugely important in leadership. We have to play to our strengths. We have to use other members of the team more effectively. In the end, it is about being genuine and authentic. It is about being true to yourself and being comfortable in your own skin, even if the skin isn't as young as it used to be. What it is emphatically not about is becoming negative and cynical or talking down the job or the profession.

It is not just about valuing the wisdom and experience of our more experienced school leaders, it is also about finding ways in which those leaders, who really don't have the energy any more for the full-time role, can go part-time through a job share or use their skills in other ways – for example, as a mentor to their successor or becoming mentors/coaches for others rather than just retiring. The expertise of school leaders who are coming towards the end of their career should not be lost entirely to education.

Courageous leadership

Succession planning can be done. By working together, we can significantly alter the landscape of future leadership and its development. The system needs new ways of working and new challenges. The job needs to be reviewed and the workload needs to be reviewed, but what often happens is that we cling on to the old because it is familiar.

One of my heroes, Leonard Cohen, once wrote a song that included the line: 'There's a crack, a crack in everything, that's how the light gets in.' School leadership is the best it has ever been in this country but the cracks are beginning to show. This also sheds light on new possibilities: are we going to play it safe or are we going to go for transformation?

Do you remember how, when we were young, we looked up to others like head teachers and chief officers in the police and those who ran the health service? Suddenly we now find that we are occupying that kind of role. Look around you. There is no one else. We are the people in charge. We are charged with leading the next generation of school leaders and future generations of young people. We need to work together if the next generation of children and young people are to experience the leadership they deserve. This can be done, but it will require courageous leadership.

There is an old proverb: 'People who say it cannot be done should not interrupt those who are doing it.' I think we need to get on and do it, but do it together.

Reading this speech many years later, it is clear that the school-led system was in its infancy in England in 2006. We were developing and growing things as we went along. Thirteen years later, there are far more executive head teachers and thousands more trusts, federations and NLEs, and most primary schools now have access to a school business manager. However, some of the new models of school leadership referred to in this speech are still under-developed. It is still rare to see job sharing for the head teacher role and, in my view, although there is some very good practice in places, we still do not make sufficient use of our wise and experienced head teachers as mentors for younger leaders. Although we had some success in addressing the succession planning challenge at the time, the issue is more relevant than ever, as we struggle to recruit school leaders to certain types of school. Moreover, the call in this speech for moral purpose and integrity amongst system leaders is just as important now as it was at the time, perhaps even more so.

Chapter Three
Collaboration –
Its Joys and Challenges

You need me, need you, need him, need everyone.

Lindisfarne, 'January Song'

Imperfect leaders appoint 'skyscrapers' – they know that success will only come through a great team

I felt that the National College moved forward strongly between 2006 and 2007. On a personal level, after 18 months in the role, I began to enjoy the job a little more. I had been too frightened of failure and too overwhelmed by the size of the task to enjoy it much in the first 18 months – though, of course, I tried not to show this.

By the autumn of 2006, the new senior team was in place and I felt really confident that, with the quality of leadership we now had, the organisation would fly. I had been personally involved, along with members of the board, in every appointment of the senior leaders and, in most cases, we made great choices. However, and I find this interesting, in spite of our very best efforts and the wisdom and experience of the people on the interview panel, we still made a couple of mistakes – individuals who had talent but who proved not to be a good fit for the organisation.

I think some of this was poor judgement on my part (and on the part of the others involved in the recruitment and selection process). In at least one of these cases, I think I had misunderstood our context and had not understood clearly enough exactly what was needed. Also, the context can sometimes change quite quickly. And if the context changes, then the skills that you need can change too, and unless the team can adapt (including the CEO), it can create a problem – which is not anyone's fault but it does have to be managed in as positive a way as possible.

I felt that the National College should have school leaders at its heart, with serving school principals acting as associates on our behalf to support talent management, system leadership and leadership development in the regions. We appointed Sian Carr to lead this work. Sian was an exceptional school principal who had also spent a few years as CEO of the Eastern Leadership Centre (which provided National College school leadership programmes in one region).

We appointed nine regional associates on a part-time basis (so they were still serving school principals). This proved to be an excellent idea and really helped us to connect much more powerfully with school leaders on the ground in different contexts. Soon, with the development of the NLE position, the regional associates began to play a crucial part in the brokerage role of linking NLEs with schools that needed help – in partnership with LEAs, of course. Not every regional associate proved to be brilliant at the role, but most were highly credible and effective and helped to establish a much stronger footprint for the National College in the regions.

On reflection, I think this was partly because at the time there was still a lot of top-down monitoring going on in schools – from the National Strategies, as well as LEA advisers and Ofsted – and it was a relief for school leaders to come across people in their locality whose role was entirely supportive and who were offering them genuine help with no strings attached. This was a rare thing in the public sector and clearly would come under threat during a time of austerity, which proved to be the case.

At that time, we identified that the country had an ageing workforce of school principals and that, unless some action was taken, we might not have enough leaders in our schools. We pushed hard on three initiatives:

1. A 'local solutions' approach to succession planning. At the time, this was quite a radical idea. We were still very much in the thrall of top-down national solutions such as the National Strategies. But it was clear from our research that each context was different and that there was no context-free general solution. This strategy was evidence-based as well as, from my point of view, instinctively the right thing to do. We needed schools to work together collaboratively to identify talent in their group of schools and to develop solutions to the potential shortage of school leaders that was particular to their area. Of course, an important by-product was that this strategy also encouraged collaborative and invitational leadership too.

2. The importance of the role of the school business manager, perhaps working across more than one small school, to relieve some of the administrative burden from the school principal and to make the job of school principal more doable and more attractive.

3. The exploration of new models of school leadership, such as federations, executive headships and job shares for school leaders.

This last set of proposals proved controversial as the press reported that we were saying that we no longer needed one head teacher for each school. I remember receiving a very irate letter from a school principal in a challenging part of Essex who said that she struggled to be the head teacher of one school and hardly had any time to sleep, and now I was saying that she had to run two schools. I felt that this had somewhat missed the point of the proposal, which was to try to reduce workload and stress!

As far as my own leadership was concerned, I had a lot of support and wise advice from significant national figures like John Dunford, who was general secretary of the Association of School and College Leaders (ASCL). However, one challenging relationship I had during my first few years as CEO was with Liz Reid, who was CEO of the Specialist Schools and Academies Trust (SSAT). Liz had built up SSAT into a very impressive organisation which had the loyalty and support of some of the best secondary heads in the country. Many of these head teachers identified far more with SSAT than they did with the National College and, in a sense, there was a bit of a rivalry between the two organisations, especially in the eyes of school leaders.

SSAT's annual conference, which took place at the same venue as ours but in November, had for several years been by far the biggest event of the year for school leaders, dwarfing the numbers at our Seizing Success conference. They were favoured by government, and since they gave out large amounts of funding to those schools who were awarded specialist status, it made sense for them to ask specialist schools to give back some of that money as a membership fee to pay for their professional development programmes, leadership programmes and annual conference. Even though I was CEO of the government agency responsible for the training and development of all school leaders, it was clear that, in terms of secondary schools, at least, SSAT was a bigger player than the National College and certainly had the support of the more well-known and more highly regarded school principals.

Over the years, Liz and I discussed how there was plenty of room for both of our organisations to operate and that it would send a great message to schools across the country if we could be seen to be collaborative. Liz was a formidable operator. She once asked me to speak at their annual conference (which I regarded as a great honour) but, overall, I felt that she was more competitive than she was collaborative. In the spirit of collaboration, I invited her to speak at a pre-dinner meeting of the governing council of the National College. She didn't pull any punches in her speech. When thanking her afterwards, Vanni Treves, chair of the governing council, memorably said, 'We are delighted that you have agreed to join us for dinner after your input to us this evening, but our worry is that from what you have just said to us you also want to eat our breakfast and lunch too!' I tried to get Liz on board as part of our collaborative approach, but in the end I gave up.

Later, at a leadership programme at INSEAD (the European Institute of Business Administration) in France, I attended a session in which we were asked to identify our key stakeholder relationships on a grid in terms of their importance to our organisation and their willingness to be collaborative. I placed Liz towards the bottom end of the top right-hand quadrant (not very willing but fairly important). Afterwards, the session leader revealed that the best thing to do with people in that quadrant was to accept that they did not want to collaborate and to stop trying. Giving up was actually the best thing I could have done for both us. One key piece of leadership learning for me at this point was: try to be collaborative in style but understand that this may not work with everyone; sometimes you may just have to decide to walk away and practise damage limitation. Imperfect leaders make mistakes but learn to adapt their leadership to different contexts.

As a footnote, I would like to say that Liz's senior colleagues, notably Sue Williamson and David Crossley, had a more collaborative style of operating. When Sue Williamson took over as CEO I found her to be far more collaborative than Liz had ever been. In the end, it is all about leadership and how we set the tone for our organisations.

One of the things I continued to do was to send personal handwritten cards to school leaders congratulating them on their achievements. If a school did really well in its Ofsted inspection then the school principal usually received a personal card from me. I also sent handwritten cards to every new head teacher every year and, of course, to every new NLE (and to some who weren't successful in their application but who I felt needed a handwritten response). I am convinced that the personal touch made a big difference in how the National College was perceived – as an organisation that was for school principals and believed in school principals.

I remember writing a card to a school principal in Birmingham because she had won an SSAT national award for her leadership. I had never met her but she was clearly an exceptional leader. I sent a card to congratulate her on her school receiving an outstanding Ofsted inspection report and I then sent her a card congratulating her on becoming an NLE. After the third card, I received a response saying that she liked my style. After that we had a really positive relationship. Of course, my aim was not particularly to get her to respond to me; it was for her to think positively about the National College and its work. I was learning that sometimes it takes more than one act of acknowledgement or kindness to win people round, especially if they are strong leaders and wary of those with ulterior motives.

I always spent lots of time visiting schools, but in 2006–2007 I stepped up the process of holding dinners all over the country to listen to the voice of school leaders. We would invite about 20 school principals from a region to join me for dinner. We paid for their meal and overnight accommodation. The dinner always had a focus (for example, what we should do about succession planning and talent management, how to make the NPQH more effective as a training programme, what is the best way to support NLEs, whether the concept of executive headship can work). I would chair the meeting and start things off with an outline of the challenges and then ask for comments and ideas. There were usually three issues to discuss – one for the first course, one for the main course and one for dessert and coffee. The regional associates would try to summarise what they had heard after each focused discussion and I would sum up what I had heard at the end. It served two purposes really well: it helped me to have a better and more hands-on grasp of the issues and it helped school principals to have a voice in influencing things at a national level. It also helped them to feel valued.

Imperfect leaders keep asking for advice and seeking an external perspective

By 2006–2007, Andrew Adonis, who had been the prime minister's special adviser on education, had been made a lord and was now the schools minister. I respected Andrew as he really moved things forward and wasn't as risk-averse as some ministers can be – he wanted things to move quickly and he made sure that they did. I found it refreshing. In 2007, he called me to a meeting in his office along with two people from an organisation called ARK (Absolute Return for Kids) and Sir Iain Hall – a recently retired school principal who worked closely for SSAT at the time but who had been on the National College's governing council.

Andrew was keen to set up a new initiative to fast-track talent into school principalship and he wanted an external organisation to lead it. One of the people from ARK was Baroness Sally Morgan, who had worked closely with Andrew in the Prime Minister's Office with Tony Blair. Andrew asked me to allocate some National College funding to ARK so they could set up this new initiative, which was to be called Future Leaders. I felt, of course, that I should do what the minister had asked me to do, but I was slightly reticent because there was no procurement process – I was simply being asked by a minister to allocate funds from our budget to a not-for-profit company without any process.

One of my mentors at the time was Estelle Morris (former education secretary) and when I told her about it she gave me some very strong advice. She said that I could not and must not do this without the clear approval of the permanent secretary in the DfES. Otherwise, it could be me who would face disciplinary proceedings. This proved to be excellent advice and I duly met with the permanent secretary, David Bell. He considered the issue and gave me his approval, on a pilot basis. Given the rows that took place much later under the coalition government about the allocation of funds without due process, I was so glad that I had taken this course of action. Estelle had proven herself to be a great mentor – she had watched my back.

Later on, we launched Future Leaders at a breakfast meeting at Number 10 Downing Street with Tony Blair, Alan Johnson (the then education secretary) and Andrew Adonis, as well as Sally Morgan and other school principals, including Sir Michael Wilshaw. At the meeting, I made a short speech and said that we now needed a new approach to developing leaders more rapidly into principalship because if we didn't we wouldn't have enough principals. I said that if things weren't going as well as we wanted them to, and the cracks were starting to show, then this could help us to think about new ways forward. I then quoted one of my heroes, Leonard Cohen. Tony Blair and Alan Johnson, who both had strong music backgrounds, thought that it was really funny that I was quoting Leonard Cohen (who had a reputation for being somewhat of a depressive in his songs) at an optimistic meeting about the future of school leadership. It may well have been the first time that Leonard Cohen had been quoted in a meeting at Number 10 Downing Street!

As part of the Every Child Matters agenda, school leaders were challenged to join things up more effectively than ever before, to place the child at the centre of all their thinking and to open up their schools more to the community. At the same time, Sure Start was another important initiative to ensure that young children and their families, especially those from more deprived backgrounds, could get access to support services even before the child started school.

The Every Child Matters agenda was an area of policy that I supported in principle but often struggled with in terms of impact. As director of education and lead officer for children's services in Knowsley, I remembered having too many experiences of unproductive meetings involving large numbers of people from different agencies, which took up a lot of time but with hardly any outcome. I knew that many school leaders felt the same way – they agreed in principle but were concerned about the time implications and the impact. So, part of the aim of my speech that year was to try to provide practical examples of strategies in schools that seemed to me to be really making a difference.

After some tricky conversations with Liz Reid, the development of our team of regional associates, the expansion of the NLE initiative, the provision of our advice to the education secretary on succession planning and the launch of Future Leaders, I was feeling a little more confident as a CEO. I think this comes through in my annual conference speech. For the first time it was mainly about leadership. I was trying to highlight, analyse and unpick the big-picture policy issues facing school leaders that year and give them the confidence to seize control and do the right thing for their school and community. I was also talking about the dangers of trying to do too much yourself as a leader and of the need to celebrate 'imperfect leadership', quoting myself as an example of an imperfect leader. In this speech I began to talk about the kind of leadership that I believed in and about how we were trying to model that kind of leadership ourselves at the National College. The key leadership lessons I learned that year were that I should be honest about my weaknesses as a leader, listen to advice from wise mentors and be as authentic as possible.

The conference in June 2007 was so packed that we had to use overflow rooms, with some people watching the speech on big screens in another room. I stood up, still with much trepidation, and made this speech.

Imperfect and Courageous Leadership

Seizing Success Conference 2007

This is the third annual Seizing Success conference. They have been excellent in many respects, but like all organisations – not least schools – you can't live for long on your reputation (or your last Ofsted). You have to strive to get better.

Over the past 12 months I have visited many schools, across all phases and in all regions. The conversations I have had with school leaders, with staff and with young people have prompted me to focus my speech around the leadership that I have seen during these visits. Not all of it has been excellent – you would not expect that – but it has all been compelling and real. I have attempted to group what I have observed in my visits under six themes.

1. User-centred leadership

User-centred leadership may seem a strange term to use; learner-centred leadership might be more familiar to you. But by user-centred leadership I mean leaders who see it as their core business to connect with the users of their school and to make sure that the school revolves around and serves them. The users of the school are three-fold: first and foremost children and young people; second, the parents; and, third, the wider community in which the school is situated.

Schools are the repository of all society's hopes and expectations. School is the only publicly funded and dependable institution that almost all future citizens will come into contact with for any reasonable length of time. And more is expected of them than ever before. For example, they are expected to:

- Personalise the provision for children and young people.

- Ensure that every child makes progress.

- Engage in more meaningful relationships with parents.

- Ensure that the school joins up effectively with other services in the local area to meet the needs of the child.

These are tough challenges but many schools are doing very well.

When I went into a secondary school in Leeds I saw a remarkable approach to user-centred leadership. For some time, the school had been hosting annual individual review meetings with the parents of each student, the student's tutor and the student to discuss performance and set targets. What I saw was a step forward from that – the students conducting the review themselves in the presence of their parents and tutor, talking about their areas of strength and weakness and proposing targets. Instead of being the recipient of the discussion, they were leading it. They were given the responsibility – and the parents were delighted. In some cases they had heard their child speak more about school and their learning than they had ever before.

I visited a primary school in Manchester in which 62 per cent of the pupils were on free school meals and where in just six years the same head teacher had moved it from special measures to outstanding, according to Ofsted. I was immediately impressed by the unusually rich curriculum and by the number of parents and members of the community in the school. I asked the head what was the single most important thing she had done to change the culture. She said that it was engaging the community in the life of the school, particularly through the use of volunteers and support staff who then acted as champions, not only in the school but also outside in the community.

At a technology college in County Durham, in a tough community context, I saw a school leadership team committed to the principle that no child was to be excluded. It achieved 100 per cent A*–G. Actually, so they told me, it was 101 per cent because an excluded child from another school wandered in and did the exam too!

We know that the older children get, the more the deprivation factor seems to kick in and have a negative impact on their learning. It is understandable, therefore, that some schools try to keep their students away from these external influences by building a community that is vibrant, valuing and engaging, and distancing itself from the local community. You might call this a protectionist approach – seeking to protect the young people from the negative influences in the community. Some schools, however, go further. They believe that it is only by bringing the community into the school that they can hope to minimise its negative effect and maximise the positive.

What about the leaders in the second type of school? They believe passionately not just in the children, but also in the parents and the community. They identify with that community and engage with that community and respect that community. They positively welcome the views and engagement of children and young people, of parents and of the community. They help the community to develop ownership of the school and they believe that they are a better school as a result.

2. Growing tomorrow's leaders

In many schools that I have visited this year, I have seen leaders who are doing fantastic work in growing future leaders. They regard it as one of their core responsibilities and they take a sense of pride in the number of people who have been promoted internally to senior leadership or who have gone on to be leaders in other schools.

For all of the leaders whose schools I have visited this year, the job is tough and sometimes relentless but it is also richly rewarding. The prize-winning author and broadcaster Studs Terkel says that work is about 'daily meaning as well as daily bread, for recognition as well as cash, for astonishment rather than torpor; in short, for a sort of life rather than a Monday through Friday sort of dying'.[16] There is sometimes drudgery in school leadership. But the complexity and the challenge of school leadership, combined with the joy of working with children and adults, provide it with deep meaning and life too. School leadership is not fundamentally boring.

As George Bernard Shaw said: 'This is the true joy in life, the being used for a purpose recognized by yourself as a mighty one ... I rejoice in life for its own sake. Life is no "brief candle" for me. It is a sort of splendid torch which I have got hold of for the moment; and I want it to burn as brightly as possible before handing it on to future generations.'

How do leaders keep that torch burning and influence others? As leaders we cast a shadow over our organisations, for good or ill. The longer we lead an organisation, the more it begins to mirror our own leadership style and behaviours. If we moan, the staff in the organisation are more likely to moan. If we look too busy to listen, they will look too busy to listen. If we look in a panic, they are more likely to look in a panic. If we inspire, they will inspire. If we demonstrate emotional intelligence and kindness, they will develop it too. If we challenge poor performance fairly but relentlessly, they will do so also. If we don't take ourselves too seriously, they will do the same. If they find working with us stimulating and challenging, and they feel valued and they respect us, then they are more likely to want to become leaders themselves and have the skills to be good in the role.

We are all in leadership roles because someone believed in us and encouraged us. The best leaders grow future leaders. Whenever someone moves into a different role, they are usually leaving something they are very good at to do something that they don't know if they are going to be good at. For that you need confidence, which is why good leaders build confidence in others to enable them to step up. They believe in the potential of their staff and they grow future leaders.

At a secondary school in Islington, North London there are 18 members of staff who want to become head teachers and who attend weekly leadership development sessions run by the school. The enthusiasm about leadership is palpable and is modelled by the enthusiasm and commitment of the head who introduced the programme. If even a quarter of the schools in the country were doing something like this and sharing it, there would be no need for the National College to have a succession planning strategy.

3. No set model of school leadership – context matters, local solutions

This year I have seen many schools where the traditional model of one head teacher per school is working very well. I have also been to a family of schools in Sheffield where five primary schools and the secondary school in a local area have collaborated to make joint appointments – where the coordinator for modern foreign languages across the family of schools is a primary teacher, where they have a shared coordinator for sport and music and a school business manager who works across the family of schools.

I have visited a college in Leicester which has been pretty much in special measures for seven years and is being turned round by a hugely talented executive head teacher and a very able principal, neither of whom believes they could have achieved what they are achieving if there had been just one of them. The most powerful thing I heard was from the young people themselves on the difference that the head teachers – plural – had made to their school. This makes me think that in some of our most challenging schools no single head teacher, no matter how good or experienced, can make a lasting difference on their own.

As Deborah Ancona and colleagues have said, we have come to expect huge things from our senior leaders in complex public service organisations:[17]

- The intellectual capacity to make sense of hugely complex and often potentially conflicting issues.

- The wisdom to be able to read the broader local, national and political environment.

- The creativity to develop a compelling vision which will move the organisation forward and generate enthusiasm and commitment.

- The operational understanding of strategies that will turn the vision into real action that will make a difference.

- The financial expertise to ensure that resources and public money are used efficiently and effectively.

- The managerial competence and flexibility to deal with the wide range of day-to-day challenging problems and external requirements that arise in the job.

- The toughness to challenge poor performance and take strong and decisive action where it is needed.

- The counselling and negotiation skills to deal with difficult and challenging parents and members of the community.

- The interpersonal skills to motivate staff and take people with them.

In addition, the public service leader is highly accountable for everything in the organisation.

It is time we accepted that believing one person can and should be this type of leader is unrealistic. It makes the job feel too hard and threatens the work–life balance, it fails to attract people to want to become leaders and, most important of all, it does not serve the public best – in our case, children and young people and their parents.

I support the local management of schools (introduced in England in 1988 and giving principals much more autonomy). We have better leadership in schools as a result. But the expectations on heads from government and from society have increased dramatically since then. Inspection systems, performance tables, the Every Child Matters agenda, asbestos, water testing, the nutritional standards of school meals, safeguarding and child protection, equality and disability policies. The list is endless.

I don't think that we can expect the pace of change to slow down under any government. We have to get better at managing that change and, in doing so, we have to challenge our fundamental concept of the head teacher as the person who is accountable for everything.

Our own leadership literature and research encourages participation and distributed leadership, but our culture glorifies the charismatic leader who everyone admires. And many of those around the school – staff, parents, governors, local authorities, Department for Education and Skills, National College – still seem to insist on having dealings with the head teacher. Sometimes we are our own worst enemies. The argument goes something like this (and it is an easy trap to fall into): I am accountable for everything in the organisation and if anything goes wrong it will be my responsibility. Therefore I cannot afford to let anything slip and I must attempt to make all the decisions. Moreover, my staff already work too hard and have enough on their plates – it will be quicker if I take responsibility myself.

One of the crucial things is for leaders to delegate strategic responsibility and accountability as well as management and operational responsibility. Increasingly, heads are choosing which bits they are going to lead and be accountable for and which bits others in the team are going to lead and be accountable for. This kind of approach to distributed leadership is particularly challenging in small schools where there is little capacity and delegation is hardest of all. In these cases, I believe that we need to look at federations and collaborations to share the burden and to play to our leadership strengths. In independent schools, the second most important person in the school is the school business manager who handles all the HR, finance, site management, health and safety and internal operational aspects of the organisation. If schools had that kind of support, either at individual school level or across a small group of schools, what a difference it would make to the capacity for school leaders to focus on their core role of ensuring effective teaching and learning outcomes for children.

In federations and collaborations, we are beginning to see joint appointments working very well, especially of people such as school business managers. We are also beginning to see executive head teacher models that free up the school leader in each school to focus on the core business of ensuring effective teaching and learning. I believe that many schools will increasingly look to collaborate or federate because they will see the genuine advantages to them in terms of capacity building.

But the National College is not insisting that federations are the only way to go for school leadership. We do not believe in a particular model of school leadership as the only right way. We believe that the right models are the models that work in their context – local solutions.

4. Courageous leadership

I keep coming back to courageous leadership. In these past 12 months, I have seen a number of outstanding courageous leaders who are relentless in their expectations and their belief in what can be achieved.

My wife and I bought a house four years ago and we immediately made a list of all the things that needed to be improved. In the first year we got about three quarters of the way down the list. Then we stopped. Not because we ran out of money – though that was relevant – but because we stopped noticing that it needed to change. We got used to things the way they were.

Effective leaders maintain high expectations even after the first six months or year or two years. They carry on challenging and wanting the best. They understand the culture but they don't lower their standards. Many of the school leaders I have visited this year have consistently, over many years, driven a culture of excellence – even in one case, in Redbridge, where the head had been in the same school for 22 years!

However, sometimes it is good to step back and enjoy how good the school is, appreciate it and take stock before driving on to the next stage. When walking at a fast pace up a mountain, sometimes it is helpful to stop, have a drink and a rest and look at the view.

School leaders can often come across as victims or martyrs in today's culture. If only we could have more money, if only there were fewer initiatives, if only there weren't so many constraints and so on. Although we have to work within the system we have, we don't have to be bullied by the system or be slaves to it. The criteria by which we judge our own schools don't have to be identical to the criteria that Ofsted uses.

Good school leaders believe in raising standards and in focusing to make sure that each child becomes literate and numerate, because without that they will struggle in our world. But they also have other success criteria for children and the school; criteria that they declare and talk about and, indeed, report progress on. Just because it is not easily measured doesn't mean to say that it can't be reported on and given high status. A happy school – a school where the curriculum is so good that every single child has at least one electrifying moment of learning and experience each year that they will remember for the rest of their life.

I used to work in Knowsley and this is what Ofsted said about one primary school there. It encapsulates everything I am trying to say:

> Children delight in school because learning is 'fun'. Their attitudes to learning and their behaviour are exemplary. Attendance is high. The care, guidance and support of children are exceptional and emphasise children's emotional health. Teachers squeeze every last drop of creativity from children. The rich curriculum is packed with experiences that fully engage learners. Children with learning difficulties and/or disabilities and those who speak a language other than English receive support of the highest quality and achieve equally well. Staff create a magical place to learn where academic rigour and emotional well-being happily co-exist. The charismatic leadership of the headteacher drives the whole school team to 'Reach for the Stars'.[18]

We need courageous leaders, like this head, who can take some risks and are prepared to help others to take some risks too. Who consider carefully their context and then seize the agenda and make it work well in their school.

Good leadership – courageous leadership – opens horizons and extends the vision of what is possible and then knows how to take steps to turn that vision into a reality. Leaders often have to take small steps to achieve their goals. You don't get what the academics call 'flow' – when the organisation is really performing at its very best and everyone knows it and is enthused by it – overnight. You need to take steps to get there.

Most of the leaders I have met this year have had to do very hard things. They have had to hold very difficult conversations with staff. Incidentally, one of the worrying things I read recently is that 88 per cent of heads said that NPQH did not prepare them properly on how to hold this type of difficult conversation. This is one of the reasons why NPQH has to change and will change next year. It also means that head teachers are not giving their senior staff enough exposure to handling these difficult conversations for themselves, which is how they will learn most effectively.

Good leadership is not about never having a bad day – we are human, after all. It is about getting up and starting all over again when you do have a bad day because that is what leaders do! Novelist and playwright Oliver Goldsmith said: 'Our greatest glory is not in never falling, but in rising every time we fall.' That is courageous leadership.

5. Authentic and imperfect leadership

The best leaders are aware of their strengths and weaknesses and don't try to be perfect at everything. They understand what they are good at and what they are not good at. They look for people who will compensate for their weaknesses so they can play to their strengths. They look to create a perfect and complete team rather than to be the perfect and complete individual leader. They are honest about who they are.

Let me be even more blunt and honest: my name is Steve Munby and I am an imperfect and incomplete leader.

It is unlikely that we will be able to inspire, excite or motivate people unless we show them who we are, what we stand for and what we can and cannot do. Many of the heads and school leaders I have met this year have been quick to acknowledge their weaknesses, keen to tell me it was the team not so much them that has made the difference. They have told me how others joining them with different skills and expertise were turning points for the school. They have talked about their own learning journey and how they are often embarrassed by some of the mistakes they made in the first year or two of headship. They have shown a complete absence of paranoia or self-pity.

They have also spoken passionately about the importance of understanding the context in which they found themselves and how, rather than going in with all guns blazing, they have thought carefully about the context before assuming that what worked elsewhere would work here.

A good leader tunes into the context:

> ... we have been witness to countless uncomfortable examples of executives who feel that the art of leadership is to give unfettered expression to their 'true selves' in bold take-it-or-leave-it fashion. They typically find that others choose to leave it. Leadership is not achieved by riding into town – cowboy fashion – and shooting it up. Skillful leaders, to continue the analogy, need to get a sense of the town, and to conform enough so that they are seen to be acting in the best interests of the townspeople, so they can lead change without being shot early in the proceedings![19]

Let's acknowledge our imperfections. Let's be honest about the fact that we have never liked that part of the role or have never been particularly good at it. Our staff will know anyway.

At the heart of authentic and imperfect leadership is moral purpose: a commitment to ensure that we improve the learning and the lives of the children and young people we serve. It is at the core of what drives us at the National College, and I suspect that it is what drives all of you in your own leadership. Leadership for moral purpose is not an easy option. It requires soul.

When we set up the national leaders of education/national support schools initiative we asked Peter Matthews, former HMI, to visit most of the schools to quality-assure the applications and especially to check that there was leadership capacity throughout the school, not just with the head teacher. Peter has recently written up his findings on what he saw when he visited these outstanding primary, special and secondary schools.[20] He concludes by saying that several compelling and largely common characteristics emerge. These include:

- They show strong and principled moral purpose in reaching out to help other schools, sharing what they have learned, from highly credible foundations. (I will come back to this one.)

- They are motivated by the challenge of providing the best possible educational experience for young people.

- They are thoughtful and systematic in the way they work, diagnosing the challenges and finding workable solutions. (Remember the small steps I talked about earlier.)

- They earn the trust they receive through consulting, valuing and developing the people with whom they work and believing in them. (Remember that as leaders, for good or ill, we influence others through our own behaviours.)

- They build confidence, capability and self-esteem in the people with whom they work, as well as institutional capacity through growing tomorrow's leaders. (Remember the school in Islington with 18 people wanting to become a head teacher.)

- They have inordinately high expectations, great optimism and believe in success. Nothing less than excellence is good enough for them.

- They are decisive and prepared to take unpalatable decisions if this is the way to provide what children and the community deserve from their school. (Remember the importance of user-centred leadership – absolutely passionate about the children and the community that they serve and being prepared to have difficult conversations.)

- They will find innovative and often unorthodox solutions to both systemic and more localised problems and they will not always follow expected patterns or rules. (Remember, strong on principles and passionate on outcomes for children, but open about the ways to achieve this and prepared to take some risks.)

Before I am accused of lauding the hero head teacher again, let me emphasise (as these NLEs do) that they are part of a team and the keys to their success are teamwork and distributed leadership. This initiative is about national support schools – not just the head teachers of those schools. I am also clear that there are thousands of school leaders out there demonstrating in their own leadership the characteristics on this list.

I want to finish by emphasising the first of the aspects on Peter's list: 'They show strong and principled moral purpose in reaching out to help other schools, sharing what they have learned, from highly credible foundations.'

6. Partnership working

Partnership working has been one of the key characteristics I have seen in almost every school this year – a willingness to share, to give something back, to learn from others. By working with others we learn ourselves, and by supporting others the evidence is that our own schools improve. The National College, as part of the London Leadership Strategy, paired 55 secondary schools in London who were in very challenging circumstances and in need of support with a number of leaders of outstanding schools to provide consultancy, advice and support. Not only did the schools receiving the support improve by more than the London average over a three year period, but the schools which provided the support improved by more than the London average too. A win-win for system leadership and collaborative working.

When we developed advice on succession planning for the secretary of state last year, we said we didn't think that a national strategy was what was needed. Local solutions were needed; school leaders with partner agencies working together to address the issues in their local area or in their network.

We are already beginning to see exciting collaborative developments on succession planning as part of the pilot work. In Blackburn with Darwen, it was a natural move for the collaboratives to work together on identifying and growing tomorrow's leaders. The programme included work shadowing opportunities and coaching sessions led and carried out by head teachers. Interestingly, this has proved to be a win-win strategy. At first the actions of the heads were altruistic in that they were helping to nurture new talent. However, it has now proved to be a really powerful retention tool – experienced heads are discovering that their skills and talents are needed by colleagues and it is revitalising their view of their last few years of headship.

The power of collaboration is overwhelming if we get it right. This is the approach we will be taking as a National College – and always will for as long as I am chief executive. In fact, everything I have been saying about effective leadership is equally relevant to the leadership of the National College. We have to be continually focused on our users – school leaders – so that it can truly be 'your college'. We need to address succession planning and talent management in our own organisation as well as supporting schools on this important issue. Our overall approach needs to be about varied models of school leadership and local solutions rather than over-simplistic national solutions. Our leadership development provision has to become more personalised and bespoke. We also, in our own leadership and in my leadership, need to demonstrate courage and authenticity, imbued with moral purpose.

When a range of leaders in South Africa got together to discuss what might happen to the country in the 1990s, they developed various scenarios and gave them names. One negative scenario, for instance, was dubbed 'Ostrich': a non-representative white government sticks its head in the sand, trying to avoid a negotiated settlement with the black majority. Another negative scenario was labelled 'Icarus': a democratic government comes to power with noble intentions but embarks on a huge, unsustainable public spending spree that overreaches itself and crashes the economy. The group's one positive scenario involved the government adopting a set of sustainable policies that would put the country on a path of inclusive growth to successfully rebuild the economy and establish real democracy. This option was called 'Flamingo', invoking the image of a flock of beautiful birds all taking flight together.[21]

This is an exciting time – there has never been a more important time to be a school leader. We should not be resisting the changes that are going to be coming at us in the hope that they will all go away in an Ostrich scenario. Nor should we overstretch ourselves and develop ways of doing things that are unrealistic, like the Icarus approach. We need to be long-sighted and optimistic but down-to-earth and pragmatic. Most of all, like the Flamingo approach, we need to work together as schools and as leaders.

I am asking you to keep the torch burning and to continue to inspire your staff and colleagues. It is a torch worth bearing.

It is interesting to read this speech now and reflect on just how much was expected of school leaders at this time. The personalisation agenda was at its height – the report on personalised learning, by the review group led by Christine Gilbert, was published in December 2006[22] – and the drive from government and from LEAs to join up services around the needs of the child and to reach out to the wider community was very strong. All of these were very worthy ideals and, looking back, I believe that we were right to aspire to address these aspects so the barriers to learning for children and young people, especially vulnerable ones, could be removed. But when you combined this with all the other initiatives at the time it became incredibly hard to make a lasting impact. This was mainly due to the complexity of the issues and the workload demands made on already busy teachers and school leaders. Of course, this was before the financial crisis, so there was more funding for schools and the national workload agreement meant that teaching assistants were available to help reduce the pressure on teachers but, nevertheless, it was asking a great deal of schools.

The quote in my speech from the Ofsted report shows the difference in the approach used at the time, compared to the more standardised Ofsted language used in more recent years. My own view is that it would be very rare indeed to read these words in an Ofsted report nowadays: 'Teachers squeeze every last drop of creativity from children … Staff create a magical place to learn … The charismatic headteacher drives the whole school team to "Reach for the Stars"!'

Chapter Four
Being a System Leader

When all the parts of the puzzle start to look like they fit

Then I must remember there'll be days like this.

Van Morrison, 'Days Like This'

My diary entry for the summer of 2007 shows that, even after more than two years in the role, I still had self-doubt about my ability to do the job:

> I have been thinking about my own ability to do the NCSL job. I seem to remember last year and the year before over the summer holidays I reflected on whether I was up to the job – whether it is just too hard for me. I am thinking this again this summer. Frankly, I am letting myself get too tired and it's showing – in how I sometimes deal with people and in making mistakes/errors of judgement ... I wonder if I can find a way next year to work less on Sundays – that would make such a difference to my tiredness and my stress levels ... I need to be wise, persistent, focused, collaborative, determined and kind.

In fact, the 2007–2008 academic year proved to be a highly successful one for me and for the National College.

In June 2007, Tony Blair left office as prime minister and was succeeded by Gordon Brown. The new prime minister appointed close colleague and former adviser Ed Balls to be education secretary. To emphasise that there would be an even greater focus on the Every Child Matters agenda, the name of the department was changed from the Department for Education and Skills to the Department for Children, Schools and

Families. Overnight in Sanctuary Buildings (the department's main headquarters) rainbow images were put up all over the entrance area to announce the new integrated approach. This signalled a fundamental change in focus under Gordon Brown and Ed Balls. This was my first close-up experience of how much things can change when there is a new education secretary and a new prime minister, and it proved to be helpful preparation for the outcome of the 2010 general election and the appointment of Michael Gove as education secretary for the coalition government!

Soon after this, I met Ed Balls' special adviser, Richard Brooks, and immediately struck up a positive working relationship with him. Over time (I was still a bit naive then), I came to understand that one of the best ways to influence policy and to make things happen in a positive way was to do it through the special advisers (SpAds). I also came to understand the crucial importance of being on good terms with the secretary of state's private secretary (something which Toby Salt – who became deputy CEO at the National College after Geoff Southworth retired – excelled at, irrespective of which government was in power).

It was through my relationship with Richard Brooks, rather than through more formal channels, that the National College ended up receiving such a strong endorsement for the growth of the NLE initiative and an announcement to double their numbers. The director general expressed his upset with me for 'going behind his back', but I didn't even appreciate at the time that I might be doing something against so-called 'protocols'. I later realised that the very success of the National College created its own problems with some officials. Our freedom to manoeuvre without going through the extremely hierarchical decision-making process within the department and our ability to get direct access to ministers – and, indeed, to the education secretary – was sometimes a source of consternation to officials and created resentment amongst some, who wondered why we got such special treatment. I think some of those officials were pleased when we got our comeuppance, as it were, when we lost our special status and were integrated into the department in 2012.

The NLE/NSS initiative ended up being so successful that it made the National College even more popular with the education secretary. We tracked the performance of those schools receiving assistance from NSSs and published the aggregated results. Primary and secondary schools demonstrated significant progress year on year in their examination results (admittedly from a low base). What was even more interesting was that the schools providing the support also mainly continued to improve in their examination results (from a high base).

Here was an initiative that was relatively cheap to run and led to significant improvements in struggling schools whilst also developing the best school leaders as system leaders. There did not appear to be a downside. It was a genuine win-win for the education system. This was a key part of what later came to be called the 'self-improving system'. No wonder the government began to praise the National College more demonstrably. By the time of the next National College annual conference in 2008, the education secretary had agreed to attend the event in person and even the prime minister recorded a speech to be played at the conference, praising the work of the college and thanking all school leaders for the work they were doing.

The NLE initiative was exceptionally well-managed by Toby Salt and by Di Barnes and her team at the college, well-supported by an impressive advisory board made up of head teachers such as Sir Alasdair MacDonald and Dame Yasmin Bevan. One other outcome of the NLE initiative was that most of the people who were perceived by government as the more effective and influential school principals became NLEs and, as a result, began to connect more with the National College. Thus, with one initiative we began to change two of the biggest criticisms of the National College in the 2004 end-to-end review – namely, that the most impressive heads did not value the work of the college and that the government saw the National College as more of a problem than a solution.

Imperfect leaders acknowledge their mistakes

On reflection, however, we did make a big mistake in the development of this initiative. We were right in setting a high bar, growing the initiative slowly and doing all we could to make it a prestigious honour to be identified as an NLE. But we made the mistake of requiring all NLEs to be principals of schools that had received an outstanding grade from

Ofsted. On the face of it this seemed like the right thing to do. At the time, Ofsted – under the leadership of David Bell and then Christine Gilbert – was widely respected as an independent and objective organisation. Being designated as an NLE was seen as very significant, so we needed some objective and incontestable criteria to use as the basis for our designations.

The use of the Ofsted outstanding grade as part of the criteria for NLE designation had three important drawbacks. The first was that if an NLE left his or her school to become a principal of a school that wasn't outstanding then they lost the status. They also lost their status if the school was re-inspected and was no longer judged to be outstanding. At the time, I justified this because the initiative was meant to be about the whole school, not just the NLE, and if the school was no longer outstanding then it needed to focus on its own issues rather than on helping others. I think that was a defendable position.

The second drawback was even more significant. It became increasingly clear that some principals who led outstanding schools were just not very good at helping other schools to improve, either because they could not understand the context of the struggling school or because their leadership style was to tell the other school what to do rather than to coach, advise and build capacity. They lacked what Michael Fullan has described as the all-important quality for making change happen successfully – 'nuanced leadership' – the ability to flex your leadership to the right context.[23] We discovered that some principals of good schools were far better at helping other schools to improve than some principals of outstanding schools were. On reflection, we should have set the bar at schools judged to be either good or outstanding by Ofsted, and then added additional criteria based on a track record of effective collaboration with other schools.

The third and final problem was that Ofsted changed things so that schools with an outstanding grade were not re-inspected unless there were serious concerns. This meant that some NSSs retained their status even though it could have been 10 years since their last inspection!

So, sometimes you think you are doing the right thing but it turns out that you aren't. Recognising and acknowledging a mistake is an important leadership skill. I recognised my mistake with regard to the identification of NLEs, but that was much later and by then it was too late to do anything about it. The really hard leadership skill is recognising it before it is too late.

One incident I remember well was when we were about to announce the first tranche of NLEs. Sir Michael Wilshaw had been outstandingly successful in his previous school and was at that time the principal of Mossbourne Community Academy in Hackney. He had set up the academy from scratch after its predecessor school had been failing for many years. Ofsted had graded it as an outstanding school in 2006, but it had not yet achieved any examination results because at that time it only had 11- to 14-year-olds on roll and it would be nearly two more years before the first cohort sat their external examinations. It was my role to telephone Michael and seek his reassurance that the school would do well in its exams and that it would not be a mistake to designate him as an NLE. I was really asking, 'Is your school good enough?' I got short shrift from Sir Michael! Mossbourne went on to become one of the most successful schools in the country under Sir Michael's leadership and he went on to become Her Majesty's Chief Inspector and head of Ofsted.

In late 2007, Andrew Adonis asked me to set up a visit to Singapore, in partnership with the British Council, to discuss with the minister and the officials there how we might strengthen collaboration between our two countries as far as school leadership was concerned. I agreed to make a visit and went with Susan Douglas from the British Council, who also worked part-time for the National College. I had never met Susan before but we immediately struck up a great relationship and have been good colleagues ever since. The trip involved lots of school visits and some time with the senior leaders at the National Institute of Education in Singapore, which has the responsibility for all of the leadership development for schools in the country.

The trip culminated in a formal meeting with Education Secretary Tharman Shanmugaratnam. It was a showpiece event with officials sat along both sides of the room, and myself and Minister Tharman in big chairs in the middle of the room, having a discussion between ourselves. I told Minister Tharman that I had been very impressed by what I had seen, especially with regard to school leadership, although I raised some concerns with the minister about their approach to student inclusion and special needs. He said that he was pleased with how things were going in

Singapore but he was worried in case they caught the 'English disease'. I asked him what the English disease was. He said that when his county was created, in the 1960s, it had no natural resources, only its people. The government decided to invest in its people through education and the people responded by being extremely enthusiastic about getting an education. The next generation were also passionate and committed to education and were determined to excel. 'However,' he said, 'I worry that the third generation, who are much better off than their parents, will not value education as much. That is the "English disease".' This made me think hard about the challenge of low expectations that we have amongst some of our families in England, and the kind of leadership needed to transform perceptions in schools where this culture could be prevalent.

Internally at the National College things were going pretty well. We had appointed Caroline Maley as chief operating officer and she was having a big impact. We introduced 360° feedback for all staff in order to reinforce the values of the organisation and to encourage self-awareness. We also introduced 'value of the month' to highlight our values and to encourage colleagues to recognise when individuals were great role models of that value. I had been conscious for some time that, as leaders, our behaviour is always being watched. Colleagues observe not just what we say but what we don't say (for example, they will notice if we praise someone or one team but don't praise someone else or another team). They notice even the smallest things, and it all adds up to create the culture in the organisation. But it wasn't really until 2007–2008 that I began to understand more deeply that developing a values-based culture isn't just about how leaders in the organisation live and model the values. It is also about how we incentivise the right behaviours and integrate these into our systems, such as in our recruitment and induction processes, performance management systems and those things we routinely acknowledge and celebrate.

The National College's governing council continued to hold me, as CEO, to account for our work, and I always felt slightly uneasy before and during every council meeting. By now I had realised that this was a good thing, and that if I started to feel too relaxed at these meetings then something was probably wrong! I was also giving more responsibility to my senior colleagues to present papers to the governing council and giving them feedback afterwards about how it had gone. My relationship with the chair, Vanni Treves, really did strengthen every year. I worked hard at making the relationship work and so did he. We rarely disagreed but when we did he was invariably right. I was extraordinarily lucky to have him as chair throughout my time at the college.

My speech in 2008 makes reference to the National Challenge. This was a new initiative by Ed Balls and the Department for Children, Schools and Families to intervene in, and provide support to, the schools that were struggling the most across the country. In a sense, it was an attempt to copy the success of the London Challenge nationally. National Challenge advisers were appointed to work with these schools and they were also linked to an NSS or other successful school. The problem with this initiative was that the media immediately announced that these were all 'failing schools', which upset quite a few of the principals in those schools. The challenge for me as CEO was to support the high expectations that the National Challenge embodied without necessarily criticising the principals and leaders in those schools deemed in need of support and keeping morale high – hence the reference to this in my speech.

I think that this speech moved my focus on leadership to a new level. This was partly due to my own growing confidence in the subject matter but also greatly to do with the appointment of Michael Pain. Michael was a young and talented former barrister and we employed him to do research for my speeches, briefings for school visits and in general to be my adviser. He grew into the role, but already by 2008 I think it is possible to see the difference in the quality of this speech.

By now, I was increasingly feeling assured enough to challenge school leaders to raise their game. For example, through my reference to the research on within-school variation, I made the point that we could perhaps make better use of expertise within our own organisation rather than always looking outside for examples of outstanding practice. Also, in this speech, I encourage leaders to think about how we can be at our best more often.

This is something I had been working on personally during the year with the help of my mentors. We had begun to work closely as a leadership team at the National College by asking ourselves: what are we like at our best, as leaders and as a team? These and other processes helped us to build trust within the team and it enabled me to be more confident about devolving leadership responsibility and accountability. I used to think that working for most of the day on Sundays was essential to staying on top of the workload. I began to realise that, with some exceptions, this was just not the case. This growing trust and confidence amongst the leadership team also enabled me, at last, to cut down my work at weekends significantly. I no longer felt that I ought to be doing everything myself. By changing the way I worked and by using the expertise of the team better, I ended up with less stress and was just as effective. Imperfect leaders try to build a perfect team and trust their team to lead.

My speech also talks about the need for toughness and tenderness – a theme I would come back to and embellish further in my 2012 speech, when I spoke about power and love in leadership (see Chapter 8). One thing I could not have known when I gave this speech, of course, is that years later Tiger Woods would fall from grace so spectacularly and Ed Balls would become even more famous for his appearances on *Strictly Come Dancing* and documentaries about Donald Trump as he was for being a politician!

By June 2008 we were experiencing considerable success at the National College. The Audit Commission's National School Survey showed that we were, in the views of school leaders, improving in almost every area.[24] I was feeling more confident. In front of a packed conference hall, with Education Secretary Ed Balls in the audience, I made this speech.

Lateral and Sustainable Leadership

Seizing Success Conference 2008

It is great to see that this year's conference is not only heavily oversubscribed but also that we have an input from the prime minister and, later on this morning in the flesh, from the secretary of state. We have certainly come a long way since 2005 when about 400 of us met for the first ever National College of School Leadership annual conference.

According to Ofsted, the quality of school leadership has improved again this year. Nevertheless, I believe that there are a number of serious and significant challenges for the school system in England and I want to mention three of them.

Challenge 1: Reducing variability

According to the Organisation for Economic Co-operation and Development (OECD), we have greater variation in performance between schools than in many other countries.[25] In other words, we have many great schools but a significant number that are struggling. That variation in quality exists is a major challenge to the system.

Alongside the variation between schools is an equally worrying issue – variation within schools. In England this is significantly above OECD averages and is between five and fourteen times greater than between-school variance. Let me try to clarify this: we seem to have great teachers and not so great teachers, great departments and not so great departments within the same school.

And as a recent McKinsey study demonstrates, high-quality teaching makes a difference.[26] If the same children were all taught by the best teachers in the school, it would have a significant impact on outcomes for children and young people.

Challenge 2: Narrowing the gap

The sad conclusion is that over the past 10 years or so we have raised the bar in terms of student achievement, but we have not significantly narrowed the gap. Research from Joseph Rowntree has demonstrated that children who are more able at 5, but from disadvantaged homes, are being overtaken by the age of 7 by less able children from more advantaged homes.[27]

Challenge 3: Enhancing sustainability

Fifty-five per cent of current heads are likely to have retired by 2012. This is a huge challenge to the system but also a great opportunity to further improve leadership. However, we have to ensure that leadership is attractive and that our leadership models are sustainable.

These are three serious challenges. They are complex and they are adaptive – there are no simple solutions, no magic bullets. However, I believe that school leadership has a key part to play in addressing each one. Not that schools can solve society's ills, nor that individual schools should be held to account for obesity, or youth crime, or the fact that deprivation and, frankly, class have such a profound effect on children's achievement. But within these broad constraints, good leadership is making a significant difference.

Indomitable and compassionate leadership

Toughness and tenderness. I have been to some schools in the past year that have been relentless in their focus on standards, but somehow the relationships and social development haven't been given enough consideration – too many of the young people are rebelling and certainly not discovering an enjoyment of learning. On the other hand, I have been to schools where there seems to be a great deal of emphasis on relationships but no driving energy or focus. It might be there in the school leader's head but it has not translated into focused practice on the ground.

However, encouragingly, I have been to far more schools where they seem to have that great skill of getting the ethos and culture just right. There is focus and commitment right through the organisation so the students know there is no hiding place for second best or laziness, but this is combined with humour, compassion and warmth so that the students genuinely feel valued and cared for – even when they are pushed hard or are receiving tough messages about the quality of their work. That's a hard balancing act to get right, but good leaders show just what a heady mix for success that balance can be.

And, of course, it works for staff too. The best leaders know that the secret of success is an insistence on high expectations combined with a focus on relationships, relationships and relationships. The best leaders are a mix of these tough and tender characteristics.

Lateral and inclusive leadership

Our modern school leaders share the leadership throughout their organisation. The most exciting and refreshing schools do not revolve around the head, they seem to have leaders everywhere. I visited a secondary in Plymouth and a primary in Edmonton, North London, and saw leaders throughout the schools – they were bursting at the seams with them.

However, there is a world of difference between distributing leadership and delegation. If it is just delegation, because there is lots of work to be done, this is more like distributed pain than distributed leadership. As Professor Alma Harris maps out clearly in her new book:

> ... one of the barriers to distributed leadership is how leadership distribution is viewed by principals and teachers. If it is viewed as delegation, it is likely to be met with resistance by teachers not wanting to undertake yet more work. If principals or heads equate distributed leadership with an erosion of their power, it will be perceived as threatening and therefore unlikely to happen.[28]

Distributed leadership, where it works most effectively, is neither of these things.

Just as an aside, I would like to speak for a few moments in praise of the deputy head teacher role. There is a commonly held notion that if you are a deputy it is either because you cannot go on further to headship (i.e. you are not up to the top job) or that it is not an important job in itself – it is just a stepping stone to becoming a head teacher. This is a false notion. Being a deputy head is not a deficit role, it is a critical one and an honourable one. Good head teachers know that they owe their success – and, indeed, their ability to lead their schools effectively – to their deputy heads.

Deputies are often the communicators and problem solvers; they ensure that heads stay in tune with their schools and school community. They are integral to making sure that heads know their contexts, make the right decisions and gain the confidence of others in what they do. This was reflected in a visit to a secondary school in Southampton. A senior person in the school said to me that the head was the brains of the school and the deputy was the heart. All schools need hearts as well as brains, and no single person – whether the head or the deputy – can always be both.

I always think that the relationship between heads and deputies is a bit like a finger and thumb. On their own they can do some things, but as a pair they can do great things.

At this point I would like to make special mention of Professor Geoff Southworth, who is deputy chief executive at the National College and is retiring in August after a lifetime of service to education. If I have had a successful three years as chief executive, much of that has been down to Geoff's absolutely outstanding role as my deputy – we certainly could not have achieved much of what we have achieved over the past few years without him. He has been a deputy par excellence. Thank you, Geoff.

We have been working with the social partners from the unions and professional associations to develop the headship standards. You may or may not agree that having a long list of skills, competencies and expertise for leadership is a good thing – it can sometimes lead to a tick-box mentality. Nevertheless, what is great about the current process is that these are no longer headship standards, they are leadership standards. We are not expecting an individual head teacher to demonstrate all of these things; we are expecting leadership teams collectively to demonstrate them. The future is not about super heads – it is about super teams. Modern school leadership is also about lateral leadership – leadership beyond the school and beyond hierarchies.

I also want to say something about the National Challenge. Most of the 638 secondary schools below 30 per cent for five A*–C, including English and maths, are in complex and challenging environments with no instant solutions. Many already have very good leadership – in some cases outstanding leadership – and are making good progress. It is incorrect, as well as patently self-defeating, to label them all as failing schools, as the media has done.

However, we cannot ignore the fact that so few young people are achieving the kind of exam results that will enable them to make progress when they leave school. The key solution is not in local authorities, or in the Department for Children, Schools and Families, or in the National College, or in the National Strategies. The main solution to improving schools is in schools themselves – that is where the real expertise lies. Even the most challenging and struggling schools have good practice within them, in parts.

One of the great lessons from the success of the London Challenge is that the key way of moving schools forward is through effective leadership and through schools helping each other – not in a patronising way, but in a constructive and professional way, with each learning from the other:

- National leaders of education and national support schools providing expert help to those in serious need.

- Local leaders – heads identified and trained by the National College – providing additional school-to-school support and expertise, as has happened successfully in London and Bristol and is now being developed in Greater Manchester and the Black Country.

- The profession taking collective responsibility in a local area for all the children in that area, not standing on the sidelines to watch some schools under the cosh or being labelled as failures.

If we are to improve the system and ensure all schools move forward, this notion of distributing leadership within schools and lateral collaborative leadership beyond the school – in whatever form is appropriate – has to be the presiding vision for the future of school leadership.

Leadership of teaching and learning

The National College welcomes the proposals for a master's degree in teaching and learning, about practice-based, evidence-based and in-the-classroom professional learning. It is right that teachers should be focused on improving their own teaching and that increasing prominence should be given to the skills of improving teaching and learning.

But let me be blunt: the core business of school leadership is ensuring that teaching and learning is effective in your school. It doesn't mean that you have to do it yourself or that you shouldn't be spending time on other important issues that have a more indirect impact on teaching and learning. But it does mean that you should never lose sight of what your leadership is for – ensuring that the children in your school learn effectively and helping them to become the people they might be.

We have recently carried out an analysis of the difference between schools that get a good grade in their Ofsted reports and schools that get outstanding. The key difference is that the word 'consistency' comes up again and again in the outstanding reports. A few months ago, the National College produced a research paper with Professor David Reynolds on within-school variation, based on three years of focused work in schools.[29] It showed that when school leaders seriously address within-school variation it can make a significant impact. Amongst the barriers to dealing with this variation it listed:

- Weak school management that finds it hard to confront the issue and develop mechanisms to learn from best practice.

- False modesty and misplaced egalitarianism on the part of effective teachers/departments.

- Small schools in which the range of excellence between teachers may be less.

- The difficulty in secondary schools of getting departments to see any utility in swapping practice when the subjects are so different.

These difficulties are challenging and it is going to take excellent leadership to overcome them. But school leaders need to ask themselves some hard questions: how well are we using data to raise awareness of the variation issues in our schools? Are we using CPD opportunities well enough to enable effective learning across the school to take place? As far as improving teaching and learning in our school is concerned, are the answers not so much in an outstanding school down the road but in our own school, on our own doorstep, with our own staff and our own leadership of those staff?

One question I am asked about all the time is this: do you have to be a teacher to be a head teacher? (Or, do you have to be a great teacher to be a great head teacher?) Since teaching and learning are the core businesses of a school, my view is that it helps a great deal if those in charge have a teaching background. But for me it is not a matter of principle; we should view it on a case-by-case basis. I met a school business manager in a Plymouth secondary school who is passionate about teaching and learning and already has NPQH. My guess is that he will soon be a head teacher.

What I am clear about, though, is that the best teachers don't always make the best leaders, and vice versa. In fact, some of our best teachers are intuitive teachers – they do it naturally. If something comes naturally to a person, it can be difficult for them to convey how they do it to someone who does not possess that innate skill.

Let me be personal here. I believe that I have good leadership skills, but although I became quite a good teacher, I didn't have a successful first couple of years in the classroom. I recently went on Friends Reunited to see if anyone had written anything about me. There was only one entry, and as far as I know this is the only comment in the public domain about my first few years in teaching: 'Does anyone remember Mr Munby? He wore a beard and drove a yellow Cortina. He was a nice man but he couldn't control us. It is a wonder we learned anything.' It is true. I struggled to prevent students from climbing out of the window in my lessons. I got better, but only because I worked at it, and I was never a star performer.

There are two general lessons about leadership that I learned from this: (1) intuitive and extraordinarily talented experts in their field don't always make the best leaders, and (incidentally) extraordinarily talented leaders don't always make the best coaches of other leaders; and (2) in any walk of life, including teaching and school leadership, it is possible to overcome a bad start.

Leadership of Generation Y staff

We have a succession planning challenge. We have to see this not just as a challenge but also as an opportunity. And to make the most of this we have to understand this new generation – Generation Y as it has become known – those born after 1980.[30] What motivates these people entering the profession, and what are their backgrounds and experiences?

First, they are known to value a work–life balance. A survey by the Association of Graduate Recruiters published in July 2007 found that more than 92 per cent of graduate recruiters believe they should address work–life balance to engage successfully with today's Generation Y graduates.[31]

We have recently conducted our own survey of newly qualified teachers under the age of 26, asking them what they want from their work. A 'desire to help children' was the most consistently cited driver for entering teaching. Generation Y are also technological natives and use technology to learn and to connect with others.

So, they use technology well, are strong on relationships and value work–life balance. We also know that they like working in teams, being creative, and they want and expect to be involved in what is happening in the organisation. They are also ambitious, flexible in their careers and willing to change jobs (sometimes annually) to build up their skills and experiences.

Our survey also shows that although most young people come into the profession to be teachers rather than head teachers, 89 per cent would be interested in taking up leadership development opportunities. And, crucially, 85 per cent claim that the availability of leadership development opportunities will influence their future choice of school.

It is therefore important that we make the most of the talents and attitudes of this new generation of leaders from an early age. We need to create an environment that gives Generation Y the flexibility and variety they want in work. We must enable them to build a portfolio career within the organisation.

Sustainable leadership

Over the years I have visited many small primary schools. This year one school sticks in my mind. It was a school of about 100 pupils – not that small as far as many primary schools are concerned. The head was hugely impressive – she was energetic, warm, focused, determined, visionary and good with the children, the staff, the parents and the community. I asked her two important questions. The first was: how often do you get a chance to meet with other heads to share ideas and discuss issues? The answer was very rarely indeed. The second was, do you get tired? The answer was a definite yes – she was pretty much on her knees.

The big issue for me was that not only the school but also the whole village community relied on this individual to make everything work well. And, make no mistake, it was working well. But what would happen if she left? I wondered whether, given the huge accountability that heads have, the demographic challenge of an ageing profession and a Generation Y who value work–life balance more, there would be another superhuman like her willing to step up.

You may say that the solution is to stop having so many initiatives or that government and the public should stop having such unrealistic expecta-tions of school leaders. Clearly, there are things that can be done on this, but my overall view is that whichever government is in power will continue to demand a great deal from its schools and head teachers – and under-standably so.

So, let's get real. We have to find a better way of managing the change and expectations. I am increasingly convinced that the notion of having one head teacher in each small primary school trying to shoulder all the responsibilities is a model that is no longer tenable or sustainable. This is not just about resources. We should be moving towards heads of school and strategic leaders or executive heads of collaboratives and federations. Not because it is sexy or modern but because it will make the leadership roles more manageable, it will lead to more realistic expectations of indi-viduals, it will be more attractive to the next generation of school leaders and it will be more rewarding professionally. Also, crucially, these models are more likely to meet the needs of children and communities and they make better use of our best school leadership. This isn't just a solution for leaders but a possible lifeline for villages – small schools are more likely to be able to stay open if there is a federation or executive head model.

It is time to think afresh and to challenge the accepted notion that every school, no matter what its size, should have a head teacher who is fully accountable for everything in the school and a governing body which holds that one person accountable. I am not arguing for a top-down centrally imposed model, but I am asking those heads and local authority staff here to talk to governors before a head leaves to help them consider other solutions than the standard response, which is too often, 'Let's appoint a replacement as our head teacher' without considering other models.

Which brings me on to leadership development and the future of the National College. We are now of the view that the most powerful and lasting form of professional development is done by learning in a real context – doing real work with support and mentoring. It was clear from our survey of newly qualified teachers that they feel the same way too: 86 per cent would prefer 'on-the-job' learning to going on a course.

However, we also know that to avoid insularity and the recycling of low-level thinking, and to provide challenge, on-the-job development must be supported by additional inputs, learning in groups, visiting other schools and listening to new ideas and reflection. A ratio of around 70:30 is what we think, in general, is best, where 70 per cent is devoted to on-the-job learning and 30 per cent to offsite and other forms of learning. This emphasis also has the additional benefit of not requiring schools to send out their staff on too many external courses.

Moreover, individuals who have experienced development, and who then return to unchanged schools, rarely transform that school. The culture of the organisation usually prevails over the individual. We have to ask ourselves whether leadership programmes for individuals are the best way to spend public money. We are therefore wrestling with the concept of how we might give greater responsibility to groups of schools for leadership development, with resources and materials to help to make it happen. Not for all of our future leadership development but for an increasing amount of it.

We need to ask hard questions about what the modern system needs in terms of leadership development and we want to ensure that this review is informed by the profession. This is why we will take our recommendations out on the road, to eight regional conferences, for discussion and consultation with school leaders, potential school leaders and other stakeholders. We want to get this right.

I will finish with two final characteristics of effective leadership.

Reducing variation in our own leadership

I have argued that the answer to school improvement is to look closely at other excellent schools and, in particular, at the great practice in your own school and to consider how to share and disseminate it. The same applies to leadership. We surveyed 500 head teachers and interviewed many of them. They say again and again that one of the biggest factors influencing them in their career was their exposure to role models – either good ones which inspired them to become heads or bad ones which made them determined to become leaders so they could show that leadership didn't have to look like that.

On the whole, we don't learn leadership from a textbook or from going on a course. A key skill in leadership is strategic intuition – intuition that has been honed and developed by watching and learning so that you just know in your bones that it won't work if you do it in that order, it will only work if you do it in this way. Those who lack that strategic intuition often end up getting it wrong. In the famous Morecambe and Wise sketch, André Previn accuses Eric Morecambe of playing all the wrong notes on the piano, to which Eric replies, 'I'm playing all the right notes. But not necessarily in the right order.' Leaders who lack strategic intuition do all the right leadership strategies but not necessarily in the right order.

Where do we learn that strategic intuition, and how do we develop it? We learn it partly by watching others, but we also learn it by reflecting on and copying ourselves at our best. Think back to a moment in your leadership when you were superb. You were energised, focused, compelling, selfless, courageous, intuitive. You were stunningly good. We can't be like that all of the time. We all have down times and up times, and it is important that we give ourselves permission to have those down times. But the best leaders are able to be at their best more often because they reflect on it and then they apply what they are learning in a more consistent way. Reducing variation within our own leadership – that is a great skill. Outstanding leaders aren't necessarily better leaders than the rest of us, they just operate at their best more often. That is the challenge for us all.

Leadership with moral purpose

The best leaders I have met this year have been strong on values and passionate about moral purpose. That is what gets them up in the morning. As part of our moral purpose, we have to consider the needs of others, not just ourselves. It is not just about being altruistic; it is about being determined to see all children benefit from the best education possible in order to fulfil their potential.

A head recently asked me, 'Why should I pay for my deputy to do the NPQH programme when he or she may leave the school as soon as they get the qualification?' I was swift to challenge this one: 'Our system will crumble unless we are prepared to develop leaders, irrespective of which school they end up leading. Do you want a school that empowers its potential leaders or one that traps them? Who will want to work in your school in the future – especially Generation Y – if they are not going to be developed and moved on, and even though they may move onwards elsewhere?'

Let me say one final thing about moral purpose and the National College. For as long as I am chief executive this will be what drives us: serving existing and future leaders who make a difference to the lives of children. Not skewing our work to attract funding, not competing against other agencies when schools end up missing out as a result, not blowing our own trumpet. We will do whatever we can to serve you and the future school leaders of this country. Inspiring leaders to improve the lives of children and young people. Building on our strengths and improving on our weaknesses.

There is an advert in the United States about what makes Tiger Woods such a great golfer. It says: 'Relentlessly consistent: 50%. Willingness to change: 50%.' I think that is about right for school leaders and it is about right for the National College. Together we will face this complex, changing and accountable future with confidence, determination and humility.

The direction of travel on school leadership outlined in this speech has gathered pace since 2008. There are now many more MATs, federations and executive head teachers, especially amongst small primary schools. Much more leadership development is now school based and there is a stronger focus on lateral leadership in how leaders of schools and teaching school alliances collaborate together. But some aspects highlighted in this speech fizzled out – for example, the master's degree in teaching and learning never really got going as a national initiative. This was partly because it was expensive and affected by the financial crisis and partly because of a change in government.

On the positive front, it is encouraging to see that the narrowing of the gap issue highlighted in this speech has seen some moderate improvement in the past few years. This may well be due to pupil premium funding and the way in which John Dunford, as the national pupil premium champion, and the Education Endowment Foundation, through its Toolkit, have supported school leaders in the use of this funding.

Also, although the national master's degree in teaching and learning never really got going, the setting up of the Education Endowment Foundation and the Chartered College of Teaching, and the identification of research schools and initiatives, such as researchED, are all encouraging developments and have helped to focus teachers more on reflecting upon their own classroom practice and on evidence-based approaches.

Chapter Five
Authentic Leadership

I don't give a damn about the truth,

Except for the naked truth ...

Just be for real.

Leonard Cohen, 'Be for Real'

In August 2008, I was a delegate on a four-week full-time leadership pro-gramme at INSEAD in Fontainebleau, near Paris. It was a programme mainly for the CEOs of private companies. It felt strange to be there and also a privilege. It is embarrassing to admit (especially as a CEO of a leadership development organisation) that this was the first opportunity that I had been given to attend a leadership development course. (I had experienced great mentoring and really helpful 360° feedback and so on but I had not been on an actual leadership course.)

I found the programme uncomfortable and enriching in equal measure. The highlights were:

- A thorough 360° feedback process involving a wide range of colleagues, and even a separate 360° feedback process to elicit feedback from friends.

- A great session on ethical leadership.

- Sessions on the leadership of Margaret Thatcher, Lyndon B. Johnson and Napoleon.

- Seminars on Marks & Spencer, Zara, the AccorHotels chain and Cirque du Soleil.

- Sessions on understanding behaviour in organisations, including a study of a failing Spanish bank (which reminded me of how national governments tend to work with schools!).

- A very strong focus on the health and well-being of leaders, including fitness and diet.

I realised how lucky I was to be so passionate about my work and to love my role; most of the CEOs from the private sector liked their role but weren't passionate about the work.

I returned to work in September 2008 full of ideas and energy and also determined to keep up my new regime of 10,000 steps each day – a practice later copied by many at the National College including Di Barnes, who soon after this and for many years later did all her phone calls whilst wearing a pedometer and walking around the building!

But two things happened that year to change things considerably. The first was the banking crisis and the worldwide recession. One of the outcomes of this was pressure on school and central agency budgets, as well as a great deal of concern in schools about some children whose parents were worried about their jobs or didn't have enough money to buy food or pay the rent/mortgage. We were entering an age of austerity in public services that had not really existed since the mid-1990s. Very few head teachers who had been appointed since 1995 had been faced with budget cuts, and the same could be said for those who led the civil service.

Later that year, the chair of the National College's governing council, Vanni Treves, and I had a meeting at Number 10 Downing Street with Gordon Brown's education adviser. It was early in the evening as we left and got into the lift. At that moment, stepping out of the lift was Chancellor of the Exchequer Alastair Darling. Alastair was at that time still in the middle of trying to solve the banking crisis but here he was clutching a McDonald's takeaway. It certainly changed my perceptions of what it must be like to live at Number 11 Downing Street. Probably the second most important politician and leader in the country was buying his own burger for his tea!

The second important event had begun the previous year, in August 2007, when a small child, referred to as 'Baby P', was horrifically murdered. An investigation was conducted into how Haringey children's services had handled the case. It was clear that there had been failures in communication between services and that, with better communication and more careful scrutiny, this tragic death might have been prevented. In particular, the director of children's services, Sharon Shoesmith, came under strong and unprecedented personal attack from the media. Ed Balls ordered an external inquiry to look into whether Haringey social services department was following correct procedure in general. This report was presented to him on 1 December 2008, and on the same day he announced that he had used special powers to remove Sharon Shoesmith from her post. She was dismissed formally by Haringey Council later that week, without compensation and with no prospect of being employed in education or children's services again. This sent shock waves around the 150 directors of children's services in England, most of them feeling that Sharon had been badly treated, with some fearful that they could be next.

Early in 2009, Ed Balls asked for a meeting with me and asked if the National College would be willing to take responsibility for the development of a completely new leadership programme for directors of children's services. He felt that such a programme would help to prevent incidents like Baby P from happening again. He thought it was time that the government invested in the development and support of directors of children's services, who had tough and complex leadership roles. My initial response was to say no. I said that we didn't have the expertise within the organisation to do this and that, as an organisation, we would lack credibility with directors of children's services. I was also worried about mission creep – after all, we were the National College for School Leadership.

As the discussion progressed, it became clear that I had given the wrong initial answer and that 'no' was not acceptable. I had been forewarned by Richard Brooks that this request was coming and had already discussed it with Vanni and with the senior management group at the college. So, my second response was that we would need significant additional funding and that I would need to lead the initial work personally (because I was the only member of staff at the college who had experience of being responsible for leading children's services in a local authority) until we could appoint a serving director of children's services to undertake this work. This was agreed. Later, we agreed on a new name: the National College for Leadership of Schools and Children's Services. (I was keen to keep the term 'National College' in the new name and, in the end, we didn't really use the full name, we still just called ourselves the National College.)

This was a really powerful learning experience for me as a leader. I didn't think that the National College should expand its remit, for some good reasons. I was overruled by the education secretary. We then ended up running a great programme for leaders of children's services without, I think, losing our focus on school leaders or damaging the brand. The leadership lesson for me, of course, was that once you have no choice and have agreed to do something, you don't do it reluctantly or bear a grudge but do it with all your energy and do all that you possibly can to make it a success.

Now that we had our new remit we set about developing the leadership programme for directors of children's services. We asked Maggie Farrar (who could turn her hand to anything brilliantly) and a very talented colleague, Aidan Melling, to lead on the development of the programme and they commissioned great support from Deloitte and from the Virtual Staff College, with Anton Florek and Patrick Scott playing key roles. Whilst they developed the programme, it was my role to win the confidence of directors of children's services. As I outline in the speech that follows, this involved lots of telephone calls, several shadowing visits and a great deal of networking. It culminated in a keynote speech at the annual conference of the Association of Directors of Children's Services in Manchester. I worked really hard on the speech as I knew that it was high-risk. Not all directors of children's services were convinced that a leadership programme was a good thing for them or that a school leadership organisation should develop it. One of the directors said to me at the dinner the night before that she felt affronted that anyone would suggest that she might need any leadership development! Having spent four weeks on a really helpful leadership development programme myself less than 12 months previously, I was shocked by this. She seemed to be the kind of leader who I referred to in my speech as becoming overconfident and dismissive.

My speech went down well and most directors of children's services were enthusiastic about this opportunity. This was strengthened further when we had a hugely positive response from serving directors of children's services to the pilot leadership development programme. I honestly think that the leadership programme was one of the best things we ever did at the National College.

At this time, I was also wrestling with two other leadership development issues. The NPQH was now mandatory for all new head teachers but the problem was that too many people had the qualification but were either nowhere near ready for headship or else they didn't actually want to become heads. The reputation of the qualification had therefore been diminished. During the previous year we had redesigned the NPQH based on five principles for great leadership development:

1. There needs to be an opportunity to lead. We learn how to be leaders more by actually being a leader than by doing anything else.

2. There needs to be regular and robust feedback from a mentor, peer or line manager to help us to reflect on our own leadership and learning.

3. There needs to be access to high-quality leadership in other contexts. Without this we might just be exposed to mediocre leadership and end up having low expectations of what might be achieved.

4. There needs to be access to research and evidence and to good-quality learning materials.

5. There needs to be an opportunity to discuss what we are learning with peers.

As a result, we had changed the NPQH quite a lot for the better. However, the other key change that we introduced was that we made it much harder to get on to the programme. Instead of the assessment being at the end, we introduced a tough two-day assessment at the beginning. Only if you came through this well, and only if your head teacher had stated that you would make a good head teacher within a maximum of two years, were you admitted on to the course.

This was a big risk for us. We wanted to raise the bar and to make the new NPQH not just a better programme but, as a qualification, more reliable as a predictor of good headship. But at the same time, the NPQH was compulsory for all new head teachers and we had to have enough head teachers to lead the 22,000 schools in England. The education secretary was holding the National College to account not just for the quality of school leadership but also the quantity. By making the NPQH harder, would we have insufficient head teachers? In the first year of the new arrangements the numbers admitted on to the NPQH went right down. This was a real worry. Should we change tack and make entry easier again? We gulped and decided to hold our nerve. Fortunately, the system responded quickly, prospective head teachers soon came to understand the new criteria and the numbers went up again for the next few years.

The other issue I was grappling with at this time was what to do about the National College's Leading from the Middle programme. This had been going for many years – it was introduced before I became CEO – and was a high-quality and popular programme. It was for those in schools who were not yet senior leaders, perhaps heads of department or subject coordinators. In any given year there were about 5,000 middle leaders on this programme and, largely, we received very good feedback.

The problem was that it made hardly any impact on the quality of school leadership. Middle leaders usually found that because most of the middle leaders in their school had not taken part in the programme, they struggled to transmit their learning to colleagues back in their schools and did not manage to change the overall quality of middle leadership. The prevailing culture in the school will always override the impact of an individual leadership development programme, unless the person on the programme is the school principal or unless the principal is strongly supportive of the whole initiative and it is part of their whole-school strategy.

At the National College, we began to think that it might be better if middle leadership development was led by the senior leaders in a school or local group of schools. If this were to happen, the programme could begin to shift the culture across the whole school, and leadership development would become more integral to the school's natural way of working. If so, the programme would have to take place much more locally so that participants could access it – for example, in school at the end of the school day. This is the new model that we embarked on in 2008 for the development of middle leaders. I think it improved access to middle leadership and had more impact at school level overall, but our quality assurance wasn't always good enough and we failed to ensure a consistency of quality throughout. This was a forerunner of the move towards licensing groups of schools to deliver leadership development, which took place under the coalition government from 2011 onwards (more of which in Chapters 7 and 8).

At this time, at the National College, I was pressing to create more internal alignment across the organisation. We had introduced an approach to programme management through an adaptation of a system called Prince 2 and this had helped. We had a small team of expert programme managers who we were able to deploy flexibly based on need and this gave us more rigour. We also spent some time together as a senior team, working hard on ensuring alignment and consistency in our ways of working. A year earlier, I had introduced a quarterly business review to enable me, as CEO, to have a better grasp of the issues and performance across the organisation, so that we could recognise and celebrate success and intervene early if aspects of our work were not delivering. This definitely helped our alignment as an organisation, especially when we firmed up the processes for it.

In the organisations I have led, I have always struggled to get the balance right between, on the one hand, empowerment, autonomy and trust and, on the other, the need for consistent operating systems and accountability. The more I have struggled with this, the more I think that we can never get it right and that we constantly have to ask ourselves if we have slipped towards too much enforced consistency (which can thwart innovation and disempower creative individuals) or too much towards individual and team autonomy (which can be highly inefficient and can lead to poor practice going unnoticed or unchallenged). Of course, the same issues apply in schools, and I know that heads wrestle with this often. This is now especially an issue in MATs, with many CEOs struggling with this tension of school autonomy versus consistent operating procedures.

One thing I am absolutely clear about is that there should be a strong foundation of clear values and a common mission in the organisation, which I tried really hard to reinforce throughout my time at the National College. If the organisation is really tight on values, mission and behaviours, there is more likely to be trust between colleagues and it is then easier to challenge if things begin to go wrong.

Imperfect leaders are authentic

I had always tried to model authenticity and integrity in my leadership, but now I found myself doing this in an even more conscious way. I was deliberately practising and reflecting upon improvements in my leadership so these practices would, hopefully, become more internalised and end up being intuitive. When I made mistakes, I usually admitted it and apologised to my colleagues; if I didn't know what to do, I would ask for help. In everything I said, I tried to keep focusing us back on school leaders and on improving the lives of children.

I began to personalise things in my speeches, such as the statement 'for as long as I am chief executive at the National College, we will lead with authenticity'. I also ended my speech this year with a poem about authenticity and trust. Since I knew that all of my colleagues at the National College would be either reading or watching the speech, I recognised that I would have to continue to demonstrate authenticity in my leadership – or be accused of the worst kind of hypocrisy. Speaking publicly about authentic leadership helped to keep me focused on being an authentic leader. Richard Brooks, having read my speeches, said to me, 'You are trying to model in your speeches the leadership that you want to see in schools.' He was exactly right on that one, but I was also modelling in my speeches the kind of behaviours that I wanted to see in my own leadership.

So, in June 2009, with the conference heavily oversubscribed and with Ed Balls once again in the audience, I walked onto the platform and gave this speech.

Confident, Humble and Optimistic Leadership

Seizing Success Conference 2009

The future is not what it was. Since our annual conference only one year ago, our society has experienced events that have redefined the expectations others place upon us as leaders. We have seen how a vulnerable child, Baby Peter, was battered to death, and we know that too many other vulnerable children have been harmed or have died. We have seen public sector leaders – directors of children's services, head teachers and principals – pilloried in the media. Public confidence has broken down in those who lead banks and financial services and, indeed, in our political system. A recession is making many lives more uncertain. A tighter fiscal climate will mean greater scrutiny of spending in the public sector and this, I suspect, will affect schools too.

Your leadership is now more important than ever. As leaders in today's complex world, we have many different but critical roles to play – as leaders of people, as leaders of organisations and as leaders of the wider system and community. Together, we are helping to lead the futures of millions of children and young people in this country.

This year I have visited 36 schools and children's centres and spoken with thousands of school leaders. As a result of our new remit I have not only telephoned 40 directors of children's services, but I have also attended meetings for directors around the country. Those meetings have helped me to develop the themes of my speech, and helped me to think about what kind of leadership is needed for these next few years.

Wearing the mantle of leadership

We are in danger of making two big mistakes. First, the mistake of not believing in ourselves as leaders. Being an effective leader means we have to believe in our own leadership, to fully accept that we are in charge. Most of us do this well. We may be inwardly lacking in confidence, but we wear the cloak of leadership with dignity and care.

But there are some who shy away from the responsibility. They are overly concerned with what others think of them – constantly seeking their approval or reassurance. Deep down they don't believe that they are OK as a leader. This sort of leader tends to come unstuck. They end up changing their views based on whoever last spoke to them, and when things get tough – as they inevitably do when managing change – they give in and never see through any hard decisions.

But, as leaders, we are just as much in danger of going too far in the opposite direction. The second mistake is believing in ourselves too much as a leader. Certain leaders who have experienced some success – especially if they have experienced a great deal of success – can become arrogant and dismissive of others. They stop listening and become intolerant of others' views. They start to drink their own bathwater.

Good leadership is about having confidence in your aims but also being comfortable and receptive to the input of others. It is about positively encouraging constructive and considered challenge from within and outside your own school or organisation. Having critical friends doesn't diminish our strength as leaders. It enhances it.

So, who is genuinely challenging us as leaders? And when they do, how do we respond? Do we welcome criticism or new ideas from parents, from young people, from our own staff? Or are those we work with too wary of criticising us or of challenging our ideas and proposals?

I went to a school in the Black Country recently that went into special measures a few months after a new head had been appointed – her first headship. She stepped into leadership and put the mantle of leadership around her. Through her determination and resolve she helped to lead the school out of that category. In doing so, she welcomed advice from a mentor and the local leader of education assigned to provide the school with support. She was a great role model – she showed strong and courageous leadership but she was not afraid to listen to others.

Which brings me nicely to my second point.

Encouraging others to try on the mantle of leadership

Succession is still a serious issue: it is estimated that about a third of head teachers will have retired between 2008 and 2012. We also know that about 30 directors of children's services will retire or leave each year – 20 per cent of the overall workforce.

Not only do we need to develop more potential leaders to step up, but we also need to support that group of new and inexperienced head teachers and directors of children's services and make sure that the transition is as seamless as possible. There is no better preparation for a future role than learning on the job, and I have seen excellent examples of heads developing future leaders, giving them opportunities to step up to leadership.

If we are serious about developing our successors, we should give key senior people in the organisation the opportunity to try out the most significant things we do as leaders – for example, a chance to lead on setting the school budget, to be the lead professional at a full governing body meeting or to handle a very difficult staffing issue. In the world of children's services leadership, this might be to present a key report at cabinet, to lead a potentially difficult public meeting or to chair a significant partnership meeting.

We have to step back if we are to develop capacity in others. What two or three key aspects of your leadership role will you offer to your potential successor(s) in the coming year? Aspirant leaders need authentic experiences to come to terms with leadership. Are we providing them with the right opportunities? And how are we encouraging and supporting people from different backgrounds to try out leadership?

Leading well through adversity

Ask yourself this: when have you learned most as a leader? Perhaps it was when things were going well for you and your organisation. It is always good to have time to reflect and celebrate when things are going well. On the whole, though, we learn most about ourselves as leaders when things are going not so well. It is also when we feel we have the least time to reflect.

When I was director of education in Knowsley, I led several public meetings on proposals to close or merge schools. Angry residents said the closures would tear the heart out of the community; staff were concerned about their jobs; parents were anxious about the potential disruption to their children's education. I learned a lot about myself as a leader during those meetings: how to deal with angry people in a public arena and about the need for focus and clarity of message. Most of all, I learned about the power and importance of authenticity and moral courage. I believe that I am a significantly better leader as a result.

Whatever kind of organisation you lead, you will have your own leadership-through-adversity stories to tell: a child fatality or injury, the death of a member of staff, dealing with staff unrest, a difficult Ofsted report, not achieving your targets, leading a restructure of the organisation – I could go on. In many cases there is no escape from these situations. We just have to deal with them, and we learn about ourselves by how we deal with them.

However, strong leaders sometimes deliberately choose to bring on adversity. Great leaders are willing to do the hard things, to make the tough choices, to put up with pain and difficulty to achieve the greater good, to take action to ensure long-term sustainable solutions, even if it is uncomfortable in the short term. We tackle that difficult member of staff not because we have to, but because we know that in the end the organisation will be better for it. We challenge that underperforming team or that department or that agency because we can see what the organisation needs to look like, and we know it will only get there if we take the hard decisions.

Are there areas where we are settling for comfortable inaction? Are there issues where we are being short term and only scratching the surface, but where we ought to be developing a more sustainable, long-term strategy?

Leading an aligned organisation

Great leaders are skilled at aligning the various aspects of the organisation – the goals, the culture, the performance management and accountability systems, the informal and formal procedures of the organisation – so there is a consistency of approach and the ways of working amongst the staff are focused on the outcomes that are needed.

I have seen real alignment and shared purpose across staff and young people this year. There is direction and focus and collective responsibility. Young people don't trash the toilets because they helped to design them and decided how they should be decorated. Most children and young people choose to work hard because they get more prestige for working hard than for being lazy. Ensuring an effective learning environment is everybody's responsibility in the school, not just the teaching staff's. Standards for teaching and for assessment are collectively understood and consistently applied across the school. The whole organisation is aligned and heading in the same direction.

But this is not just about achieving alignment within the organisation and reducing within-school variation. It is also about alignment beyond the organisation, with the parents and the community too.

This year, in partnership with the National Union of Teachers, the National College carried out some research on great leadership in white working-class areas (in children's centres, primary and secondary schools) which told us that connecting with the community is key to success.[32]

This was brought home to me when I went to a terrific secondary school in a white working-class area on the outskirts of Manchester. The leadership of the school clearly recognised the potential and deep commitment of the people in the school and in the wider community. They were active in identifying those in the whole community who could help to take that school forward. There was a deep alignment and sense of common purpose.

When I got back, I received an email from the head with the agenda from the latest meeting of the school's senior leadership team:

Reading test results and action planning

Attendance results and individual action plans

Raising girls' self-esteem programme

Acts of kindness

Extended schools provision

Post-16 brochure

Look for Loneliness programme

Hampers for Christmas

What a fascinating combination of different agenda items. Teaching and learning is outstanding at this school and attainment is on a rapidly upward trajectory. But it isn't just what is happening in the classroom that makes this such a great school; it is also how the school relates to its parents and community, and how they help it in return.

This year I also visited a primary school in Oldham – a different context but still very challenging circumstances. The head and her team entered into a partnership with the local housing association to help the pupils find ways to improve their environment. Together they had galvanised the whole community in support of high aspirations – within and beyond the school. The children's understanding of the learning process was excellent and the deep learning going on – consistently in all classrooms – was some of the best I have seen. The parents and the community were engaged, the learning opportunities were rich and of an extremely high-quality and the support for children's well-being was greatly improved. This was achieved, yet again, because of a focus on consistency and a real alignment across the staff, the school community and the wider community.

This concept of alignment also applies to children's services. In Lord Laming's report on the protection of children, he said that the structure of integrated children's services was the right one but it had not always been implemented well.[33] He added that there was a need for those who lead children's services to just get on and do it. However, unless there is real alignment between those who are supposed to work together in the children's trust, then just doing it becomes extremely hard, especially when you don't manage some of those services.

Professor Alma Harris, on behalf of the Training and Development Agency, has just completed some research on where the Every Child Matters and the extended services agenda works well and where it does not. She found that the quality of local authorities made a key difference. In less effective authorities, the absence of a clear infrastructure meant that there was an over-reliance on systems, procedures and paperwork to make things happen. This way of working generated backlog, frustration and blame. In contrast, those authorities that were succeeding had realigned themselves to deliver on the five Every Child Matters outcomes, changing structures, processes and cultures in the meantime. They had a single standardised referral process – everybody knew where to go if there was a problem – and a culture of collaboration and trust.

This alignment is happening in some local authorities. Schools, the health services, children's services and the voluntary sector are aligned around common goals. It is not just a collective vision; there are also agreed ways of working to achieve better outcomes. People don't retreat into silos and there is an energy and focus that engages the key players.

But achieving alignment is one of the hardest aspects of leadership, especially in complex organisations. As leaders, you set the tone and lead the culture. Is your organisation aligned? Do the systems, ways of working and procedures (informal and formal) enable your organisation to work smartly, consistently and collectively in the interests of the children and young people you are here to serve?

The secret to a world-class education is a mixture of some top-down, some bottom-up and, most importantly, a great deal of lateral development and sharing of effective practice between teachers, leaders, schools and local authorities. The difference good leadership can make should never be underestimated, and if we get this sharing and distribution of expertise right it can really make a difference to the whole system.

This notion of system leadership – of leaders and organisations working together to reduce variation – is a concept whose time has well and truly come. I am talking about outward-facing leadership; leadership that is not bound by individual institutions but is concerned about the whole system and prepared to do something about it. England is leading the world in this. The recognition by the government that this is the way to improve the school system is a huge compliment (and challenge) to the current generation of school leaders.

This is about the future of leadership in this country: partnership working, bringing organisations and leaders together in the interests of every child, the profession leading itself, local solutions and lateral leadership rather than top-down centralised approaches. If we succeed in aligning these things then we really can do great things together. It is my expectation that the 21st century schools white paper will really embed this notion of lateral, collective leadership to improve the wider system.[34] I hope that it will:

- Formally recognise the role of leaders who lead more than one school or institution, including executive heads.

- Encourage greater collaboration between schools locally and between schools and others so that we can more easily align the system towards better joint outcomes.

- Support a local-solutions approach to the development of new models of collaboration and federation, with the National College having a key support and brokerage role.

- Further enhance the important role that national leaders of education, local leaders of education and school improvement partners play in system leadership. The system leading and improving itself. The best leaders leading the system.

I want to say a little more about the National College's extended remit.

In December, the college was given responsibility for the development of directors of children's services and aspirant directors of children's services. The college's DNA will inform how we shape this – through partnership, through local solutions, through the profession leading itself and driven by our common moral purpose.

This is hugely important work and we need to get it right. It is fundamental that those leading children's services have access to high-quality professional development and support. But it will not distract us from our focus on school and children's centre leaders. We are proud of our reputation for delivering great school leadership programmes and services. We intend to work hard to keep it.

We will also use to its fullest the opportunity to bring our provision for children's centres, schools and children's services leaders closer together, to allow for leadership development across the children's services system to improve outcomes for children. If we can get the alignment right, this extension to our remit is an excellent and exciting opportunity.

Those who lead children's services need great leaders in their local schools, and those who lead schools need great leaders in their local authority. When that partnership and collaboration work well, children and young people benefit most.

This extended work is the single most important change to the National College since its inception in 2000, and to mark the significance of this change we will now have a new name: the National College for Leadership of Schools and Children's Services. We don't want any new acronyms and we don't want you to have to remember the new formulation, so we hope we will just be known as the National College.

Optimistic and cheerful leadership

One aspect of good leadership is optimism – the ability to elicit hope amongst those with whom you work.

This year I visited a challenging school in Thurrock. In her first two years, the head had had to have some really difficult conversations with some staff about their performance. She had worked hard to raise classroom standards and bring in staff with the necessary expertise, but she admitted that there was a way to go. She was still working hard to build capacity and engage parents, and the school buildings were tired. This was a hard job.

We walked around the school and she told me about the achievements and the future potential of her students. When I mentioned the buildings, she said she was very keen to get new ones, but right now they would have to settle for being Lewis Hamilton driving a Ford Fiesta! She was clear about the challenges and the direction in which the school was going, and was optimistic about its future. She also told me that she now had the best leadership team in the region. Isn't it funny that many heads tell me that their leadership team is the best in the region or even the country? Provided that you think you have a great leadership team, that is good leadership. You are demonstrating and articulating your belief in them.

The great leaders, like this head in Thurrock, who achieve meaningful change and improvement are innately optimistic. Their staff told me that, through the bad times, when things looked bleak, the leader had a vision and excelled at telling the story of how they were getting there.

One of our chief roles as leaders is as storytellers. Our role is to paint the picture of what the organisation is and what it can do. We tell the story of what we are going on to achieve – what the future looks like. We help others, internally and externally, to see an optimistic future, a future that they can aspire to and believe in, a future they can help to shape. That is our job.

There is one key caveat: optimism is fundamental to good leadership but it must be grounded in reality. As leaders, we must stay focused on what outcomes matter and know where we are on the journey.

When I was 15 (in the equivalent of Year 10), I was fifth bottom of the fifth set in French, which was the bottom set. A few years ago, my dad gave me copies of my old reports and I was particularly interested to look up what my French report said for that year. My teacher had only written one word: 'Cheerful'. Colleagues, when you are fifth bottom of the bottom set a year before your O levels, being cheerful is not enough. You have got to work harder, improve and deliver. I needed to take some realistic concerted action. I actually did that and scraped my French O level.

Part of our role as leaders is not to be blindly optimistic, it is to prepare people for tough times, to be honest about bad news and the challenges ahead. Some leaders always give out messages of tough times and problems. No wonder their staff feel ground down and unhappy. Others can be over-optimistic and hide problems ahead until it is too late. Pragmatic optimism is the key here.

But in the end, as leaders, we need to have some cheerfulness. If we don't have that – at least for some of the time – we will not be great leaders. I recently saw one of my heroes, Leonard Cohen, in concert and he said that he had spent much of his life studying the great philosophies but cheerfulness kept breaking through. Cheerfulness is an essential element – it prevents our leadership from becoming too heavy and too intense, which can put people off too. Let's make sure that it breaks through quite a lot in our leadership.

Leadership based on trust and authenticity

I worry sometimes that some children and young people are being lost. The child most at risk in our society is the child who has never made a trusting relationship with an adult. The challenge to you as a leader is what to do in your organisation to enable these relationships to develop. Are you sure this happens in your school? Does every child have a trusting relationship with at least one adult?

But it is not just trust between young people and adults; it is also between adults and adults. Does every adult in your organisation have a significant other adult who is trusted and can provide support? What about the trust that exists between you and your leadership team, and between your leadership team and the staff in the organisation? What about the trust that has been established between those who lead schools and those who lead services for children?

If we want people to trust us as leaders, there are two dimensions to address: one concerns integrity, ethics and authenticity, and the other relates to competence and reliability. As leaders, we need to demonstrate both. Leadership is a task where humanity is at the heart. People are intensely motivated by the personal relationships they have with their leaders and by being recognised for what they are trying to achieve. People in organisations are ultimately driven by two things – the need to be admired and the need to be understood

The leaders who elicit the best performance from their staff are those who can make everyone know that they matter. The worst kind of leaders are always looking over your shoulder when they are talking to you to see if anyone more important is walking into the room.

Conclusion

There are tough times ahead. The order of the day for all of us will no doubt be efficiency savings, focus and impact. I am up for that – it is only right that in times of hardship the public expect greater value for money, as well as services that are able to respond to social challenges and prepare us for a more sustainable future.

But this can also be a time of innovation. That too is the mark of good leadership. At a time of austerity it is easy to go for across the board cuts. It is harder to think through ways of being more efficient and imaginative in how we deliver within a tighter budget. But in doing so, we should be working with colleagues to think through the solutions now so we don't rush rash decisions later.

How should we deal with the challenges ahead? Well, each leader must do what is right in their own context, but I hope that it will include:

- Wearing the mantle of leadership with dignity and with humility.

- Drawing on all the talents from within and beyond your organisation, and encouraging others to wear the mantle of leadership too.

- Providing strong, determined and aligned leadership through adversity.

- Leading with optimism and cheerfulness and telling the story.

- Building capacity and trust through authentic leadership.

These approaches need to be deeply integrated. It is a meal, not a menu.[35]

I said at the beginning that the future is not what it was. But the future can be thought of in two ways – either as a place which is predetermined or as a place we can shape. We are only just beginning to realise and understand what can be achieved for every child and young person if we align things within and across our organisations so that our collective focus is on their individual outcomes. We can set a 'new order' of alignment and achieve what in the past we haven't even thought possible. This new leadership – beyond organisation, beyond hierarchies – may seem daunting to some but it is possible and it is the future. There are an increasing number of leaders who are already making it a reality.

Before 1954, almost everyone in the world of sport was of the view that it was not humanly possible to run a mile in under four minutes. Roger Bannister proved everyone wrong. But the really interesting point is this: within 18 months, 54 people had done the same thing and half a century later it is the standard of all male professional middle-distance runners. Working together, we can create and shape our future and set new standards in our own and in our collective leadership.

Finally, for as long as I am chief executive at the National College, we will lead with authenticity. We will hold on to our values and our principles, stay focused on what we do best, and lead with genuineness and integrity. What people want most of all from their leaders is to trust them and for them to stay true.

Let me finish with a poem that encapsulates this:

The Contract
A word from the led
And in the end we follow them –
not because we are paid,
not because we might see some advantage,
not because of the things they have accomplished,
not even because of the dreams they dream
but simply because of who they are:
the man, the woman, the leader, the boss,
standing up there when the wave hits the rock,
passing out faith and confidence like life jackets,
knowing the currents, holding the doubts,
imagining the delights and terrors of every landfall;
captain, pirate, and parent by turns,
the bearer of our countless hopes and expectations.
We give them our trust. We give them our effort.
What we ask in return is that they stay true.

William Ayot

Let's stay true and earn that trust. Thank you.

This speech was made less than a year before the general election of 2010, so most of the new policy issues that I make reference to have proven to be of limited relevance. The white paper on 21st century schools was indeed published and, with its focus on a pupil guarantee, a parent guarantee, a broad curriculum entitlement, a balanced scorecard for school accountability and the expansion of academies and of trusts, it was potentially groundbreaking. But it was barely published before a new government changed things.

One really interesting comment in the speech is that I say that England is leading the world in lateral system leadership – leaders leading beyond their school. I think that was true then and in many ways it is even more true now. What is not true now is that schools like the secondary in the white working-class area of Manchester are likely to get an outstanding judgement from Ofsted. Since 2012, that particular school has been judged inadequate, as the Ofsted focus moved towards more hard-edged outcomes and has valued less the Every Child Matters agenda and 'acts of kindness'.

Chapter Six
Leadership at Times of Change

You'd better start swimmin' or you'll sink like a stone

For the times they are a-changin'.

Bob Dylan, 'The Times They Are A-Changin''

This diary entry from 2 January 2010 sums up the challenges of 2009–2010 for me and for the National College:

> 2010 is going to be a year of uncertainty and a test of my leadership. It is going to be a tough one for me – possibly even traumatic. By next summer we will have a new government – probably a Conservative one. It will inevitably mean change for the National College. If we survive (and I think we will) we may be merged with the Training and Development Agency or we may lose responsibility for children's services leadership, or we may have our budget cut significantly, or we may be asked to do some things that I don't agree with. Trying to hold on to moral purpose whilst at the same time being politically astute is going to be a real challenge.

It turned out to be quite prophetic since each one of these predictions came to pass, some more quickly than others!

In the autumn of 2009, with the general election only eight or nine months away and the Conservatives holding a 10-point lead in the opinion polls, we were determined to do all we could to influence the Conservative Party, especially Michael Gove (the shadow education minister) and Nick Gibb (the shadow schools minister). We knew that Michael Gove was no fan of so-called 'quangos' (a generic term used to describe non-departmental public bodies such as the National College). Moreover, he believed that the size of the state and the civil service had grown too big under the Labour government. We also knew that although the National College was supported by a large number of school principals, including many of the most influential, it had been closely associated with New Labour and was therefore a possible target for closure, or at least for radical change in its role and function.

We organised seminars at the National College and in London to discuss the future of school and children's services leadership. We invited to attend and to speak those thinkers and educationalists who were known to be favoured by the Conservatives. This would enable us to understand more what the Conservative Party's thinking might be on education and, hopefully, get the message back to Michael Gove that the National College could be a positive benefit to any new government.

By this time, I had a new mentor – Sir Michael Barber. Michael had been really helpful to me and generous with his advice when he was head of the Prime Minister's Delivery Unit. When he had later gone on to be a partner at McKinsey, he and his colleagues had provided the National College with some external challenge and support. I was delighted that Michael agreed to mentor me. He was another of my education heroes. I was a huge admirer of his analytical skills and his reading of situations, as well as of his humour and honesty. I knew that he would be invaluable in providing me with wise and politically astute advice, and that proved absolutely to be the case.

The Civil Service Code, which was strongly enforced by the Prime Minister's Office, stated that no civil servants were allowed to have meetings with Michael Gove or Nick Gibb until directly before the general election. I was not aware of this at the time, or that it applied to people in non-departmental public bodies, like me, so in October 2011, Vanni Treves and I had a rather surreal meeting with Michael Gove and his adviser, Dominic Cummings. It took place in the Portcullis House cafe. (Portcullis House is where most MPs have their offices but shadow ministers do not have big offices so the cafe meant we had more room.)

Vanni and I did our best to communicate what the college did and the important role it played. We talked a lot about the NLE initiative (which we knew he would like) and the role that the National College had played in the very successful London Challenge. We described the National College as being like Sandhurst but for school leaders. This was a phrase Tony Blair had used years before. We argued that no government would think of closing down Sandhurst and nor should any government consider closing down the National College. Michael Gove was charming and listened intently, but Dominic Cummings looked bored and left early. Meanwhile, off the radar, Toby Salt was having drinks and informal chats with Nick Gibb, since they both lived quite near to each other in West Sussex.

Once I realised that the ban on contact with opposition parties applied to me and to colleagues at the National College, we had to be much more careful and rely on people like Vanni to meet with them. This was not the first time, and it wouldn't be the last, that Vanni's influence proved to be very significant.

The general election took place in May 2010, and David Cameron, the leader of the Conservatives, became prime minister of a coalition government with the Liberal Democrats. Michael Gove was appointed secretary of state for education and Nick Gibb became the schools minister. The Department for Children, Schools and Families was renamed the Department for Education, and all of the rainbow posters in Sanctuary Buildings were taken down overnight. I was there to see the new education secretary enter the building to rapturous applause from the civil servants gathered in the main atrium.

This kind of behaviour from civil servants is something that both shocks and impresses me. Civil servants will be completely loyal to one secretary of state, falling over themselves to advise, protect and support him or her, then they will immediately switch enthusiastic allegiance to a new secretary of state, who may well want to undo all of the work of the previous incumbent. I understand how this forms the very bedrock of an independent civil service, but I must admit that I struggle with it personally – which is one of the reasons why I found it very difficult when I became a civil servant in 2012.

There was significant concern amongst school and children's services leaders as to what the new education agenda would be. We all anticipated a big shake-up but we weren't sure exactly what would happen.

Almost immediately, Michael Gove announced that the General Teaching Council (GTC) would close and so would the British Educational Communications and Technology Agency (BECTA) (which supported the use of technology in schools). We wondered if the National College would be the next quango selected for closure.

Everything went silent. There were no replies to my emails to senior officials or to special advisers. During this period, I often adopted a new strategy to try to get information. I would walk into Sanctuary Buildings (headquarters of the newly renamed Department for Education) and stand near the lifts. I would then lean on the bannister overlooking the atrium and cafe area pretending to be on my mobile phone. If someone important who might know something walked past, I would casually ask them if there was any news.

By now we were only three weeks away from the annual Seizing Success conference. We had planned a VIP dinner for many of the most influential educationalists in the country the night before the conference, and we were keen that the new education secretary should attend the dinner and then make a speech to the conference the next morning, as Ed Balls had done for the previous two years.

One day as I was once again loitering on the balcony in the Department for Education, in walked Sam Freedman (policy adviser to the education secretary) followed by the secretary himself. I stopped them and asked Michael Gove if he was coming to our conference, and whether he would speak at it and also come to the VIP dinner. He said yes. I went away very much encouraged and worked on the final preparations for my speech. I knew that it would be by far the most important speech I had made in my professional life.

There was a great turnout at the VIP dinner. Almost every single significant educationalist was present. After the main course, Vanni Treves made a speech. He thanked Michael Gove for attending the dinner and said that the National College had been wondering what our fate would be under the new coalition government. He said that since Michael Gove had announced that the GTC and BECTA were going to close, and hadn't said anything about the future of the National College, he was going to take it as a positive sign, especially since the education secretary had also agreed to join us for dinner. 'But,' he added, 'the thought has occurred to us that maybe this is his strategy: have dinner with us the night before and then announce our closure in the morning!' Vanni continued, 'We asked our colleagues at the GTC and BECTA whether the education secretary had had dinner with them the night before he announced their demise. Fortunately for us they said that he did not. So, we are very much looking forward to hearing what you have to say to us in your conference speech tomorrow morning.'

Michael Gove took this speech in good heart and said that having dinner together was not always a positive sign of support. He declared that his family are from Scotland and are related to the Campbell family, who provided hospitality for the MacDonalds at Glencoe – and then massacred them in their beds overnight! The education secretary was absolutely charming that evening and I felt a bit more optimistic that he would probably be supportive at the conference in the morning.

The Seizing Success conference was of the utmost importance in 2010. It was going to host the first major conference speech by the new education secretary. I would be speaking first and Michael Gove, who would be in the audience, would be following on immediately after me. The school and children's services leaders present would all be feeling uncertain about the future. What could I say to help and inspire them whilst not alienating the new education secretary? How would everyone respond to what the new education secretary would be saying? How could I find the right words for this unique occasion?

For some time, I had been reflecting on the concept of leadership as service or 'servant leadership'. This kind of leadership is about leading with humility. It is about being driven not by ego or power for its own sake, but by moral purpose. Servant leadership challenges the orthodoxy of the strong hero head teacher powerfully driving things forward in a charismatic way, and instead considers how leaders focus on meeting the needs of others and on doing the right thing. I concluded that if I chose servant leadership as the focus of my speech, it would enable me to talk about leadership as public service.

All of us who work in the public sector are public servants and whether we agree or disagree with a particular government's policies, we need to respect the fact that they are the democratically elected government of the day and have a right to change policy in education in ways that they see fit. Our job as leaders is to challenge, to question and to influence when we can, but once the proposals have become law, we are responsible for implementing those policies. But there is an even higher call upon us as servant leaders – namely, the importance of leading with moral purpose and, within the boundaries of the law, doing the right thing for the children and young people whose needs we serve.

I struggled with this speech more than any other. I worried in case the delegates at the conference might interpret servant leadership as weak or subservient leadership. I worried that people might think I was saying that we had to change our views on everything now that we had a new government and, like civil servants, enthusiastically do whatever the new education secretary demanded. This is why I also wanted to get into this speech that we not only serve the government of the day as public servants, but we also we have a moral duty as servant leaders to do the right thing to meet the needs of the children and young people in our schools. This is leadership with a moral purpose, leadership that shows humility and selflessness, leadership that puts others first – our colleagues, of course, but most of all the students.

Fundamentally, this speech was very personal for me. I had to decide how I, as a leader and as CEO of the National College, could show leadership at this time. I knew that new education policies could be introduced that I might find uncomfortable or be unable to support. But I was a public servant – funded by taxpayers and accountable to the elected government of the day. How could I lead and model the kind of leadership that was now needed?

On a June morning in Birmingham, I knew that I was speaking as much to myself as I was to the delegates when, having had very little sleep, I stood up in front of a very full conference hall, with an unprecedented 2,000 delegates in attendance and the media lined up in the front row, and made this speech.

Servant Leadership

Seizing Success Conference 2010

A few weeks ago, I visited the old Apprentice House at Styal, in Cheshire. The children who lived there almost 200 years ago – many as young as 8 – had a harsh life: 14-hour days working in the mill, six days a week, sleeping two to a bed and 60 to a room. But there was one thing that was relatively new: they had the chance to go to school for a few hours on Sundays. This marked an important change in their lives and the lives of many other children. Instead of their childhood being entirely dedicated to serving adults, increasingly some adults were dedicating their lives to serving them. This was the early beginnings of public service in education.

Over time, the right to education and learning became universal. And great professions emerged – teachers, social workers, general practitioners, nurses and others – passing on the baton and continuing the journey to improve the education, health and well-being of children and young people.

Our work today may seem very different to those Sunday school teachers of the 19th century, and maybe the phrase 'a life dedicated to the service of others' isn't the sort of language we regularly use in our competitive individualised world. But being a leader in schools, children's centres or children's services is not a take-it-or-leave-it kind of job. We work not just to earn money; we also work because we are committed to making a difference to children's lives.

The new government is clear that it wants school leaders and all those leading services for children to be more enterprising in the years ahead, creating new ways of doing things in the interests of children and parents, and taking even greater responsibility for narrowing the gaps between the haves and have-nots. As leaders, we are more than ready to step up to the task. However, in order to succeed we must retain the strong notion of leadership as service.

What is leadership as service or, as we might call it, servant leadership? It is absolutely not subservient leadership based on some Victorian upstairs–downstairs concept. It is fundamentally about a mindset. Instead of saying, 'What do I want?' these leaders ask themselves, 'What is wanted of me?' They lead with moral purpose. They see it as their fundamental duty to do everything in their power to act in the interests of those they serve – in our case, children, young people and their families. They become leaders because they believe that one of the best ways to make a difference is to lead.

Leadership as service is not just the prerogative of the public sector. Some of our best business and sports leaders have a deep faith in the people they serve and a commitment to making a positive difference to people's lives.

Those leaders who are driven by serving children and families possess a number of important characteristics. They:

- Develop others.
- Are careful stewards of resources.
- Understand the context of those they serve and manage change well.
- Are learners.
- Collaborate.
- Are resilient.
- Hold courageous conversations.

These qualities – which are at the heart of servant leadership – are going to be more important than ever in the coming months and years.

Empowering and developing others

In the past year, I have visited more than 40 schools and four children's centres, and I have shadowed or spent time with six directors of children's services and their teams. Again and again, I have seen leadership that is a demonstration of leadership as service.

One stunning primary school was in Bourne, Lincolnshire. Every classroom was buzzing with children who were engaged and enthusiastic. Standards were high. The relationships between children and their parents and the school were terrific. It was obvious that every member of staff was focused on serving the children, but the head teacher was not only serving the children but also the team around her. It appeared that most of her efforts were focused on giving her staff the right tools and professional development so that they could lead and take responsibility.

I've talked about legacy leadership in previous speeches – planning so that the torch is passed on to others – but great leaders who develop others tend to be servant leaders because they focus on the needs of others.

At Weatherhead High School in the Wirral, the primary role of the assistant head was to lead professional development. I was struck by the belief she had in her colleagues and in young people, and the enthusiasm she had for what they could achieve. The school had produced its own development framework for staff and was delivering much of its own training. It was also working with the local authority to deliver the framework to other schools. It felt like almost everyone on that school staff was supporting and encouraging someone else to get better.

If our leadership is all about the difference we make, rather than our own self-importance, then we will be quick to empower others and push them forward, to give our colleagues the credit for what they do and to be constantly looking for ways to develop the talent in our organisation. In almost every school or children's centre or children's services department I have been to this year, the leaders have been insistent that I meet their teams and hear about the great work those teams have done.

Of course, there are some things that you have to front as a leader, but the servant leader is quick to find ways for others in their team to be in the limelight and to receive the accolades.

Being careful stewards of the resources available

The £170 billion budget deficit is the great challenge of our time and every public sector leader will need to address it. Meanwhile, the families and children we serve are also having to deal with increased financial and social pressures.

If you have been a head teacher for less than 10 years and your school has not had falling rolls, you won't have experienced these challenges before. I have great hope that the pupil premium will help to make things more manageable and ensure that disadvantaged pupils do not lose out. However, about 25 per cent of schools are already funded at the minimum funding guarantee and 3 per cent of primary schools and 9 per cent of secondary schools are already operating at a deficit. Even a small reduction in funding will be hard.

Meanwhile, local authorities are planning for significant reductions to the funding they receive from central government. As budgets are reduced and the commissioning role of the director of children's services becomes even stronger, with less responsibility as a direct provider of services, the need to support our most vulnerable children will be paramount. I hope that schools will work together to play an active part in supporting those children.

Arm's length bodies and agencies, like the National College, have either been closed or are having to make significant cuts, with the college losing £16 million this year. This will mean redundancies as well as reductions in what we are able to do.

But let me focus on the school efficiency agenda and its implications for leadership. Across all schools, an average of 54 per cent of expenditure is spent on teachers, 26 per cent on other staff costs (including support teachers), with the remaining 20 per cent on non-employee related items. This means there may be a need to look for efficiencies in the non-staffing budget.

One interesting question, then, is whether federations and collaborations can reduce costs. There is now compelling evidence from 37 school business director projects that clustering and pooling resources to recruit and share a business manager across groups of primary schools could potentially achieve gross financial savings of £277 million if these clusters were to be developed nationally.

Core staffing cuts will increasingly need to be considered, including the size of school leadership teams. The average secondary school now has five deputy or assistant heads compared with 3.4 in 2001. This growth has partly been to accommodate the increasing demands placed on autonomous schools, but it is an area that heads and governors will want to consider if they need to reduce costs, and, given the age profile of the senior teams in schools, may be an attractive place to look for savings. However, the downside is that it will significantly increase the pressure on heads (more may choose to retire early), worsen the negative perceptions of headship and may reduce the pool of potential leaders on senior teams ready to step up to headship.

What this means is that we will need to make sure that our senior teams provide value for money, that we are not carrying any passengers and that we make the best use of our teams, as individual leaders for their areas and as a collective team. The kind of curriculum that we offer will also need to be considered. It will require significant expertise in curriculum-based budgeting and a real grasp of individual lesson costs.

But this is not just about understanding our budgets better. It is also about developing bold new ways of doing things, to identify at a local level new models for working that are less about top-down standardisation and more about people working together to make a difference. We can get ideas from the front line. In schools, teachers, support staff, midday supervisors, governors, parents and young people themselves may well have great ideas to save money that we haven't considered.

Understanding the context of the people we serve and managing change well

Change is not new. Indeed, the Romans had their own mantra: *Tempora mutantur, nos et mutamur in illis* (Times change, and we change with them). I thought that with the secretary of state in the audience it would be a good idea to use some Latin!

In times of change and uncertainty we, as leaders, need to be really good at reading our context and knowing when to be transformational and when to focus on gradual improvement. Many academy leaders have done this well, but not all. In the early days of the academies movement there was a big push from government to appoint innovative and creative leaders. In some cases this fell down badly. What was usually needed in those first few years was not innovation and creativity but leadership that could ensure the basics were done well – restoring order and managing behaviour. There needed to be a focus on teaching and learning, and people needed to be held to account for their performance. Some of those early leaders of academies did not survive.

Nevertheless, I believe that outstanding school leaders are nearly always great risk-takers and creative leaders. The key is knowing what to change and what to leave and, crucially, when the timing is right.

This brings me back to servant leadership. Servant leaders demonstrate a deep understanding of their context. They identify with the children and the communities they are working in and they do what is right for them. And because they understand the need to take people with them, they are good at managing complexity and change.

None of us need to be surprised by what happens when we lead change. We understand that some will be enthusiastic adaptors and activists, others willing participants, yet others bystanders and some will be opposers. We can expect that some people will hold on to the way things have been done in the past and will grieve over the change. This is why, as leaders, we need to be good at celebrating endings before moving on. Others need to see some manageable steps for the change and require leaders who will scaffold the change and help them to understand what is happening.

Others need to see the outcomes clearly – what the change will do – and need the leader to be the vision keeper. People will support the hardest changes if they can see that they are conducive to the progress they wish to see. And they are far more likely to support the change if they have trust in you and in your leadership.

The big challenge for many of us is that we have led successfully in times of plenty. Can we lead successfully in this new environment? Are we up for the challenge, or are we just a one-trick pony unable to adapt to a new context?

Being a learner

I wonder why so many people, especially in the media, seem to think that leadership skills are in a different category from teaching, musical or scientific skills or sporting prowess. Many imply that it is intuitive – you are either a leader or you are not. It is not about practice; it is about instinct. Indeed, some believe that getting better as a leader is like getting taller in adulthood – impossible. But becoming a better leader never ends. It needs to be constantly striven for and practised.

The best leader keeps driving forward, as a leader, learner and reflector; as someone who, as it were, 'works out' in their leadership and rehearses and tries out new ways of doing things. Having a bad day, reflecting upon it and then coming into work the next day optimistic again – even when you don't feel like it – is what leadership is all about.

And, of course, we learn most about our leadership from others, which brings me on to my next theme.

Being collaborative

One of the great things about the developments in school leadership in recent years has been school-to-school support. We have the second most devolved system of schooling in the world, according to the OECD, and the new government's proposals for more academies, more free schools and more freedom for schools will reinforce this.

National leaders of education, local leaders of education and professional partners who provide mentoring support for new heads are all part of this growing movement of sector-led school improvement and school-led leadership development. But with more freedom and autonomy comes more responsibility – and there are two important but related dangers here, both of which are bad for the system.

The first is isolationism. We know that school-to-school support works and that using the expertise of excellent school and academy leaders and their staff to build capacity and provide expert support in other schools is central to improvement. Supported schools tend to improve rapidly and the schools providing the support continue to do well and make progress. Moreover, when schools work together with other schools, the continuing professional development (CPD) is two-way and supports wider staff development.

The second danger is the opposite: empire building – strong schools and great heads taking on school-to-school support for the wrong motives. Instead of being driven by moral purpose, they are driven by the status of being an NLE and the need to build an empire. If the work is good and delivers better outcomes for the children, then the motives of the lead school are irrelevant. But if it is not driven by moral purpose, the profession will not accept it and it will be seen as a deficit model of school improvement.

The national and local leaders of education work has moral purpose and the concept of 'service' is at its heart. This will need to continue if we are to develop this notion of school-to-school support further. Collaboration is one of the hallmarks of servant leadership. Servant leaders want what is best for those they serve and they know this can only be achieved through working with others.

Being resilient

Many of you will have seen Eddie Izzard undertake his 43 consecutive marathons earlier this year. How did he do it? He had never run a marathon until a few weeks before he started. I think there were two reasons why he managed to succeed:

1. **Determination**. He made a decision that overruled all other factors. He announced that he was going to run 43 marathons in 51 days and, as far as he was concerned, it was going to happen. That same resolve can give us, as leaders, the resilience to see us through the hard times. It is amazing what we can make happen if we truly believe that it is going to happen. Servant leaders are determined

because they know how important the work is and how much it matters to the people they serve. Failure is not an option.

2. **Help from others.** Eddie was successful because he got help – help from his team, who supported him all the way and on whose expertise he relied heavily, especially the physiotherapy and medical staff. But also support from the public. What really kept him going was the number of people who joined in the run, from marines to pensioners. People wanted him to succeed. If we want to retain resilience, being determined on its own is not always enough. We need the help of our colleagues and our friends or family to get us through.

I decided to do a job swap when I was director of education in Knowsley. I wrote to all schools in the borough and asked who would like to swap jobs with me for the day. One reply was from a Year 5 teacher in Tower Hill in Kirkby, a tough part of Knowsley. She asked me to teach her class and to have a go at midday supervision. I said yes, although I had never taught in a primary school before. Then the *Times Educational Supplement* asked to send a reporter to see how I got on. I swallowed hard and again said yes. The midday supervisor slot went well and then I taught the class for the afternoon – first the literacy lesson and then religious education (RE).

I soon realised that my RE lesson, so carefully planned, was not going to work. Instead, I told the story of how, when I was their age, I ran into the kitchen to push open the glass swing door but, instead of the door opening, my hand went straight through the glass. I looked at my hand and all the outside was in and all the inside was out and there was blood everywhere. I still have the scar (I showed it to them). That was when the lesson began to take off …

I then asked them what were the two things that I most wanted at that moment. They got the first one straight away – a doctor to sew up my wrist. It took a while but eventually they got the second one – I wanted a hug from my mum. Then I said, 'I am now director of education for all the schools in Knowsley, and do you know what I still need sometimes? A hug from my mum.' We then had a great discussion about the importance of family and friends. The lesson went well – and the *Times Educational Supplement* did a really positive story. (At the end of the lesson one child stopped me and asked, 'How do you keep the electricity going in all the schools?' I said it was one of the toughest parts of the job.)

I tell this story because without the support of friends, family and colleagues we will struggle as leaders. We need a hinterland and our own networks of support – and sometimes a hug from someone close to us. Servant leaders have the humility to learn from others and ask for support from others. And precisely because they have those qualities, most people are keen to provide that support for them.

Holding courageous conversations

The poet David Whyte talks about the importance of courageous conversations. Servant leaders are more likely to hold these difficult conversations because they know that ultimately it is the outcomes for children that matter, and children rarely get a second chance. They hold people to account, have high expectations of them and challenge underperformance and mediocrity, not because they like power but because young people deserve the best.

Servant leaders will also be more willing to give and receive honest feedback with colleagues because they understand the true value of authentic and trusting relationships. They know the danger of letting things fester when they need to be discussed openly.

So, are we having courageous conversations with those we lead and with our colleagues, or are we avoiding them? Do we have an uneasy feeling about one of our key professional relationships? Perhaps we know we should do something about it, but we are just too busy and it is very hard to raise it. Is it time we had that courageous conversation?

And what about our personal lives? Are we having courageous conversations with our partner, our children or our parents about how things can be better and how we truly feel? And are we having courageous conversations with ourselves about what we really want and the kind of future that we really see for ourselves?

Conclusion

The future will be a challenging one, and for some of us it may be the most demanding time of our careers. But it is during times of uncertainty and change that great opportunities come about to build the foundations for something even better. There will be less bureaucracy, less central prescription and fewer barriers. We can build new partnerships and alliances, we can be genuinely innovative and we can seek out new opportunities to make a difference.

Your challenge will be to manage tighter funding while achieving even better outcomes for children, by managing change well, showing collaboration, demonstrating resilience and holding courageous conversations. Underpinning all of that – the fundamental element – will be to approach every challenge and opportunity with the strong notion of service for which you are renowned.

Finally, let me say a few words about the National College. We fully understand that national agencies like us should be first in line when it comes to reductions in spending. But I also want to say this: for as long as I am the chief executive, the National College will hold on to its moral purpose and be here to serve. Of course we will challenge leaders and not necessarily give you an easy time, but we will be evidence-based in our judgements – we are not a lobbying group or a union. We are here to deliver on behalf of the government of the day. We are here to champion leadership for children and young people. We are here to make sure that we have the best leadership that our children and young people can possibly have. We exist to help children achieve what they might achieve and to help you all to be the best leaders you can be. That is what I mean by leadership as service.

When we asked leaders in schools and children's services which leader across the world and in all walks of life they admired most, the most common response was Nelson Mandela. He led his people through huge uncertainty, showing great courage, determination and optimism. He visibly grew as a leader as he got older, becoming wiser and more tolerant. He showed that collaboration is not weakness but requires strength. He saw it as his mission to engender trust and confidence where there had been hatred and enmity. And he certainly knew how to have courageous conversations.

When it was clear that he would become the president of a new South Africa, he said: 'I stand here before you filled with deep pride and joy – pride in the ordinary, humble people of this country ... I stand before you humbled by your courage, with a heart full of love for you all. I regard it as the highest honour to lead the ANC at this moment in our history.'[36] Servant leadership personified.

Like the early pioneers of our school system a century or more ago, our role is to lead change within the context that we now find ourselves. To believe that things can be even better for children and then to lead in such a way as to turn that vision into a reality. For the past six years, our annual conference has been called Seizing Success. Never has that term been more apt than this year. Let's pick up the baton of leadership, recommit ourselves to our moral purpose and seize success for the children and young people we serve.

Postscript: In his speech immediately afterwards, Michael Gove said that he had enjoyed my use of Latin and wondered whether people were expecting him to be making a speech announcing the end of the National College. Instead, he said, 'I am a fan of the National College and of Steve and Vanni's leadership. I come not to bury the National College, but to say "Hail Caesar".'

Looking back years later, this was a very important speech. It was an attempt to balance hard-edged issues – such as the need for efficiency – with the overall message of doing the right thing for our children. It was positioning the CEO of the National College as a public servant and thus accepting the new government and their right to lead. It stated that we were willing to look for efficiency savings in our own budget, willing to give out tough messages and looking to make the most of the positive opportunities in the changes that were going to be introduced by the new government, but that in doing so we would not compromise on our core mission or on our overriding moral purpose. In essence, I suppose I was asking school leaders to do the same.

As far as policy issues are concerned, it is interesting to note that I was predicting less central prescription and bureaucracy under the coalition government. In a number of respects that was true, but not in others. New tests were introduced, a new national curriculum, the English Baccalaureate, tougher examinations, an Ofsted framework that would change two or three times in the next five years and a huge number of schools forced by central government to become academies, with no choice over which academy trust they must join. Arguably, we have ended up with more central prescription rather than less.

Chapter Seven
Resonant Leadership

Well, this world is cruel with its twists and turns,

But the fire's still in me and the passion it burns.

Van Morrison, 'Precious Time'

My diary entry in August 2010 shows how aware I was of the challenges ahead, how uncertain things were for the National College and how concerned I was that I might find myself out of a job:

> The huge spending cuts in the public sector require between a 10 and 20 per cent reduction in the Department for Education's budget – that will fall mainly on central costs, I am sure. Combined with a Cabinet Office review of arm's length bodies, things are looking very precarious now. Either we will survive as a separate agency (not as a non-departmental public body but as an executive agency) with a massive cut of about 60 per cent in our budget or we will be merged into a single workforce agency with the TDA and the Children's Workforce team at the Department for Education. It is going to be an extremely tough time and I may end up out of a job at the end of it, either because there is no job for me or because I will need to resign and walk away because the job is unattractive or unacceptable ... If I am not chief executive at the National College it is hard to know what kind of job I could do. I hope I don't have to become a consultant ... I think that all I can do is try to be the best leader I can be, to be collaborative in style, to be open and honest, to be optimistic about what can be done and to be clear about my bottom lines and resignation issues.

Shortly after my return from a holiday in Greece (to celebrate our fifth wedding anniversary), I was informed formally by a senior official in the Department for Education that the National College would be closing and would be integrated into a new workforce agency with the Training and Development Agency (TDA) and the Children's Workforce Development Council (CWDC). I was deeply upset at this decision as I believed that the National College's clear focus on leadership had been key to its success in recent years. Vanni Treves was even more upset than I was and demanded an immediate meeting with the education secretary. This was not granted but instead we had a meeting with the director general of schools, Jon Coles.

I had known and admired Jon for many years (he had been the official who led the work of the London Challenge on behalf of the DfES, to great effect) and I knew that he would be completely professional as well as empathetic. Vanni told Jon in no uncertain terms what a disaster this would be, how the National College's best people would leave and so on. Jon responded by saying that he was not aware that a final decision had been made about the future of the National College and that he would investigate and get back to us. I immediately emailed Sam Freedman, with whom I was forming a good working relationship, and asked if a definite decision had been made. He said that he did not think a final decision had been made and that it might not be too late to get a different outcome.

In the end, the earlier 'decision' was overturned and it was decided that the National College and the TDA would not be closed but that the CWDC would. It had been a whirlwind few weeks.

Soon afterwards the relationship between the education secretary and the National College seemed to be strengthened further because Michael Gove invited Vanni Treves and myself, along with Toby Salt, to make a presentation about the work of the National College not just to him but to his whole ministerial team. It was extremely unusual to get the chance to present to the whole ministerial team and we saw this as a huge vote of confidence. The meeting took place at Portcullis House – where we had experienced our first meeting with Michael Gove a year earlier – but this time it was not in the cafe but in a very large and impressive room. As I walked through to the meeting room, I looked down and saw David Miliband – who until a few months ago had been foreign secretary but was now an opposition MP – walking into the cafe, presumably to have a meeting. Such is politics!

I want to acknowledge that at this time I was becoming a fan of Michael Gove. I didn't agree with everything he was pushing. I had some particular concerns about the free schools policy, which at the time had a strong focus on the schools being parent-led and my worry was that they would lack the necessary professional expertise. I also had concerns about what I regarded as Nick Gibb's narrow view on education. But I found Michael to be genuinely concerned about the education of children from more deprived backgrounds, passionate about the importance of good leadership in schools and a charming, respectful and engaging minister with whom to work. In the autumn, we set up a dinner for him and the children's minister, Sarah Teather, to meet with some children's centre leaders and early years specialists and, again, I found him to be open and genuinely interested in the children's centres' and early years' issues. I later changed my view about him completely.

During this period, we were lobbying hard behind the scenes to influence the forthcoming white paper, mainly through dialogue with officials and with Sam Freedman. We were asked by the education secretary if we would take responsibility for the training and development of school governors. I was very reluctant to agree to this, as I saw school governor training as a local issue rather than as the responsibility of a national body, but we agreed that we would take responsibility for the development of chairs of governors and for children's centre leaders.

When the white paper, *The Importance of Teaching*, came out in November 2010, it represented a huge endorsement of the National College.[37] We were given a new role to accredit teaching schools and to support a local and national network of teaching schools. It stated: 'The National College has done some extremely important work in strengthening school leadership in England. It is vital that this should continue, and we want to enhance the College's role, asking it to train chairs of governors and leaders of children's centres' (p. 17). It also stated: 'We will work with the National College to double the number of National and Local Leaders of Education by 2015' (p. 18). The white paper even formally endorsed our new approach to devolving responsibility for the development of middle leaders to groups of schools. It also asked us to strengthen further the NPQH, which would remain mandatory. Considering the huge uncertainty of the last 12 months, this was in many ways an absolute triumph for the National College.

In a formal letter to Vanni Treves a few days later, the education secretary wrote:

> I want to reassure you and all of those working in the College that I am clear that the College is fulfilling a *hugely* important role, that you and *everyone* who works at the College are genuinely committed to improving the quality of leadership in our schools and that the College has been making a real difference in achieving this. I am truly appreciative of everything that the College has accomplished and believe that the College should be proud of its work.[38]

The one serious downside was that the white paper also stated: 'Consistent with our wider reforms of arms length bodies, we will also streamline its governance so that it becomes an executive agency' (p. 27). I had serious concerns about this decision. Vanni and I had done everything we could to fight against it. In the end, I am not sure why the decision was made, but I suspect it was because Michael Gove was not strong enough at that time to resist the pressure from Sir Francis Maude and the Cabinet Office to make quangos more accountable and also because the officials could not (understandably) see a downside to making the National College more like the Department for Education. In the end, this decision proved hugely damaging to the National College and was, in my view, one of the main reasons for its ultimate demise.

Imperfect leaders worry about getting it wrong today (sometimes too much) but they are even more concerned about getting it right tomorrow

The National College had some very significant challenges in 2010–2011, and I confess that I did not manage them as well as I should have done. We lost responsibility for the leadership of children's services and also had a significant cut in our budget, meaning that we needed to lose quite a large number of staff. I led a restructuring and downsizing of the leadership team, with them all having to apply for their jobs and go through an interview process. In the end, two valued colleagues – Ken Gill (who had led the work on commissioning and our international work) and Catherine Fitt (who had led the work on children's services) – decided to leave, one to promotion elsewhere and the other to early retirement. I was left with an extremely strong leadership team of Toby Salt, Maggie Farrar and Caroline Maley. But we also had to restructure the rest of the organisation, and I made the mistake of not keeping as close to this as I should have done. Morale began to plummet, with people feeling uncertain, worried and let down.

It was a tough time and, in spite of my public optimism, I think that many at the National College began to think that things would only get worse from now on and that they should get out while they could. It is relatively easy for people to have confidence in a leader when things are going well and your own job is not at risk, but that confidence can drop away rapidly during times of uncertainty and downsizing. Fifty members of staff applied for voluntary redundancy and, to be honest, I felt pretty helpless. All I could do was hold my nerve, rely heavily on Caroline, Maggie and Toby for support and advice, see the restructure through and hope that we would come out stronger on the other side.

This was a time of very considerable policy change in education as the new government shook up the system. They granted significant financial incentives for schools to become academies (academies are more autonomous state schools independent of local authorities, rather like charter schools in the United States). They announced that they wanted 50 per cent of secondary schools to become academies by 2012 which would lead to massive structural change. They also announced new accountability measures and a new national curriculum. The system was in overdrive trying to cope with the change. Whilst some school leaders were hugely positive about the new approach towards a 'school-led system', others were more wary and many just felt overwhelmed.

One of the biggest changes was the introduction of teaching schools. These had been the brainchild of George Berwick and had been piloted in London and Greater Manchester. They were based on the same principle as teaching hospitals – namely, that there should be some schools clearly identified as demonstrating outstanding professional practice where those training to be teachers or school leaders and those wanting to improve their practice could receive high-level professional development.

We were delighted that the National College was given the responsibility to lead on this work and we asked Andy Buck – who had been leading on the National College's City Challenge work – to take this on. Andy was a hugely talented educationalist and former head teacher and he led the work with enthusiasm and charm. We developed the notion that it should be about teaching school alliances rather than just teaching schools. Only schools with a track record of collaboration could apply to become teaching schools and only as part of an alliance with other schools. This was the recommendation that had come out of the last Fellowship Commission.

Each year we set up a Fellowship Commission, asking 20 NLEs to work together intensively on a national policy issue (which had been identified by ministers and officials as one on which they would value some advice), calling in expert witnesses, talking with specialists and policy-makers. After an intensive week of working together, the Fellowship Commission then made recommendations directly to ministers and senior officials. These recommendations and the accompanying report often had a significant influence on government policy, and this was true in 2010–2011 when the Fellowship Commission was asked to consider what the national policy should be on school-to-school collaboration and teaching schools. It recommended that the focus should be on teaching school alliances.

The concept of teaching school alliances led by a teaching school was a stroke of genius because it meant that any teacher or school leader could be involved in leading professional development, providing they were very talented and their school was part of the alliance: their school didn't have to become a teaching school for them to be involved. This kept the bar high on quality but made the whole process more inclusive and also meant that any teacher could become a specialist leader of education (SLE), working beyond their own school for some of the time, even if their own school was not judged to be good or outstanding.

There were some problems with the teaching school model. The first problem was that we probably asked them to do too much. We developed the 'big six' priorities which teaching school alliances were asked to address: (1) initial teacher training, (2) professional development, (3) SLEs, (4) school improvement and NLE work, (5) leadership development and (6) school-based research. Even though we stated that teaching school alliances could prioritise from the list, it was a very demanding set of activities. In addition, we probably didn't fund them as well as we might have done, which meant that some of them ended up competing with other teaching schools for income streams instead of collaborating. Moreover, we didn't withdraw accreditation quickly or often enough when teaching schools failed to make an impact. Finally, we didn't have many teaching schools in areas where we needed them most. This was because, once again, we linked teaching school accreditation to the Ofsted outstanding grade, and there were far fewer schools with an outstanding grade in more deprived localities.

Nevertheless, I think teaching school alliances were generally a very good thing and I feel proud to have been involved in helping to create them. At their best (and there are many examples of this) they embodied a powerful movement towards voluntary collaboration between schools that focused on better outcomes for children and young people.

In the spring of 2011, Graham Holley left his role as CEO of the TDA. His two deputies also left, partly due to the move of the headquarters from London to Manchester. The department had tried to recruit a replacement for Graham but without success. I suggested to senior officials that rather than leave the TDA without someone to lead the organisation, I could take on the role as acting CEO until they found a permanent replacement, with Toby Salt becoming acting CEO of the National College.

I suggested this for two reasons. First, because I wanted to help out and, second, because I knew that Toby was ready to lead his own organisation and I thought that a time as acting CEO of the National College would be great experience for him. The senior officials, including the acting permanent secretary, thought this was a good idea and suggested it to Michael Gove. The answer from Michael was negative. When I enquired as to the reason, I was told: 'Michael thinks you are a great professional but you are not what he is looking for.' I later came to understand what this meant: Michael did not regard me as 'one of them' – my background and instincts did not relate to a Conservative Party approach to the world. I didn't move in the right circles. I was not sufficiently 'on message'.

This proved to be a pattern of behaviour for the coalition government from 2011 until 2015, with people like Baroness Sally Morgan (a former colleague of Tony Blair at Number 10) being asked to stand down as chair of Ofsted in 2014. It also explained, in my view, why other very talented senior officials in the Department for Education, such as Jon Coles (director general for schools) and David Bell (permanent secretary), who had worked so well as civil servants with the New Labour government, found it increasingly uncomfortable to work in the department under the coalition government and left within two years.

At the VIP dinner the night before the 2011 Seizing Success conference, we had a great turnout of influential educationalists and we were delighted that the education secretary was, once again, in attendance. That dinner proved to be one of the most memorable evenings in my time at the National College. After the main course, Vanni welcomed everyone and, in particular, the education secretary. He said that he had been reading articles in the *Times* by Michael Gove's wife (the journalist Sarah Vine) and had been upset to read that, in her opinion, her husband was not a good driver. He said that governing council members of the National College were concerned about this and didn't want him to have an accident, so they had clubbed together to buy him some P plates to put on his car (P plates are for people to use when they have just passed their driving test and are not yet confident drivers).

Having presented the plates to Michael, Vanni went on to say that he was also concerned to have read that Michael was untidy and some-times left his underpants lying around the bedroom. Vanni continued: 'Members of the National College governing council have got together, secretary of state, to buy you a spare pair of underpants in case you can't find yours, as they might be lost in the bedroom somewhere.' Before pre-senting Michael Gove with a pair of pink underpants, Vanni added that he hadn't been sure what size to get so he had telephoned the office at the Department of Education and asked them, 'What size underpants does the secretary of state wear?' The reply was that it was not part of their role to know this. 'So,' Vanni said, 'we settled on medium.'

I have to say that the jaws of many people at that dinner dropped, especially the civil servants, as Vanni made this speech – they had never heard anyone speak so disrespectfully to the education secretary. Everyone wondered how Michael Gove would react, but to his great credit he responded with a combination of wit, eloquence and good humour. It was a very memorable evening.

Imperfect leaders are aware of their own weaknesses

The theme of my speech that year was resonant leadership. Again, it had been a theme I had been thinking about for a long time, especially the bit about resonant leaders being grounded and comfortable in their own skin. I saw this aspect of leadership in people like Geoff Southworth and Maggie Farrar, people who were energy givers and life enhancers. I was not convinced that I was yet in that category, although I wanted to be. I felt that I needed to slow down sometimes and to be calmer and wiser. Again, this speech is sending messages to me about my own leadership as well as to the delegates.

The other aspect for me that was so important was the link to collaboration across the system – the idea of the resonant leader creating a larger orchestra that is not discordant but is collaborative and plays together in tune. Already I was becoming concerned that the school system was breaking up, with an increasing number of isolated academies doing their own thing and many choosing to be competitive rather than collaborative.

With the education secretary again in the audience and due to speak immediately after me, I walked onto the platform in Birmingham to a full conference and made this speech.

Resonant Leadership

Seizing Success Conference 2011

A few months ago, I went down to the coalface of a working mine at the National Coal Mining Museum in Wakefield. As I descended, I thought about what it must have been like for those young men making the same journey, all those years ago, starting out on a life of back-breaking toil.

The highest paid and most physically powerful of the miners were the rippers. They used their physical force to hack into the stone and break new ground. If you were a young lad starting out in the mine, giving a ripper a bag of sweets now and again could earn you protection from the bullies. Nobody wanted to fall out with a ripper.

That notion of leadership by the physically strongest and the most muscular is no longer a requirement for leaders today. We don't expect it in our prime ministers or, indeed, in our secretaries of state. Nor is it a requirement for school and children's centre leaders or, fortunately, for chief executives of national agencies. We now expect different leadership skills.

As Gandhi reportedly said: 'I suppose leadership at one time meant muscles, but today it means getting along with people.' Today we consider our best leaders to be those who draw on their character, their passion and their values – people who foster relationships and shape the environment around them for the greater good. This particular kind of leadership has never been more important.

Much has changed in the education landscape since our conference a year ago. The Department for Education is predicting that by the end of 2012 about 50 per cent of secondary schools will have become academies. There have been hundreds of applications for free schools. We are going to have a new national curriculum, a new test for reading at the end of Year 1, the English Baccalaureate, a new approach to school improvement, a significantly revised Ofsted framework, a consultation on the admissions code, an emerging new policy on special educational needs and we are about to have a foundation years policy statement. The National Strategies have gone and school improvement partners are disappearing. And all of this during a time of severe pressure on public spending.

At times of change and uncertainty, the leaders who are going to succeed are those who see change not as a threat but as an opportunity to shape something to be even better. This is our time to really make a difference. Over the past year, as I have visited schools, children's centres and local authorities and have spoken with leaders about their challenges and heard about their worries and their successes, I have become increasingly convinced that what is needed most is what I want to call resonant leadership.

What do I mean by this term? If you strike a musical triangle wrongly it judders and makes a horrible noise, but if you strike it well it resonates perfectly and a pure note rings out. Resonant leaders are able to strike a pure note, so they, their teams and their organisations resonate. Rather than muscle-bound rippers forging ahead on their own, resonant leaders are more like conductors of orchestras – they energise those around them. Knowing which notes to strike as we respond to the scale of change becomes crucial, as is the ability to keep those we lead motivated and focused on what will best serve the interests of children and young people.

There are five key characteristics of resonant leaders:

1.   They know themselves and develop their own leadership style.

2.   They motivate and energise others.

3.   They focus on improvement.

4.   They collaborate.

5.   They develop a compelling narrative.

1. Resonant leaders know themselves and develop their own leadership style

Resonant leaders tune in, as it were, to their own frequency. A tuning fork has to be grounded if it is going to reverberate appropriately. For leaders, this means that if we are going to be really effective, we need to be self-aware and comfortable in our own skin.

As Alma Harris and Andy Hargreaves say in *Performance Beyond Expectations*, great leadership can be charismatic and ordinary, autocratic and shared, top down and distributed.[39] There is no one model that works and the National College does not propound a set theology of leadership. The key is to be tuned in to the kind of leader you are, to know your own strengths and weaknesses, to develop the leadership that works for you in the context you are in – not what worked for someone else who is a different kind of leader in a different context.

Although we can learn a lot from working with and alongside great leaders, we should not aim to become copies of them. Each of us has our own personal way of making change happen. It is a combination of our expertise, our personality, the context we find ourselves in and the core values and beliefs we hold.

The leader who has learned to understand herself or himself has an open rather than a closed mindset. Carol Dweck says that leaders with fixed mindsets believe that intelligence and ability are set in stone. They repeatedly affirm their superiority, they avoid risks because they see failure as a weakness, they get their thrills by doing things they are already good at again and again, and they make a decision to do something (or not to do something) based on whether it will make them personally look smart or dumb. They appear confident but are, in fact, deeply insecure. In contrast, leaders who are self-aware and who have an open mindset are more confident but less opinionated; they welcome professional challenge and know that they don't always have the answers.[40]

2. Resonant leaders motivate and energise others

As with the conductor of an orchestra, our role as resonant leaders is to help those we lead to understand their connection to the bigger picture and the part they play in it, to motivate and engage, to be energy creators and to help all those we lead to work together to create a resonant culture.

Resonant leaders are exceptionally good at prioritising their presence and at demonstrating empathy at the right time and in the right context. This can come across as intuitive – and maybe it is – but I also think that this is a finely tuned skill that really can be practised and learned.

Resonant leadership is also about ensuring that the organisation is set up to get the best out of people and to motivate them. It is about how we make sure that everyone is tuned in to the ways of working in the organisation. It is about how we reduce disharmony and create a resonant culture.

Our job as leaders is to create an environment with resonance, like an orchestra, where everyone knows their part and plays their part well. If we want to change behaviours, we need to make it more interesting and more personally rewarding to play the new tune rather than the old one.

Seven weeks ago, I decided to employ a personal trainer as a means of getting fit and losing weight. He has put me through my paces a lot. After the first session he asked me, on a scale of 1–10, how I felt – where 1 was very relaxed and 10 was so tired I could hardly speak. I said, '9½ and I feel sick.' Every week he has increased the pressure and the weights, every week he has monitored my progress and given me feedback and encouragement, and, crucially, I have begun to get a sense of progress.

Gradually, what was once highly unusual behaviour (which is me in a tracksuit doing exercise) is becoming habitual. You are what you repeatedly do and gradually your brain hardwires your behaviour and learns a new habit. Success breeds motivation which breeds more success. Our role as leaders is to create an environment where people are encouraged to practise and model those good habits, and where they are able to see how those habits contribute to individual and collective success.

Precisely because we are in leadership positions, we are being watched by our staff all the time. Because of our role, we have a disproportionate influence on those we lead. Whatever we are feeling, however we are behaving, reverberates through the workplace.

3. Resonant leaders focus on improvement

Knowing yourself and motivating others will get you so far, but unless you achieve better outcomes it will all be for nothing. Musicians know that a performance should never become introspective and self-serving, but instead needs to impact on others. In education, our leadership is not for its own sake, but to make a difference to the lives of children and young people – and that is how our leadership should be judged.

The notion of transformation has been overrated. It is time to speak in praise of improvement rather than transformation. Of course, an organisation that does not innovate will die, but so will an organisation that innovates too much. Think of all the education initiatives you have been involved in over the years. Now think of how many have had a lasting and deep impact. In the venture capital world, we should not expect more than one in five new initiatives to be successful, so why should that be any different in education?

There are cases when dramatic transformation is the only sensible and reasonable solution. When I went to be director of education in Knowsley we had the second worst GCSE results in the country. After a year of my leadership we had the worst. In contexts like that doing more of the same is not an option. But too often we can get enticed by the notion of radical transformation because it is exciting and different and new. In reality, most of these initiatives end in little or no impact and, come the next initiative, are often quickly forgotten. What sounds like a great idea in Whitehall or at a think tank in London, or even at the National College in Nottingham, does not necessarily work effectively when tried out in Scunthorpe or Seaham or Exeter.

We need two things. First, more evidence-based policy development founded on hard evidence of what works. That is why I am so excited about the development of teaching school alliances. The whole idea behind them is that developments in the future will be led by practitioners, based on what works and what has proved to be excellent practice. Practitioner-led research, practitioner-led CPD and practitioner-led leadership development. We will be moving much more strongly to learning about what works on the ground and trying it out in practice rather than top-down initiatives. Second, we need to focus more on the development of staff to improve the quality of teaching.

In an international study undertaken recently by the college, with Michael Barber, Fenton Whelan and Michael Clark from McKinsey, we looked at eight school systems and found that head teachers in all of the countries worked for an average of 60 hours a week.[41] However, the distinguishing feature between the high-performing heads and the rest was what they did with that time. The highest-performing heads dedicated a significantly greater proportion of their 60 hours to the business of developing their staff to improve teaching.

In her excellent new book, *Student-Centered Leadership*, Viviane Robinson confirms that focusing on these outcomes is the right approach. Her findings show the kinds of leadership practices that have the most effect on student outcomes:

0.84: Leading teacher learning and development

0.42: Ensuring quality teaching

0.42: Establishing goals and expectations

0.31: Resourcing strategically

0.27: Ensuring an orderly and safe environment[42]

She argues that many school leaders have become side-tracked from focusing sufficiently on teacher development.

How seriously are we taking teacher development in our schools? How far are we focusing down on the detailed slog of improving quality in the classroom, or are we too easily side-tracked?

How good are we at investigating what the successful teachers are doing in our own schools and then asking them to share it? To what extent do we encourage deep investigation into the specificity of the practice and get beyond the rhetoric?

Resonant leaders seek to build on best practice, but they also know how to encourage, motivate and energise their staff. They are good at developing powerful relationships and at building trust, but they also avoid the low-risk socialising that can lead to overly comfortable relationships that then make it harder to hold higher-risk discussions with staff about their performance. They can readily challenge underperformance and they make sure that pupils' interests are not sacrificed for the comfort of adults.

Interestingly, our research tells us that those in their second headship are more likely to move at pace on performance management and account-ability systems and to take tougher decisions more quickly. This tells me that effective performance management is as much about confidence and skill as it is about knowing the procedures.

If we want to create and develop a culture of continual improvement, we need to focus more on improvement than on transformation, identify the bright spots in our organisations and build on them, focus relentlessly on developing capacity to improve teaching and learning, and be excellent at developing an effective performance management culture. What is more, that improvement culture will be even more successful if it has a strong emphasis on collaboration.

4. Resonant leaders are collaborative

If we want the whole system to improve then we need to be outward fac-ing, resonant leaders developing a deeper and more powerful sound, not just in our own organisations but across a much wider group. We have to create, as it were, a bigger orchestra and enable that larger group to play in tune. There is a concern that 22,000 schools and academies and 3,000 children's centres doing their own thing without working together may create discordance in the system, may not make use of the best practice and talent effectively and, ultimately, may not serve our children and their families well.

We all know that collaboration is easier in times of plenty but harder when resources become scarce. In the savannah, when the watering hole begins to shrink, the animals start to look at each other differently. In spite of the challenges, we must not step back from being collaborative. All of us in leadership roles need to be part of networks and collaborations based on reciprocal altruism and trust; it helps us to be personally and professionally resilient.

Resonant leaders also recognise, in an increasingly complex world, that leading and working with others will ultimately make their organisations stronger and more effective in the face of challenges. I welcome the fact that this secretary of state is enthusiastic about collaboration, through strategies such as converted academies working with other schools, through teaching school alliances, through the work of national and local leaders of education and through the development of chains of high-quality academies. The growing number of chains of academies and hard federations offer great opportunities for leaders and for the system. These formal collaborations make the best use of good leadership and expertise. They tend to lead to stronger governance, they can open up exciting opportunities for succession planning and career progression, and they can help to secure efficiencies in the system.

Many schools and local authorities are looking at how they can develop new collaborative arrangements. I was in Wigan a few weeks ago, where the local authority is commissioning groups of schools to work together and take collective responsibility for school improvement. In Buckinghamshire, the local authority and almost all of the schools have together developed the Buckinghamshire Leadership Academy – and it is going from strength to strength. In Greater Manchester, groups of schools made up of national and local leaders of education and teaching schools have got together to form a board – in partnership with the National College and with the local authorities – to further embed the collaboration developed under the Greater Manchester Challenge and to provide high-quality school-to-school support across the region.

Having said all that about exciting examples around the country, I worry about the complacency I am still seeing amongst some school leaders who are waiting for someone else to create the new collaborative culture for them or carrying on as if all the old systems and support networks will still be in place. Colleagues, in terms of collaboration and creating the new landscape, it is no use waiting around for it to happen to us, it is time to be proactive. But we also need to be careful and choose the right kind of collaboration that will work for our context.

What can we do individually and collectively to help create an effective collaborative culture within our organisations and across the wider system?

First, the mission and motive must be based on moral purpose. Collaborations and chains will not have lasting support if they are about empire building or self-service. Second, we need to model effective collaboration by proactively seeking out opportunities that are purposeful and based on shared need. We must make sure there is a clear need for the collaboration, and we must choose, together, what the sharp focus should be. Third, we must enter into collaboration as partners – as learners and sharers of our own practice. Our mindset must be to give and receive. No matter how good we perceive our own organisation to be, we should welcome new ideas and challenges.

At the National College, we want to do more to un-tap the potential of collaboration. That is why teaching school alliances and the new specialist leader of education role are going to be such an important step. I have to admit that we have been bowled over by the interest from schools wanting to become teaching schools. By April, we had well over 1,000 expressions of interest and we received more than 300 formal applications. The fundamental role of the teaching school will be to identify and draw upon great practice across the alliance of schools and enable leaders and staff to spread the influence of their skills and expertise.

One example where we will see this inclusive approach come over strongly is through specialist leaders of education. We know how critical senior and middle leaders are to school improvement, and, for the first time, these leaders will be formally recognised. By harnessing this wide pool of talent we are making a big step towards a system-wide culture of leadership and improvement.

5. Resonant leaders create a narrative that others can believe in

Our colleagues must believe that under our leadership we can take them to a better place. Our narrative must have resonance with those we lead – it must make sense to them in their context and in the changing world they are experiencing. It requires us to see the big picture and the changes that are coming, to look again at our context and our community, and to create a vision that provides real meaning for those we lead. It must create resonance out of potential dissonance.

This is very tough because the context is rapidly changing. I know that over the past two years I have struggled at times to create the right narrative for the organisation that I lead and, yes, I have felt stressed and challenged, as I know many of you in this hall have too. I have had days when I have struggled to see a way forward. It can sometimes take time for us to see how to make the right connections and develop the appropriate narrative. It is not poor leadership to struggle with this – it is normal – but it would be poor leadership to struggle forever.

The good thing is that if we are resonant leaders and if we have built up trust and empathy with our colleagues, then they will be understanding if we need a little time to develop the right new story for the future. The other great thing is that we don't have to go into a darkened room to think or go up to the mountain top on our own to receive a blinding flash and come down again with a new vision. We can develop that new vision and new narrative together with our colleagues.

A few weeks ago, I went to Woodside secondary school in Haringey, North London. This is a school that five years ago was achieving 8 per cent A*–C (that does not include maths and English, by the way). Today it has been judged by Ofsted to be outstanding, and rightly so.

At the beginning of the evening, four Year 11 students who were just about to start their GCSEs made speeches about what the school had meant for them over the past five years. Each spoke warmly about the relationships and friendships they had formed and the memories they will treasure about their time at the school. There was a strong sense of family and aspiration that was intensely moving. Something profound had taken place that had deeply affected the culture of the school. Those students were helping to write a new tale and it was clear that the head teacher had, in the course of those students' time at the school, led the turnaround of the culture to one of ownership, belonging and purpose. She reinforced the sense of community. She and her staff had helped to do to this with new stories, new ceremonies and new traditions – ceremonies and traditions that reinforced all that was now positive about the school.

Most of what I have said so far has focused on the school/academy context, but I believe that all of the key messages in this speech also apply to the early years context, to sixth form colleges, to the local authority context and, indeed, to the National College.

As far as early years is concerned, as we await the foundation years policy statement in July, I am convinced that we need to develop a more sophisticated and consistent system leadership approach. We need to ensure that the National Professional Qualification in Integrated Centre Leadership really does help children's centre leaders to be resonant leaders with their own style, able to energise and engage others. It is important that the early years sector continues – as it always has done – to make the interests of the child paramount, and that leadership development should be inextricably linked with improvement. The future of leadership in early years settings is undoubtedly collaborative. My hope is that the foundation years policy statement will empower early years leaders so they can view that context and then develop their own narrative that is resonant and meaningful for those they lead.

Finally, the National College. We take seriously the trust that has been placed in us by the secretary of state and the confidence that so many leaders have in us. It has been a great privilege to have carried out the work we have done with directors of children's services, although that is now going to be carried out elsewhere, and we are excited about our new remit for chairs of governors. But we are under no illusions about the challenges ahead. We have a much-reduced budget and we cannot be complacent or wait for change to happen to us. We have therefore developed a new narrative – a narrative in which you, as leaders, will all play a key part.

Our aim is to gradually reduce the college's role and for leaders of schools, academies and children's centres to take greater responsibility for their own improvement, as the college licenses them to develop leaders themselves. We will still have an important role to ensure high-quality leadership development, but it will be a different role as we help to build capacity in the system to become self-improving. The best leaders find that they slowly do themselves out of a job. Just as you must create the narrative that inspires and empowers those that you lead to take forward the vision and become great leaders themselves, so we as a college have developed a narrative that we believe will empower and inspire school and children's centre leaders to increasingly lead improvement in the system.

As Tom Peters says, 'Leaders don't create followers, they create more leaders.' Stepping back and letting go is always a challenge – but that is what resonant leadership is about. It is time for myself and the leadership group at the college to demonstrate resonant leadership.

Conclusion

If we are to be resonant leaders, we need to know ourselves and be authentic. We need to tune in well to those we lead and be present for them when they need it most. We need to focus on improvement in general, and on better outcomes for children and young people in particular, and to do that through effective collaboration. And we need to be great at reading the context and the changing world around us, helping to provide the narrative and vision for the future – a future that has resonance for those we are privileged to lead. We are not on our own. We are not going back to the muscle-bound model of the ripper down the mine leading in isolation. It is not all about the hero head. It is about leadership teams and a whole orchestra playing together.

It is important that we remind ourselves that we are part of a much bigger canvas. In modern Africa, the word *ubuntu* is used to describe the way in which generosity of spirit connects us to the energy and affirmation of a larger community. As Desmond Tutu says: 'A person with *ubuntu* is open and available to others, affirming of others, does not feel threatened that others are able and good; for he or she has a proper self-assurance that comes from knowing that he or she belongs in a greater whole and is diminished when others are humiliated or diminished.'[43]

We are all part of that community and it is up to us to work together in the interests of the children and young people we serve. This is the moral purpose that binds everyone in this room together. This collective purpose is what energises us and what prevents us from becoming weary. It is what gives us the ability to elicit hope and create energy in others.

My wife and I went on holiday to southern Spain over Easter and visited the town of Ronda, which is built over a huge gorge. We had both had a tough term and were relaxing in a cafe high up on the hill, lost in our own thoughts about the challenges of the term past and the term about to commence the following week. Then to our astonishment an eagle swooped down almost to our level. We could see it hovering there with its wings outstretched. It looked at us momentarily and then in one majestic movement soared upwards high into the sky. It was not afraid. It was not trapped. It was not a victim. It was not tired. It could see the big picture all around and yet could focus deep down with an eagle eye into the valley below. It was confident and in control. It was an emotional moment and the message was such a powerful one about leadership. It renewed our sense of hope for the future and for what can be achieved.

This is no time for carping or cynicism or fear. This is no time for complacency or for being the victim. It is time to be true to ourselves as leaders and to sound that resonant note. The last verse of a poem by William Ayot says:

> This is your time.
>
> For standing up to be counted, for being yourself,
>
> For becoming the sum and total of your life,
>
> For finding courage, for finding your voice,
>
> For leading, because you are needed now.
>
> This is your time.

It is our time.

Looking back on this speech, it is interesting to note that it is less about national policy than many of my previous speeches were. Perhaps this was because the change happening in terms of policy was so significant that I felt that I should focus more on the kind of leadership needed at this time rather than addressing particular policy changes – and, of course, I had to attempt to keep the education secretary onside. It is interesting that the requirement for new academies to work with other schools was never reinforced and was soon dropped, leading to many converter academies becoming isolated. This point about the dangers of isolated autonomous academies is picked up later in my 2015 speech.

Chapter Eight
Power and Love

You've got to get up every morning
With a smile on your face.

Carole King, 'Beautiful'

My diary entry in August 2011 shows that I was more confident in 2011 than I had been in 2009 and 2010, but that my confidence was about to prove unfounded:

> As far as work is concerned, I still mainly enjoy it. The annual conference went well again and so did my speech – though there are some who think that I am getting too close to the secretary of state. It is really hard to manage to stay in that territory between being close to government and being close to school leaders. A tricky balancing act.

In fact, 2011–2012 proved to be my toughest year at the National College. The 40 per cent reduction in our budget meant that the restructure needed to cut deep, and at the same time we were preparing to become an executive agency and part of the Department for Education, which happened formally in April 2012. Most of our great staff stayed but we began to lose some talent, as some people decided that the college was going to change for the worse or simply that they didn't want to become civil servants.

The politics was also becoming increasingly difficult, as most of my ministerial meetings were now with Nick Gibb, the schools minister. I tried my best to work well with Nick but I really struggled. He could be very charming and I knew that his views were genuinely held, but he seemed to only be interested in certain aspects of education and was totally convinced that he was right, based partly on his own schooling experience. When the government proposed getting rid of the national curriculum levels and leaving it up to schools to decide how to assess students' progress, I asked him what would happen if a child moved school before the age of 11 or before the age of 16 – how would the new school know where to pitch the work for that child? His answer was, 'Give them a test, a mark out of 100 and then a position in class, of course – that is how it worked in my day.'

Toby Salt and Vanni Treves were better at relating to Nick than I was. We tried to improve the relationship by having dinner with Nick one evening – Vanni, Toby and I – at an Italian restaurant to discuss in a more informal environment who we might invite to be on the National College's new advisory board (we weren't allowed to have a formal governing council once we became an executive agency). The dinner was not without some tension. Nick asked Vanni who his political heroes were. Vanni asked him to go first and he replied, 'Margaret Thatcher and Ronald Reagan.' Vanni responded with 'Clement Attlee and Winston Churchill.' I don't think that Clement Attlee was a name that Nick was hoping to hear.

We managed to gain some concessions from the Department for Education, as we negotiated our move to becoming an executive agency. We held on to our name, the National College for School Leadership, our logo, our brand, our website and our email addresses. We were very keen to avoid school leaders thinking that we had just been swallowed up by the department. All of these small victories were hard won and tested Toby's excellent negotiating skills, as he was leading the work for us.

I always prepared very thoroughly for any meeting with Michael Gove, Nick Gibb or Lord Hill (the academies minister) and also for my meetings with the special advisers. To be honest, Sam Freedman, Michael Gove's senior policy adviser, continued to be a delight. He was honest, thoughtful, listened to any ideas or proposals I might have and helped me to understand the thinking that was going on in the department and, especially, in the education secretary's office. In contrast, my meetings with Dominic Cummings (one of Michael Gove's SpAds) were always extremely challenging. I knew that I had to have something interesting or important to say to him otherwise he would soon look bored and end the meeting. Personally, I found him to be moody at times but obviously extraordinarily bright. I wondered why a man as charming as Michael Gove continued to have such a close working relationship with someone who, on occasions, could behave so objectionably in meetings. I also remembered seeing something similar with one of Gordon Brown's SpAds when he was chancellor.

Why did they do that? If, as a leader, you appoint a senior colleague to work closely with you and they behave badly, then it is inevitable that people will watch their behaviour and think that you are endorsing it. They will judge us by the colleagues we appoint and by the friends we keep. If someone who is representing us behaves badly then it is our job to challenge that behaviour. Questioning the behaviour of a senior member of your team is one of the hardest things a leader has to do. I have always struggled when holding those conversations, but I have tried not to avoid them, even when tempted to do so. I suppose that is why they are called 'difficult conversations'!

As far as the role of the National College was concerned, we agreed with the officials a broad approach for how we were going to reduce our budget year on year. The agreement was that we would build capacity over time to enable the school-led system to gradually take more and more responsibility for leadership development. I was a strong supporter of the idea of a school-led system and I genuinely believed that it was the right thing to do, as long as it happened gradually and with enough quality assurance built in. The agreement was that the National College would gradually step back as teaching school alliances stepped up and as we further developed our new licensing approach for leadership development – whereby groups of schools were licensed to deliver our training and development programmes.

This was a huge undertaking for the National College; we had to close almost all of the existing commissioned leadership development programmes whilst also creating an entirely new business model based on licensing. At the same time, we created a modular curriculum that applied to each of our licensed programmes at different levels of complexity. This was a vast exercise and we did it from scratch. Incidentally, I initially resisted the idea of a modular curriculum, fearing that it was too complex and too sequential in its expectations of career progression for school leaders. My colleagues had to work hard to convince me to change my mind. I learned, again, that it is better to be right at the end of the process than to be seen to be right at the beginning.

The advantages of the licensing model are that it is led by people who know the realities of school leadership – school leaders themselves – and it is more likely to connect to the issues in their local context. It recognises that leadership development must be embedded in day-to-day experiences, that formal leadership programmes are only a small part of learning, and that leadership development should be connected to a dynamic work environment and actionable practice. Under this model, the idea was that leadership development would become the normal way of working within a group of schools – part of the day job. As Michael Fullan would say, 'the learning is the work'.[44]

However, looking back on it now, I can see that the dangers of this model are many. It may fail to address the needs of the whole system as it focuses on local and individual needs. It may recycle existing practice and current ways of doing things rather than encourage innovation. It may mean that schools get distracted and lose sight of their core purpose, which is teaching and learning for children and young people. But the main concern was always that – without robust quality assurance and without refreshed ideas, materials and research – the quality can become very mixed and school leaders can end up with an ad hoc approach to school leadership development. If they are lucky, they get a really good licensed provider; if they are unlucky, they get a mediocre one. That was why we agreed with the officials that the National College would perform a quality assurance role and retain sufficient capacity and expertise to commission research, and make sure that the materials used were refreshed and kept up to date.

Unfortunately, when this role was removed from the National College two or three years later, England ended up with a much more mixed approach to school leadership development – with some great practice and some not so good.

Imperfect leaders have an ego but they try to keep it under control

On 1 April 2012, I officially became a civil servant and joined the schools group as a director, reporting to the acting director general of schools, Stephen Meek (Jon Coles had recently left to become the CEO of the United Learning MAT). I wanted to be positive about becoming a civil servant but I was worried that I would hate it. My fears were completely founded. The Department for Education had many very bright people in it, it seemed to me, but their focus was on policy rather than on implementing change. There were endless policy papers and briefings for ministers. 'Please the minister' seemed to be the main motivator for middle-ranking and senior officials.

There were also numerous review meetings to monitor the performance of a particular initiative or programme. These meetings always included a 'RAG-rating' (red, amber or green) for how well each aspect of the programme was going. The discussion seemed to be more about rating the performance and less about how to change the performance. Most officials appeared to lack an understanding of how the system operated at grass-roots level (i.e. in classrooms and schools), had limited understanding of change management processes and lacked any authorisation to do much apart from have meetings about things. I sometimes thought that for the officials, the meeting was the work. If they had a busy day with lots of meetings then that was a good and effective day.

There were two specific incidents that brought my frustration to a head. The first was when all the directors in the schools group were asked to discuss and agree on a common vision and mission for the group. I knew from the start that this was nonsense. All my experience of working in local authorities over many years told me that when you group together different teams that perform completely different functions and decide (for administrative purposes) that they should form a group under one senior manager, then no amount of discussion or tinkering will lead you to a common mission and identity – unless, of course, that common mission and identity is the same for the whole organisation.

Everyone understands that for line management and logistical purposes each leader of a team needs to report to someone, but I had learned from my own mistakes as an assistant director in Blackburn with Darwen that trying to create a false common mission to give us some coherence and distinguish us from other groups in the department was pointless. Moreover, there was no clear rationale as to why a certain team was in the schools group as opposed to any of the other groups in the department (incredibly, the schools group was separate from the academies group at this point!). It was no surprise to me that this ended up as a futile endeavour.

The second and more disturbing incident was to do with performance management. The National College had for many years run a reasonably successful performance management system linked to 360° feedback for all staff. Any bonus for staff was based on the collective performance of the whole organisation, linked to our balanced scorecard. Now that we were part of the Department for Education that system had to be scrapped, at least for senior managers. All senior staff had to be identified for the 2011–2012 financial year as either weak performers, average performers, good performers or exceptional performers, and this judgement would determine the financial bonus they received. The problem was (and this was non-negotiable) that a certain proportion of the senior team had to appear in each of the categories, so a certain percentage of my team had to be judged to be weak performers and a certain percentage had to be deemed outstanding, irrespective of how well the team had performed that year. In my view, this was a performance management system gone mad and I struggled to tolerate it.

Overall, though, I guess that I struggled because I was used to being the CEO of my own organisation. I was used to being able to make decisions and accustomed to dealing directly with the governing council. Some of my frustrations must have been about ego and loss of power.

Imperfect leaders welcome and seek out external challenge

I had been thinking a lot about power this year and the importance of using it wisely and effectively. It seemed to me that if we are to be effective as leaders then we need to move things forward with pace but we also need to take people with us. I was reflecting on this in my own leadership in 2012. I was having my own inner turmoil about power and the loss of it. Also, the drop in morale during the National College restructure had re-emphasised to me the importance of trust and of being there for people in times of uncertainty.

I was also observing close at hand the approach that was being taken by the education secretary and the coalition government. I saw so much dramatic change taking place in the education system within just two years of the new government. The school system was being transformed – for better and for worse – with a huge rush to become academies amongst secondary schools, the formation of MATs and teaching school alliances, and a new curriculum. There was an even tougher accountability system, with some qualifications no longer counting as 'GCSE equivalent' and thus not being included in the school performance tables. The English Baccalaureate was brought in as a new accountability measure (which had the impact of narrowing the curriculum) and the Ofsted grade of 'satisfactory' was replaced with 'requires improvement'.

The government was clearly driving change, but I began to wonder if they were doing enough to take the profession with them. In the early days of the coalition, I felt that they were trying to form a 'broad church' and to work collaboratively with other key players in the system (head teacher associations, a wide group of school leaders, etc.), but, increasingly, I felt that they were now talking to a narrower group of people who usually agreed with them. Michael Gove was starting to refer to those who disagreed with him as the 'enemies of promise'.

This groupthink approach is dangerous for any leader, and I know that there have been times in my own career when I have been guilty of only listening to the voices of the people with whom I agreed. We need external challenge in order to help us make the right decisions, and if we are going to take a critical mass of people with us, then we need to be invitational in our approach and go out of our way to build trust. This is what I was starting to feel was lacking in the current government.

This year, I decided that the theme of my annual conference speech would be power and love. I deliberately moved the timing of my speech so that it was not immediately before the education secretary's – my attempt to not be seen as overly close to Michael Gove. It ended up being my last speech to the conference as CEO of the National College and some people who heard it said they felt that I was saying goodbye. It was certainly not a deliberate message that I was trying to convey, and at the time I did not know that I would be leaving the role. But if I was to have a final speech to sum up what I had been trying to do at the National College over the previous eight years or so, then I guess that doing my best to combine power and love in my leadership would be very apt. So, on an afternoon in June 2012, with the education secretary already having done his slot and departed, I made this speech.

Power and Love in Leadership

Seizing Success Conference 2012

I watched the film *Invictus* recently. It is set at the time of the 1995 Rugby World Cup in South Africa when rugby was seen as the sport of the white Afrikaners rather than the black majority. Nelson Mandela, the new president, made a key decision – he put on the green jersey of the South African team. What a gesture! In that act he demonstrated his power. He was the president. The eyes of the world were upon him and he made a bold decision. But he also demonstrated his love for all the people who made up the new South Africa. In one huge symbolic moment he was saying, 'We are all South Africans now.' It was an act full of power and full of love.

My theme is the importance of getting the balance right between power and love.

This is my eighth annual conference speech and every year I reflect on changes and on some of the most interesting and inspirational things I have seen and heard during my visits to schools, children's centres, local authorities and academy chains. What has struck me this year has been the contrast between those leaders who feel a real enthusiasm for changes in the system – citing new opportunities to shape things for the better – and those who feel that their work is not valued or that their school or organisation might be put into some kind of category as they see the accountability bar raised. And then there are those who feel neither excited nor frightened, just uncertain.

There is no doubt that the changes are profound. Just as we look back now on the Education Acts of 1944 and 1988 as watershed moments, we will look back on this period in the same way. The system will be radically different a few years from now. Whatever type of school or organisation you lead, the message from this government is that you can choose your own path – but with that freedom comes accountability.

When Mandela became president of South Africa it was a moment when he had to demonstrate real mindfulness about how he was going to manage his new-found power and responsibility. As leaders, we have similar challenges. Our context is changing and those we lead are watching us. As more is expected of us, how should we use our power and increased autonomy?

Should we emphasise being decisive and strong, leading with authority and driving things through at pace? Do we nail our colours to the mast and step out in front and say, 'This way – follow me – now,' or is now the time in our leadership to be more inclusive and empowering? Do we need to develop radical ways of operating and seize the moment to make an even bigger difference, or is it time for calmness and a sense of perspective?

Adam Kahane is an experienced adviser on solving complex national and international problems. In his new book, he says that to address our toughest challenges we must exercise both love and power.[45] By power, he means the drive to achieve one's purpose, to get the job done, to push things to a conclusion. By love, he means the drive to connect things, to bring people together, to unify. He argues that if we chose either love or power, we will get stuck in recreating existing realities, or worse. If we want to create new and better realities – at home, at work, in our communities, in the world – we need to learn how to integrate our love and our power.

As Martin Luther King says: 'power without love is reckless and abusive, and love without power is sentimental and anemic'. I believe that at this time of great change and in an increasingly devolved system, we as leaders should not choose between power and love. We must choose both. Martin Luther King goes on to say that the 'collision of immoral power with powerless morality ... constitutes the major crisis of our times'.

Why does this strike me so strongly? I have often spoken of the importance of moral purpose and have committed myself to this being the hallmark of the work of the National College. But in an autonomous system, moral purpose takes on an even greater significance. Moral purpose is not just about having good intentions, about being well disposed towards children and young people, about wanting the best for them. It is also about having the single-minded determination to push things through to make a difference. Moral purpose is more important than ever, but this is not just about morality. It is about purpose too. It is about power as well as love.

There are four tensions that we need to navigate when balancing power and love in our leadership. The ones on the left-hand side here are characteristics of power, authority and decisiveness. The ones on the right are characteristics of love, inclusion and empowerment. My strong view is that they are false opposites and that the best leadership has both.

Power	**and**	**love**
Being a pace-setter	and	being a coach
Being challenging	and	being open to challenge
Being competitive	and	being collaborative
Being consistent	and	being adaptive to context

Being a pace-setter and being a coach

Daniel Goleman argues that although pace-setting is an important leadership style and is sometimes just what is needed, it won't provide lasting improvements unless you also adopt other leadership styles.[46] I have become a runner (of which more later) and know that you can only follow a really fast pace-setter for a certain time before you get left behind. As leaders, if our only style is pace-setting, we may find that we have stepped out on our own and nobody is following – instead, they are criticising us from the sidelines.

The answer is not necessarily to reduce the pace, it is to also have strategies to support those we lead in coping with the pace; to be a coach as well as a pace-setter. There is an Old African proverb: 'If you want to walk fast, walk alone. If you want to walk far, walk together.' The dilemma for leaders is this: what happens if we want both? Walking far is great – we all want that, but we will only have the ability to ensure lasting, long-term improvements in our organisations if we collaborate and walk together with others. Coaching and collaboration take time, and if we walk far but too slowly, it may be too late and the children and young people in our care may have missed out.

And what happens if the government is pace-setting too and is in a hurry to make a difference? What does that mean for our leadership? The tension between the pace-setter and the coaching approach is real, but it is not either/or for us as leaders, but both. Have we got the balance right?

Being challenging and being open to challenge

I remember when I worked for a local authority many years ago and was called to the director of education's office for a breakfast meeting. It was a big thing to be asked to attend a meeting with the director; I was nervous but at least I was looking forward to my breakfast. When I arrived at his office there was a long table with him at the head, his senior officials sitting along each side and a chair for me at the end. It was at this moment that I realised that it was indeed a breakfast meeting, but the director of education was the only one allowed to have a breakfast! The rest of us sat there, watching him eat, and duly received our instructions on what needed to be done in the local authority. It was an uncomfortable and challenging experience, and then I left the room – still hungry! This man was a great strategist and over the years I came to appreciate his strengths far more, but at the time I didn't want to follow him or emulate him.

This example shows the exercise of power in a poor way, but actually some of the best leaders I know are extremely strong leaders. They brook no compromises on certain things, and rightly so. But they focus their use of power on the right things. A challenging leader keeps us focused; we know exactly where we stand.

Crucially, a culture that relies entirely on motivation through fear and challenge can only take leaders so far and its positive aspects are short lived. Here is what a leading medic in the United States said recently:

> If you look at people after coronary-artery bypass grafting, two years later, 90% of them have not changed their lifestyle. ... Even though they know they have a very bad disease and they know they should change their lifestyle, for whatever reason, they can't.[47]

Heart disease is a serious illness, but it still isn't enough to persuade people to change, even when supplemented with hard factual information about the risks.

These people aren't just frightened of letting their leader down or being told off by a challenging boss. They know that their life chances are in jeopardy if they don't change their lifestyle – and many do in the short term, but hardly any manage to shift their behaviour in the long run. Fear, accountability and data are not enough. We will just have an exhausted and demotivated staff feeling done to and done in.

The secret is not to reduce the challenge. Our colleagues want a job that challenges them; they want challenging performance management and they desire feedback. The key is that alongside the challenge we should also demonstrate that we welcome challenge ourselves and are able to model a more open and engaging style of leadership.

The best heads I have seen this year are very challenging, but they also don't take themselves too seriously. They encourage their teams to question their thinking and they go out of their way to make it OK for their teams to challenge them.

What we need is neither a challenging leader nor a leader open to challenge. We need both. We need leaders who are strong, challenging and confident, and who are vulnerable and open to challenge.

Being competitive and being collaborative

Most of us are accountable for what happens in the organisations we lead. Our role is to do the best we can to improve things. If other similar organisations do a lot better than the one we lead, then questions will be asked, and if performance declines significantly over time, then our job is on the line.

So, of course there is competition between schools and between organisations. We would not be strong leaders if that competitive edge wasn't there. Competition stops us from being complacent and keeps us on our toes. We learn from the performance of others and realise that we could do better ourselves.

Being held to account is a positive thing and being benchmarked against external criteria is a way of supporting improvement. I have no doubt in my mind that over the past 20 years or so increased accountability has improved quality. Schools in this country are, overall, significantly better places, providing better teaching, better leadership and higher standards than they were when Ofsted and school performance tables were introduced. During the whole of my teaching career I was only observed once. I didn't even know what the school's exam results were, never mind being held to account for the performance of the children in my care.

But without collaboration our education system has no hope of being successful. If we have schools and children's centres competing and not collaborating, we will get greater variation in quality. Overall the system will not improve.

Just as I believe that competition for the sake of competition is unhelpful, so too is collaboration for the sake of getting along. The worst kind of collaboration is the sort that sees schools huddling together and keeping one another comfortable. I have seen some of that in my travels around the country this year: collaborations that appear to be strong on love but not on power – lots of warm activity to very little effect. I have also seen others that appear to be in danger of being the opposite – strong on power but not on inclusivity and love.

The most impressive forms of collaborative practice are those that are inclusive but are also focused on outcomes, on raising the bar and achieving real solutions for improvement. Earlier this year I visited some Bradford secondary heads who have formed a trust. They have agreed between themselves that they will all take part in peer review of each other's schools, with support from an external reviewer, and share the findings. They have also agreed to disclose all their performance data. I watched with huge admiration as they all sat together in the same room and saw each school's achievement and progress put up on a big screen. It was uncomfortable for some of the heads but they all stayed and discussed two things strategically: what were the overall messages the data was giving out concerning the issues for Bradford as a whole and how might they address them as a group? And what could they provide collectively for the schools and the departments that needed support the most? A great example of powerful and courageous collaboration.

So, our collaborative leadership needs to be challenging and to have a competitive edge as well as being inclusive and genuinely supportive of others. It needs power and love if it is to be successful. As those who are involved in teaching school alliances know, collaboration requires lateral leadership, the ability to deliver through influence rather than through instruction and the ability to demonstrate authority without having any formal power. At a time of greater autonomy, we need these kinds of leaders more than ever.

Being consistent and being adaptive to context

To what extent can solutions and good practice be applied across the board, or are they context related? Robert Hill's important publication, commissioned by the National College, suggests that, at their best, chains of academies are highly effective; they tend to make faster progress than individual sponsored academies. They often have decisive governance and leadership with clear decision-making, they have a focus on the professional development of teachers and they provide exciting career opportunities for staff by enabling them to spend time working in other academies. They also often use consistent systems for things like tracking pupil progress, managing behaviour, performance management and even for some aspects of teaching, expecting all the academies in the chain to introduce and implement those systems.[48]

If you have a tried-and-tested system that has clearly worked well and delivered results, why should other schools not use that system rather than try to invent their own, especially if it is based on sound evidence? But in education, we have this deeply engrained culture that ignores the evidence and too often rejects what works in order to find out for ourselves. Can you imagine a hospital or a GP practice refusing to use the latest proven practices for treating a patient because they prefer to make their own mind up about what works?

Context also matters. Think of the late Brian Clough. He took over two very mediocre football teams in the 1970s and won the first division title with each of them, even winning the European Cup with Nottingham Forest. But in-between those two roles he went to a very successful football club, Leeds United, and failed spectacularly. What went wrong was that he tried to adopt the same dominating and challenging style of leadership that had worked so well at Derby County, but at Leeds he had inherited professionals at the top of their game who had just won the league title. The strategies that had brought him such outstanding success in his previous leadership role did not work, and he did not adapt his leadership to the new context.

We all know far too many examples of heads who have been successful in one school but unsuccessful in another. Context does matter. One of the criticisms of some of the academy chains is that they do not take enough care to connect with their local community and understand their particular contexts and challenges. Even if they are good systems, without ownership, without nuance, without connecting to the different context, you may find yourself – as the pace-setter leader – out on a limb. Systems need people to implement them and without goodwill your bright new system may soon be in trouble.

Now a few words about primary schools. The size and scale of the primary leadership challenge is massive. There are about 18,000 primary schools. The future is surely not thousands of standalone schools, each doing its own thing.

At the National College we have been using scenario planning with a group of primary head teachers to address the challenge that autonomy presents. In every scenario, the answer is the same – collaboration. School improvement needs to be done together, not in isolation. But in each scenario, the challenge of collaboration takes different forms. Is it the entrepreneurial, business-minded head collaborating by buying and selling services with other schools? Is it the collegiate head, balancing the vision and ambition they have for their own school against the competing demands of others in the same federation or partnership? Is it the CEO or executive principal of an academy chain collaborating with the heads of the individual academies?

There may be important differences between these different models of leadership, but there is one inescapable message: if your only model of leadership is one based on high levels of direction from above or one based on being in control of everything yourself in your own isolated school, then the future is unlikely to hold much more than increasing frustration.

As I said at the beginning, the landscape is changing for all of us, not just for primary school leaders. So, how should leaders in whatever kind of setting they are in be preparing themselves for a world which, whether they like it or not, is going to be very different from the one they have now?

Remember Brian Clough – the key is adaptive leadership. We need leaders who can adapt their leadership to different circumstances. How do we make that happen? The hardest habits to change are the ones that have made us successful.

In the end, it is hard to get the balance right between consistency and adaptability. If I decide I need to be consistent, am I really just being stubborn and complacent about the changes around me? If I decide that I need to be adaptive, am I really just being weak and trying to avoid conflict? This is the tension that we have to manage.

Towards a self-improving system

If the profession is to be trusted to run schools – and it is the secretary of state who has put that at the heart of his mission – then we have to ask what this means for how we, as leaders, conduct ourselves with other leaders and colleagues.

What I am proposing is that now is the time, more than ever before, for leaders to demonstrate both power and love across the system. We need leaders who are demonstrating authority, pace and a commitment to systems that work and are combining it with inclusivity, collaboration and contextualisation. If we are going to have a new kind of professionalism based on power and love, we might hope to find some of the following things high up the list:

- A profession that sets high standards, taking seriously the evidence of what works.

- Enthusiasm for excellence, even when it is achieved by our competitors.

- Accountability that starts with those we serve – children, young people and their parents.

- A commitment to continuous improvement, for others as well as for ourselves.

If we are to have a profession demonstrating its power, independence and autonomy wisely, we need to see leaders stepping up to lead a self-improving system. Leaders who are strong and proud, who challenge mediocre practice, who drive tirelessly towards improvement, who are determined to make a difference. Leaders who are pacey and authoritative and who understand that children only get one chance at school.

But if we are to have a profession that is demonstrating love as well as power, we also need to see leaders who are respectful of what has happened before, who build on the achievements of former teachers and leaders, who are inclusive and engaging, whose egos don't get in the way of the great endeavour, who are quick to praise others rather than seek it for themselves. Leaders who can be trusted by others because they are open to challenge themselves, who are empathetic, collaborative and filled with a passion to make a difference for all children and young people, not just the ones in their own organisation. As the whole system shifts and turns, we need that kind of leadership more than ever before.

It is this new kind of professionalism, as much as anything else, that could go on to shape the real watershed moment we are living through. This is an era that won't be defined so much by the policy changes taking place – unprecedented though many of them are – but by what we, as leaders, make of those changes and how we seize the opportunity to redefine our approach and ensure more children succeed.

In closing, I want to bring this all back to the personal again and say a few words, leader to leader. It has been a challenging year for me. I have overseen a reduction of almost 40 per cent in the staffing and in the budget of the National College. I have had to wrestle with the tensions of power and love too. As I said at the beginning, Nelson Mandela needed to practise mindfulness in his leadership on becoming president of South Africa. So, we too, all of us, have to reflect on our powers and our responsibilities.

Everything I have talked about today depends on mindfulness in our leadership. It is impossible to achieve the profound balance between power and love if we are not reflective. I have found that running has given me some of that quiet reflective time. You don't have to be a runner, but how are you, as a leader, building in that opportunity to take a step back and listen? How are you practising mindfulness?

In the end, we all make decisions about the kind of person and the kind of leader we choose to be. I want to end my speech with an extract from a poem called 'Anyway', which I think sums up what I have been saying today. It is about being strong and empathetic. It is about being your own person and your own leader. It is about power and love.

> The good you do today, people will often forget tomorrow.
>
> Do good anyway.
>
> Give the world the best you have and it may never be enough.
>
> Give the world the best you have anyway.[49]

I think it is time for all of us to step up as leaders, to demonstrate power and love, to show renewed determination to give the world the best we've got and to do what is right for the children and young people in our country.

Looking back at this speech, I can see that I was starting to distance myself more from the government. Some even accused me at the time of using the speech to covertly criticise the leadership style of Michael Gove and Sir Michael Wilshaw, the head of Ofsted. I suppose that I was getting concerned about leadership style and tone at a national level but I was also equally concerned about some leadership approaches in schools. I was signalling a worrying trend that developed even more in the next few years of some leaders of MATs and, indeed, some leaders of local authority schools, allowing their new powers and freedoms to go to their heads and letting their egos get in the way of the great endeavour. The abuse of power by some well-known head teachers and CEOs was one of the themes of my 2017 conference speech, and it is interesting that I was highlighting these dangers as early as 2012. It is also interesting that the Bradford collaboration between schools that I highlighted so positively and optimistically in this speech ended up, ultimately, being unsuccessful when judged against the changing Ofsted framework.

Chapter Nine
Starting Over

The birds they sang at the break of day.

Start again, I heard them say.

Leonard Cohen, 'Anthem'

By the summer of 2012, I knew that I couldn't carry on for much longer in the role within the constraints of the civil service:

> The reason I have become increasingly frustrated in the job at the National College hasn't been the staff at the college (who continue to be excellent – and wonderful people too) or even the politics (though that has been challenging and Nick Gibb has been particularly challenging); it has been the bureaucracy of the civil service and the accompanying loss of autonomy that this has brought. I know that, even under great leadership from an outstanding CEO, the college can never ascend to the heights it has known as an organisation for as long as it stays as an executive agency.

In summer 2012, Toby Salt was appointed as CEO of Ormiston Academy Trust, taking up his new post in the September; he had done a great job for the National College. We had already lost the highly talented Andy Buck, who had taken up a very senior role working with Jon Coles at United Learning. Then, in July 2012, I was interviewed for the role of CEO of CfBT Education Trust.

It was a huge decision for me to apply for another role. Being CEO of the National College was the best job I had ever had and I had loved it.

But I was failing to provide the enthusiastic and optimistic leadership that had been one of my strengths in the past, so it was pretty obvious that I needed to leave. I think knowing when it is time to go as a leader is a tough one. Some leaders get bored too quickly and look for a new challenge too early, before they have seen change through, leaving the organisation to pick up the pieces. Some leaders stay too long, even though they are no longer having the positive impact they used to have, staying either because of a feeling of loyalty or because of personal insecurity and fear of change. It is very hard to get it right.

I spoke about these issues in more detail in my 2016 speech, 'Grown-Up and Restless Leadership' (Chapter 11). For me, it was obvious that I needed to leave when I did. Looking back years later, I still think that I got the timing about right, but it was a huge wrench and part of me still kicked against it.

This is not a book about the National College but about my own leadership journey, so I will be brief in outlining what happened after I left. Maggie Farrar, who became my deputy after Toby Salt's departure, stepped up as acting CEO when I left in November. Toby Greany, the excellent director of policy and research, joined the leadership team, as did the ever-professional Di Barnes. Along with Caroline Maley this was a very strong team and I knew that, under Maggie's leadership, the organisation would be led with authenticity, integrity, determination and focus, and the team would do all it could to ensure that the college was successful as an executive agency. Maggie and the team did a brilliant job in very difficult circumstances.

What happened next surprised me at the time but, on reflection, I should have anticipated it. Charlie Taylor had been an impressive head of a special needs school in Hillingdon. He was educated at Eton and moved in the 'right circles'. He was appointed to the role of 'behaviour tsar' to the Department for Education and then in 2012 became CEO of the TDA. A few months after I had left the National College, Michael Gove and his team decided that, rather than appoint a new permanent CEO they would formally combine the TDA with the National College in one organisation under Charlie's leadership. There was no selection process for the CEO of the new organisation – just an announcement.

Maggie and her team were informed after the decision had been taken. The education secretary had found someone who fitted the bill for him: an experienced head teacher, someone he trusted and someone who would be 'on message'. Charlie had gone from being the head teacher of a small special school to the much bigger role of CEO of the TDA, and within a year or so he was now being asked to bring together two completely different large organisations. It was a huge task, but the education secretary was convinced that Charlie was the man to do it.

It didn't end well. The two organisations were combined under the new name of the National College for Teaching and Leadership. Maggie steered the ship courageously and authentically until the merger and then left, later becoming a very successful national and international consultant and facilitator. Jane Doughty, whose knowledge of the design of leadership development provision was unrivalled and who had been at the National College from the beginning, also left. Caroline Maley, who had little respect for the new leadership, departed to spend more time with her retired husband, Tom. Di Barnes had already left to join Toby Salt at Ormiston Academy Trust. Soon afterwards, Toby Greany took up a professorship at the London Institute of Education. The leadership group as I knew it was no more.[50]

It did not take long for senior officials to begin to worry that the organisation was not being well led. At the annual Seizing Success conference in June 2013, I sat at the back of the auditorium to hear Charlie, seemingly without notes, give probably the worst speech I had ever heard at the conference. The organisers had to suspend the conference hashtag on Twitter because of so many negative comments.

The National College for Teaching and Leadership was starved of funds and its research arm virtually disappeared. Learning materials were not refreshed and the quality assurance function was significantly reduced. Charlie became ill and eventually left to join Michael Gove at the Ministry of Justice in August 2015. On 1 April 2018, the National College for Teaching and Leadership closed down completely and what was left of it was integrated into the Department for Education. Of course, school leaders had observed the gradual decline of the college, but by the time it was closed it was too late to mourn. By gradually running it down, the National College disappeared quietly, whereas closing it in 2010 would have caused a furore.

Imperfect leaders are self-aware

I think that I did well during the selection process for the CfBT role, including in an informal meeting with the chair, Philip Graf, who I warmed to immediately. But I then messed up very badly at the final formal interview. I think this was partly because I still wasn't sure that I wanted to leave the National College and partly because, for whatever reason, my attitude was all wrong. I actually ended up having a row with one of the members of the panel during the interview! It was a very poor performance and I didn't deserve to get the job.

I knew I had let myself down so I was very surprised to receive a phone call from the recruitment agency to say that Philip Graf wanted to meet with me again in the next few days. I said that I was on the road, with speaking commitments and school visits in the diary, but Philip agreed to drive to Lincolnshire from his home in London and have dinner with me in the hotel where I was staying. Over steak and chips, he asked me how I felt the interview had gone. I said 'very badly' and he asked me what I thought I had done wrong. I explained that I had been too confrontational in my response to some challenging questioning and had failed to show good listening skills or humility. He then said that the board would like to offer me the role of CEO at CfBT. I was again very surprised. He said that the key to appointing me was my own self-awareness – had I not been aware of what I had done wrong then they would have looked elsewhere. What I didn't know at the time was that I was the clear favourite walking into the interview, and if I had just been myself with the right attitude it would have been a straightforward appointment. As it was, my referees – Sir Michael Barber, Sir David Bell and, especially, Vanni Treves – had helped to convince them that I was the right person for the role.

I was now starting again as a leader of a very different organisation and I had to think my way into the context of my new role. My diary entry from August 2012 reads:

> I am still unclear about the kind of CEO I need to be at CfBT ... I have been making some notes about the things I need to do as a leader, based on what I have been like at my best in the past ... I will need to listen carefully and be very invitational in my approach, whilst quickly achieving clarity about the way ahead and then articulating that in a clear and inspirational way. I will need to get the key people on board

but be prepared to do tough things if needed. It is an exciting and scary challenge. Will I be up to it?

The organisation I became CEO of in November 2012 had a large number of strengths. It had a strong moral purpose, good values and dedicated, committed and professional staff. It was committed to research – one of its core aspects – and it had a good international presence. It had started off many years before as the Centre for British Teachers, with a focus on recruiting and deploying teachers from the UK to teach overseas. My predecessor, Neil McIntosh, had been CEO for 22 years, and under his leadership it had gone from being an organisation with an £8 million turnover to an organisation with a £150 million turnover, with responsibilies including leading the National Literacy and Numeracy Strategies in England on behalf of the government.

By the time Neil left, however, CfBT was in decline. It had been running a significant deficit for two consecutive years and this was eating into its reserves. It had a very wide portfolio of work:

- Ofsted inspection work across the whole of the north of England.

- The provision of most of Lincolnshire County Council's support for schools, including the music service and special needs support, as well as school improvement.

- A long-standing contract to provide teachers of English for all the government schools in Brunei.

- Inspection support for schools in the Middle East.

- Careers advice for young people in London schools.

- Education of young people in secure units/young offender institutions.

- Ownership of a group of small private special schools for excluded young people (as a separate company called 'INCLUDE').

- Careers advice for adults in the north-east of England.

- Three small independent preparatory schools in the south of England.

- A British international school in Cape Town.

- Other contract-based operations in Kenya, Oman and India.

With a turnover of just under £100 million and staff located all over the world, it was a complex and diverse organisation. In addition, CfBT was the sponsor of a separate MAT (called CST) with 21 geographically dispersed academies in England, and I became the chair of the CST board.

Imperfect leaders are learners

It was clear to me from pretty early on that, in several aspects of this new role, I was out of my depth. I had very limited experience of international work, especially in the developing world. I didn't know what great contract work in the developing world looked like, so how could I lead it? I also struggled to work out how to generate and create a coherent culture, common values and a sense of mutual trust when the organisation was spread out all over the globe. Even holding a senior management group meeting (which I introduced, as it didn't exist) involved several people dialling in via video-conferencing from other parts of the world. It also required careful planning due to the various time differences (there was a seven-hour time difference between London and Brunei).

But the main gap for me was that I had no experience of leading – or even working in – a commercial organisation. CfBT was a not-for-profit organisation and a registered charity but it had no donations or grants; it had to earn all of its income from operating within a commercial environment. Throughout my career in the public sector I had just been given an annual budget and then I had tried to manage within that budget. Now, unless we brought in more income, the organisation would ultimately close. I was extraordinarily naive. I didn't even know what a profit and loss account looked like, and I certainly had no idea how to turn a loss-making organisation into one that was making a good and healthy margin.

I had to rely on the kind of things that had served me well in the past – invitational leadership. I asked one of the trustees, Philip Wood – a very experienced former CEO of a business – to be one of my mentors. I met individually with each of the trustees and asked them what they thought I should do and what they thought was needed. I invited in some external consultants to look at our structure and our set-up and to advise on what might need to change. I worked closely with the chair, Philip Graf, and sought his views regularly. I set up a task and finish group, made up of internal staff, to look at each of our key issues and to draw up some recommendations.

By spring 2013, I was ready to have a special meeting with the full board of trustees to set out a vision and strategy for the future and to ask them to critique it. From the start, my instincts were to streamline the organisation (as I had done at the National College), to re-clarify our brand and mission and to ditch some of the work that was not our core business. I brought forward proposals to sell off our group of small private schools for excluded students (INCLUDE) and also to move out of the market in adult careers advice. My logic was that we should focus on a smaller number of things and do them well – our school inspection work, our school improvement work, our running of mainstream schools and our work to support the education of young people rather than adults.

This decision proved partly successful and partly almost disastrous. We successfully sold off the group of private schools. But when we tried to pass on to other providers the contract for the careers work with adults in the north-east of England, we couldn't find anyone to take it on. So, against my own judgement but following the decision of the board of trustees, we decided to go ahead and bid for the contract again. Not only did we win it but we won an additional contract too. A year later, when things were very tough indeed and we were losing other major contracts, the contract for the careers education work with adults came to our rescue and kept us on top of the cash flow. Without it we might have been in real trouble.

I had learned something very powerful: sometimes approaches which have worked well in the past don't always work well in a different context. Having a wide portfolio of work may not help with brand identity, but it can certainly keep the organisation afloat if the bottom falls out of the market in aspects of your core business. My diary entry in April 2013 emphasised how challenging I was finding the role:

> I have been doing the job for four-and-a-half months now and it is proving to be exciting, stressful and scary. Sometimes I think it will

be a disaster and that I won't cope with the pressure, and at other times I think I will come through the hard times and it will be a great organisation. Only time will tell.

The tough times continued for me, as I soon led a wholesale restructure of the organisation, designed to reduce costs considerably and enable us to be in a position to balance the books. This led to many redundancies and a great deal of upset and uncertainty in the organisation. My diary entry in January 2014 (14 months into the job) reads:

> ... work is very, very hard. Mainly because I don't necessarily have the right people working with me – I am also leading a wholesale restructure of the organisation – which is extremely challenging. To cap it all, I am operating in a commercial and international environment that is unfamiliar ... I think I need to renew my hope and my absolute focus on doing what is right for the organisation – providing challenge and support and inspiration to colleagues. Leading from the front, whilst empowering others. If it doesn't get any better by this time next year then I will need to consider whether to stay on as CEO – it is not doing good things for my health or for my mental well-being.

In spite of the challenges, there were also a great number of positives to build on at this time.

In 2012, I believed that there was a need in the system for an organisation that would support school-to-school collaboration, including peer review. I knew the need was there, but I just wasn't sure whether the initiative would be commercially viable. We brought a few people together to think it through and, crucially, I asked Maggie Farrar if she would be willing to lead the work (on a part-time basis). She agreed, and we also involved Jane Doughty and, later, Jane Creasy, who had both been at the National College. We started off with a small pilot of about 30 schools in different areas of the country in 2013 and we put in some upfront investment. To my great delight this initiative – which we called the Schools Partnership Programme – turned out to be very popular with schools and was commercially sound too. At the time of writing there are now well over 1,000 schools engaged in the Schools Partnership Programme.

What lessons did I learn from this?

- Encourage innovation and new ideas.

- Invest in the ones that are the most compelling and seem to have the greatest potential.

- Start small and 'test and learn' as you go.

- Appoint great people to lead the work.

- Use a robust programme management approach to ensure it is appropriately managed and costed.

- Invite other highly effective and influential leaders from around the system to be involved in shaping it (invitational leadership).

- Champion it as CEO when needed but mainly step back and let others lead it.

In March 2013, I made my first visit to Brunei in South East Asia. One of the unforgettable experiences I had was being taken by speedboat to Temburong District (it is hard to get there by road) where we visited a school on the edge of the jungle. CfBT had three English-speaking teachers employed at the school. When we got there, I was informed that the school was slowly sinking into the swamp and that some of the buildings were no longer in use. Because of this, the school was doing a morning shift and an afternoon shift in order to make the best use of the buildings that were still usable.

The three teachers from CfBT were having to do the afternoon shift, which meant they could not leave the village during the week (the last boat left before school finished for the afternoon). I asked them how they felt about teaching in a potentially dangerous building that was slowly sinking, being trapped in the tiny village all week and living with wild animals around – including crocodiles in the river. I expected anger or frustration but I got neither. 'We love it here,' they said. I think it takes a certain kind of mentality to enjoy that kind of environment, so I was glad to hear that our recruitment strategies had been so effective. I have visited many so-called 'sink schools' in my career but this was my one and only visit to a sinking school! It was my first experience of Brunei, and it was of great personal encouragement to me to know that what we were doing was making a difference to the children in schools in that country.

Later that year I visited Kenya to find out more about the work we were doing to get 81,000 girls who were not currently attending into school.

I found the whole experience very moving. The issues were deeply entrenched. Many girls did not attend because there was no water in the school and therefore no toilet except a hole in the ground. Some did not attend because their parents thought that they shouldn't be educated, or that they were of more use at home, or because if they went to school they would come under bad influences. Indeed, many of the teachers (and even sometimes the head teacher) did not want to be in the school either – they had often been placed there against their wishes and would have preferred to teach in the towns or cities.

I was overwhelmed by the courage of the team of CfBT staff who were travelling to remote communities on mopeds, knocking on doors – at personal risk to themselves – to try to find ways of encouraging the girls to come to school. The issues seemed to be highly complex and intractable. The enthusiasm and commitment was there, but how could we possibly help to turn this around?

After the 2013 Seizing Success conference, Charlie Taylor and Michael Gove had decided that the National College should no longer run conferences for school leaders. I could tell that Charlie didn't feel comfortable in that big conference environment, but it was still a shock to hear about this decision, given the popularity of the conferences and their success over the years. Apparently, they both felt that the event was not sufficiently 'on message' and that some speakers did not talk positively enough about the government's agenda and may even have criticised some of it. Also, there was a view that the state should step back as the self-improving school system stepped up. So, the argument went, it was time for the National College to step back also and allow schools themselves and/or the market to organise leadership conferences.

Once it became clear that the Seizing Success conferences would no longer happen, I was approached by the company who had administered all nine previous conferences on behalf of the National College to enquire if I would be willing to help them set up a replacement conference, rather than let the whole thing disappear. I had a number of worries. First of all, how would the Department for Education and the education secretary react? I approached the department and was assured that they would not mind if others, such as CfBT, stepped in. My second worry was the financial risk. It would require quite a lot of upfront funding, and there was a risk that no delegates would come and we would make a significant loss. My third worry was that not many people in England had heard of CfBT and it might be better to partner up with the professional school leader associations, the ASCL and the NAHT. I approached the two general secretaries and, after some discussion, they both agreed to form a partnership with CfBT to put on a replacement for the Seizing Success conferences.

The first ever Inspiring Leadership conference took place in June 2014, sponsored by CfBT, ASCL and NAHT. It happened at exactly the same time of year that the Seizing Success conferences had taken place and in the same venue. It had also been agreed that I should make a keynote address on the Thursday morning – the usual time for my keynote when I was at the National College. In preparing the speech, I received great help from Tony McAleavy and Matt Davis who worked at CfBT. I also had excellent support from Michael Pain, who by then had left the National College and was running his own consultancy company.

Having been on a huge learning curve myself for the past 20 months as CEO of CfBT, it made a lot of sense for the theme of my speech to be about the leader as a learner. In it, I am transparent about some of my own challenges as a leader in my new role. Also, now that I was no longer accountable to the education secretary, I began to feel more comfortable in openly challenging the policy agenda and in questioning some aspects of Ofsted and the drive towards academy status as a good thing in itself.

Learning-Centred Leadership

Inspiring Leadership Conference 2014

Many of us will have seen Daniel Day-Lewis' portrayal of the great American president Abraham Lincoln last year. In the first dialogue in the film, Lincoln sits in the rain talking to soldiers – black and white – serving in the Union Army. America is in the midst of civil war. His gaze fixed, he asks question after question. He listens intently as they tell him of the recent battles at Poison Spring and Jenkins' Ferry, of the horror and brutality on all sides.

He is immediately presented to us as a learner, portraying humility, curiosity and a desire to understand the people and the world around him. He is one of the most important men in the world and yet he is still a learner.

Lincoln is considered to be amongst the greatest – if not the greatest – presidents. And he left a fantastic legacy: the abolition of slavery. His beginnings were humble. His father was an illiterate labourer, his mother died when he was nine and he had little formal schooling. Yet from an early age Lincoln possessed two important traits – intense curiosity and a love of learning.

As president, he deliberately surrounded himself with rivals and advisers with a wide range of perspectives because he knew they would challenge him, help him to be a learner and help to make him a better leader. As he said: 'I do not think much of a man who is not wiser today than he was yesterday.'

The success of our education system depends, more than ever, on our ability as leaders to be learners and to know how to enable those with whom we work to be powerful learners too. That is why my theme is learning-centred leadership.

Not only is learning at the core of what happens in our classrooms and in our schools, but it also sits at the foundation of a self-improving education system. It is by learning from one another – as teachers and leaders – that we will generate the professional confidence and empowerment to chart the destiny of our education system and, like Lincoln, create a legacy that is transformational.

What do I mean by learning-centred leadership?

1. Learning-centred leaders have a compulsive interest in making sure that all the children and young people in their care become powerful learners.

2. Learning-centred leaders establish a community whereby all staff develop and improve their professional expertise.

3. Learning-centred leaders are effective and enthusiastic learners. They have an insatiable well of curiosity and constantly analyse how they can improve their own performance.

4. Learning-centred leaders help to lead the system and support future learning. They are committed to the sustained success of children in all schools and to the development of education generally. They aim to leave things in much better shape than they found them and they expect the same from those who come after them.

Let's look in more detail at each of these four aspects.

1. Leaders who ensure powerful learning for children and young people

We all know what an impact great teachers can make. We also know that, for disadvantaged pupils, the influence of teacher quality is even more profound than it is for those who are not so disadvantaged.

Inspiration is an important part of what the most effective teachers bring. In his seminal book, *Visible Learning*, John Hattie suggests that when people are asked to identify the teachers who really made a difference, most will think of just two or three who have genuinely inspired them and have had a profound impact.[51]

CfBT's own research into inspirational teaching has found that, across different contexts, inspiring teachers consistently exhibit certain key behaviours.[52] Regardless of the age of the children taught or the subject, our observations showed us that almost all of them:

- Demonstrated genuine warmth and empathy towards all students.

- Created a sense of security about learning – encouraging experimentation and the ability to make mistakes without damaging self-esteem.

- Used highly interactive whole-class instruction with extremely skilful use of questioning.

- Encouraged students to communicate frequently with one another on task-orientated issues.

- Developed metacognitive skills, with students given substantial opportunities for reflection on their own work.

Where this research becomes really interesting is that we asked the students to tell us about the experience of being taught by an inspirational teacher. Young people were given a whole series of statements about these teachers and asked to say whether they agreed or disagreed. In all classes, irrespective of age and context, they came up with remarkably similar descriptions:

> My teacher believes that all students can do well.

> My teacher believes that learning is important.

My teacher seems to like teaching.

My teacher expects me to do well.

My teacher is interested in what the students think.

This list is predominantly about mindset and attitude – and we have a right to expect this from all teachers.

As learning-centred leaders, our role is to ensure that all children in our school have the opportunity to learn well. Much of this is about how we recruit and develop our staff, but it is also about how we, as leaders, communicate our commitment to helping every child become a powerful learner. School leaders have a responsibility to be deeply knowledgeable about what works in terms of classroom practice – it is the core business of the school. It is beholden on you as a head teacher or principal to know enough about the emerging evidence of what works to ask challenging questions, to signpost colleagues to recent evidence and to remove barriers to learning if they occur.

You may or may not be the expert on teaching in your school, but your role is always to provide the relentless focus on high-quality teaching and learning for every child. In those schools where all children succeed – including the most disadvantaged – we know that the fundamental belief in every child as a learner begins at the top. School leaders set the tone, for good or ill. If you believe every single child can and will succeed, your colleagues are likely to believe that too.

It is easy for leaders, and therefore schools, to be knocked off course – to be distracted from the core business of learning. One side effect of our high-accountability school system, combined with our relative autonomy to make decisions, can mean that we have a great deal of stuff to deal with that requires leadership and decision-making. It is easy to become side-tracked by other quite legitimate demands. Initiatives and proposals for change from the government of the day – usually perfectly sensible in isolation – can create huge challenges for an individual school trying to make sense of them all. Incidentally, one of the reasons why the London Challenge was so successful was that the strategy, the resources and the focus was a key priority for the government for an extraordinary eight years. Most policy initiatives last between 18 months and three years before the next one comes out.

It is also very easy for leaders to become bogged down by the 'tyranny of stuff' – to flit from one task to the next, to lose focus on what is most important. As leaders in schools, we have to be the guardians of the emphasis on 'always better learning'.

174

The coach and motivational speaker Humphrey Walters tells a story about the victorious England rugby World Cup team in 2003, and how they had to focus on the key things that would make a difference and remove all distractions. He uses the analogy of taking all the furniture out of a house – including all the things stuffed in drawers and at the back of wardrobes – and only putting back what is necessary.

This is a powerful point. What might decluttering your own school or organisation look like? How focused are you on what is absolutely crucial?

2. Leaders who enable all staff to develop their professional expertise

It is much easier to improve when you start doing something than when you've done it a thousand times before, when habits have formed and you're in your comfort zone. Teachers make a lot of progress in their early careers but this improvement plateaus. This is the real challenge for professional development – how do we get the so-so teachers to improve to be as good as the rest? Is it just about practice?

It is not as simple as that. In recent years, the notion of 10,000 hours of practice to achieve mastery has taken hold. However, Daniel Goleman tells us that the rule has been lost in translation:

> The '10,000-hour rule' – that this level of practice holds the secret to great success in any field – has become sacrosanct gospel ... The problem: it's only half true.
>
> If you are a duffer at golf, say, and make the same mistakes every time you try a certain swing or putt, 10,000 hours of practicing that error will not improve your game. You'll still be a duffer, albeit an older one.[53]

As Goleman goes on to say, 'hours and hours of practice are necessary for great performance, but not sufficient'.

We know – for example, through the excellent work of David Hargreaves – that the prevailing model of sharing good practice somewhat misses the mark: sharing good practice is effective for the sharers but not as good for the recipients. The best get better and the so-so teachers stay where they are. Instead, he says, CPD is most effective where it amounts to joint practice development between colleagues. This is professional learning that is engrained into the life and practice of schools and the nature of partnerships between schools.[54]

We also know that there is a growing shift towards more evidence-based approaches in education. The advent of the Sutton Trust and Education Endowment Foundation's Teaching and Learning Toolkit has made a huge contribution here. It is unprecedented that teachers and leaders can access evidence based on many thousands of research projects from all over the world and then apply it within their own classrooms.[55]

The questions we need to ask are: are we giving sufficient time and resources to our teachers and leaders to engage in research? Do we provide the right opportunity and climate for them to reflect on their own learning, to investigate how they can improve and work with others in a focused way on that improvement journey? This would be a big leap for many schools in this country, but it is an important step if we are to build a profession that is responsible for its own improvement and that looks to itself for answers.

I want to say something in particular about inspection. I am a fan of Ofsted – the English education system is much better as a result of inspection – and when public money is being spent, we need strong accountability systems. But I also understand that the current system is extraordinarily high stakes – it can make or break a school and make or break a head teacher's career. If you get 'outstanding' it opens up a new set of opportunities for you and your school – system leadership roles and more. However, if you get 'requires improvement' twice over, or if you get 'special measures', then it can mean you are out of a job, that you may struggle to get another headship or ever be seen again as a credible school leader.

This high-stakes system is creating a culture in too many schools where compliance and adherence to frameworks comes at the expense of professional enquiry and innovation; where professional learning isn't so much profession-led as led by what Ofsted expects.

Don't misinterpret me. Teachers and leaders need to be accountable for the impact their teaching has on learning. We cannot and must not deprive children and young people of high-quality and high-aspirational education – and strong accountability and inspection procedures are at the heart of that. But, we must remember that Ofsted is a regulator. Its job – which it does well – is to report on school performance and effectiveness so that government, parents and the public can hold schools to account. Its job is not to inspire, to promote innovation and creativity.

Can you imagine Quentin Tarantino or Danny Boyle developing a new film and looking to the regulator for advice on structure and style? Of course not. They would take account of the regulator and make sure that they perform within the guidelines, but they wouldn't look to it for inspiration. Nor should school leaders be dependent on the Ofsted framework for their view of what an exceptional school looks like. Inspirational learning-centred leaders look to research evidence, seek out examples of brilliant practice in other schools, take a thorough account of the Ofsted framework and then develop a compelling vision for their school that will excite and inspire the children and the staff.

By developing greater ownership of professional learning based on evidence, we will see less dependency on top-down solutions and, as happens with the medical profession, we will see a more confident and self-improving profession looking to itself for the answers.

3. Leaders who are enthusiastic learners themselves

Like Lincoln, we need to embody the constant pursuit of ideas, evidence, challenge and knowledge. We need to be focused on our own self-improvement as leaders, learning from other leaders and from the evidence of what works.

This is harder than it sounds. In his book *The Righteous Mind*, Jonathan Haidt argues that we always interpret evidence and situations by using our intuition. He says that we decide what we think by gut feel and then cast around for evidence to back up what we already believe.[56] This, of course, explains why we will never have a truly evidence-based education profession. People who go to Finland or Singapore or Shanghai or Ontario to see what they can learn from the education systems there tend to come back with their own gut feelings reinforced. The practices they see strengthen the views they already hold.

Relying on our own judgements and our own gut reaction to things can serve us well, but it can also be very dangerous. In leadership, we must do all we can to avoid isolated subjectivism and to welcome external perspectives. We must be deliberate, enthusiastic and proactive learners.

I worry about complacency in leadership – at school level, at system level and, of course, in my own leadership. What happens when we become complacent? Well, we think that what we are doing and how we are leading is fine. We are still working hard, but we've lost our drive and focus and our determination to improve things. We have stopped asking ourselves the really hard questions. We are not actively seeking out what is not going as well as it might and confronting it, and we are not seeking out external challenge as much as we used to. The most worrying thing about complacency is that we normally don't realise we've got it until it is too late.

Our role as leaders, therefore, is to be constantly asking ourselves questions and challenging ourselves. If we are to lead successful learning organisations we should model a strong passion for curiosity, for asking the 'why' question more often and for developing an evidence-based problem-solving strategy.

But being a learner and being open about being a learner can be a challenge for some leaders, especially when we are trying to instil confidence amongst those we lead. Some are wary about admitting that they are learning as a leader because they want to appear strong.

Interestingly, Brené Brown argues that it is the people who admit to their vulnerability who are happier and more successful. They are more likely to take risks and share their worries, and thus empower others to feel able to share their worries too.[57] People will forgive leaders who make mistakes and admit to them, but they hate a cover-up or a blame culture. It takes confidence to admit to being a learner and to being vulnerable, and those who do so are probably more self-confident than those who give the impression that they know all the answers.

If we are to create a genuinely self-improving system, we need a critical mass of leaders who are as willing to be open about their areas for development as they are about their strengths; leaders who are willing to discuss their needs, as well as their triumphs, with their colleagues in other schools. This must begin with school leaders who are the most accomplished in the system. If you don't model this approach, you can be sure that others who are less confident will struggle to do so. That is my challenge to you and to myself: are we modelling learning-centred leadership and setting the tone for a self-improving system?

It is hard to get the balance right. As leaders, we need to demonstrate that we are learners, ask for help and admit that we don't know the answers to some of the issues we are dealing with; but, at the same time, we need to exude confidence and clarity so that those we work with feel that we know what we are doing. Those we lead need to see our vulnerability but they don't want a paranoid leader, a self-pitying leader or a whimpering wreck of a leader.

I have been on a very steep learning curve over the past 18 months or so – leading a complex education charity working in more than 40 different countries and contexts. I have sometimes felt out of my depth, unclear as to what to do, aware of my own lack of knowledge in key areas and not even sure where to go to get the right expert advice and support. But at times like this, when you feel embattled or uncertain, I have found that it is important to remember three things:

- Hold on to your core values and principles.

- Go back to the people management approaches that have worked well for you in the past.

- Be an enthusiastic but focused learner.

This brings me on to the really, really hard aspects of leadership. Those moments when our stomachs turn to jelly. When we know we have a difficult set of actions to take, meetings to hold or conversations to have, and we want to stay in bed. It may be to announce redundancies, tackle competency, meet with angry parents, suspend a member of staff or – and this is one of the toughest things we ever have to do – manage things after the death of a member of staff or a child in your school. As leaders, we learn how to cope in these highly challenging contexts by reflecting on our own practice.

When I was director of education in Knowsley, we decided to consult on closing a large number of secondary schools at the same time. I led the public meetings and at first found the anger, the upset and the personal attacks hard to deal with. I actually burst into tears at the end of the first meeting. But I gradually developed my expertise at handling these situations – reflecting on my mistakes and trying out different ways of managing the meetings. Eventually I became quite confident about them. Detached involvement is the essence of leadership. Reflecting on how we approach particular situations, being mindful of what we are doing (in the moment) and then reflecting later on what went well and what we could have done differently is how we learn to lead.

Leadership in difficult situations is also about an attitude of mind. Feeling good is a skill. You can control it. It is possible to approach difficult situations and difficult people with joy, provided you are clear about your values and the processes you are going to use. As leaders, we need to walk into the wind, not run away from it. You know that moment when you enter the staffroom and it all goes quiet – that is when you stay rather than leave. Spend time in the places in your organisation where you feel least welcome and tackle difficult issues honestly, transparently and with empathy.

I learned that one of the best ways to manage those difficult school closure public meetings was to turn up early and make people a cup of tea when they arrived. I was also the last to leave. Once you accept that crises are going to be the norm for this part of your leadership, embrace them, adjust your stress levels accordingly and welcome the complexity. As a learning-centred leader, we can draw upon the fact that we often learn most from the most difficult challenges. As I have said, feeling good is a skill.

One of my education heroes, Tim Brighouse, says that there are four characteristics needed to lead change successfully:[58]

1. Regard crises as the norm and complexity as fun – learn how to feel good in stressful situations.

2. A bottomless well of intellectual curiosity – like Lincoln and Einstein, show constant curiosity.

3. A complete absence of paranoia and self-pity – be a vulnerable, learning leader but not a paranoid one.

4. Unwarranted optimism.

4. Leaders who help to lead the system and support future learning

Learning-centred leaders believe in supporting learning not just for the young people and the staff in their school but also more widely. They demonstrate a commitment to collaboration beyond their school to the development of the profession and, crucially, the learning of the next generation of leaders.

Let's look at the transformation of London's schools in recent years. They have improved at a greater rate than schools in the rest of the country by a significant degree, at primary and secondary level, and the gap between London students eligible for free school meals and the rest has narrowed more rapidly than elsewhere. This is a great success story.

Central to the transformation was the work of the London Challenge, but other reforms also contributed, such as Teach First and the work of the best academies and the best local authorities. The London Challenge pioneered the essential concept that school leaders have a real, shared moral responsibility for the well-being and educational attainment of young people, not only in their own schools but also as part of a collective pact between leaders at a local level and across London.

Developments in London moved the thinking forward about 'sector-led improvement' and the role of school leaders as system leaders – this was picked up strongly and developed further by the National College. System leadership and school-to-school collaboration are increasingly embedded in our ways of working. They have moved far beyond London – from small primaries in rural Lincolnshire working collaboratively to become more sustainable, to places such as Greater Manchester where schools are committed to supporting each other. There are now more than 1,000 national leaders of education and, from a standing start in 2010, there are already 549 teaching schools across 450 alliances.

The system can go one of two ways over the next few years: we could see either more fragmentation and more tension between schools or a further significant shift towards robust and meaningful collaboration.

There are broadly two types of collaboration between schools at present. The first is hard-edged multi-academy trusts. They have quite a good track record of effectiveness, although the quality is patchy and some of the bigger ones are overstretched. But at least accountability is clear and everyone knows where they stand.

The second is a loose collaboration or network where schools want to work together to share practice and learn from each other. Many of these networks do good things and serve an important purpose. They plan professional development, they share ideas and they visit each other's schools. But the danger is that it may not be hard-edged enough – the difficult conversations about performance don't take place, the focus is not challenging enough and insufficiently based on outcomes. It is a club that you can simply leave if it gets uncomfortable.

Why does this have to be either/or? Why are multi-academy trusts the only solution? Why can't we have hard-edged, formal collaboration that is outcome focused and holds each school to account but is also inclusive and collaborative? That doesn't require the schools to become academies but does require a formal agreement from governors that they will not walk away? That builds high challenge as well as support into the process?

I have mentioned some of the challenges of my new role at CfBT, but one of the really exciting parts is that in the UK we are trialling a new collaborative approach to school improvement which, amongst other things, involves self-evaluation, moderated peer review and some joint professional development across each school partnership. It is led by schools themselves – school leaders who are determined to get on the front foot and develop the right strategies for the future rather than just rely on the strategies that have served them well in the past.

It is not just based on the inspection framework but on research about great teaching and exceptional schools. It is genuinely developmental, but it is also hard-edged, robust and enables the difficult conversations to take place. There is a focus on accountability but also, crucially, on capacity building. And there is a commitment to collaboration, coherence and moral purpose rather than isolationism and fragmentation. It is learning-centred leadership in action.

When you walk into Sanctuary Buildings you see the photographs of education secretaries of old. For all of us in education, we have become used to defining change and progress by the name of the secretary of state in power at the time. We talk about the Butler reforms, Baker reforms and Blunkett reforms. The current secretary of state is one of the most radical and reforming education ministers we have had.

However, with more autonomy, collaboration and self-regulation, we have an opportunity to change the fact that educational progress and reform is so associated with, and dependent upon, the politicians of the day. It is less the case in the legal profession and the medical profession, and it is time it was less so in education. Governments have an important role in education, but on aspects such as pedagogy and school leadership it is for us – as a learning-centred profession – to be the pioneers and to best prepare our system and our children for a future we haven't seen yet.

That will mean some difficult conversations about performance amongst ourselves. We will need to embrace evidence-based approaches to education and engage in serious discussion and evaluation about what actually improves outcomes for children, rather than what we think might work or what we would like to work. We will need to welcome professional challenge and be positive about being held to account for how well we meet the educational needs of our young people and our communities. It will mean embracing autonomy and collective responsibility in equal measure and, in particular, committing ourselves to achieving high standards for all, rather than just high standards for our own school. Most of all, it will mean committing ourselves to providing inspirational teaching and inspirational leadership rather than merely responding to regulatory control.

The system leadership challenge is a global challenge, however. How are we, the leaders of the profession, ensuring that we shape an education system that improves all children's learning, wherever they live or go to school?

Last October, I visited a low-cost private school in the slums of Nairobi. Here, amongst the rotting vegetables, the narrow dirt tracks and the corrugated iron shacks was a tiny school in a space not much bigger than an average classroom in the UK. There were 250 children crowded into small run-down wooden huts. In one classroom, I watched an unqualified teacher, coached by someone from CfBT, give a good lesson to 20 enthusiastic children thirsty for learning.

Without education, these children have no real hope, but they are having their life opportunities transformed through going to school. None of their family has ever been to school, but here they are as enthusiastic learners. And it is not just in the slums of Nairobi that teaching is making a difference. As I was driving through Nairobi on that same visit in October, I saw a sign for the name of a school. It was called Soon Big Brain Academy. Learning-centred leaders are leaders in hope and show unwarranted optimism, even in challenging contexts.

Finally, I want to talk about the system and the culture that we leave for the next generation of leaders and teachers.

In his book *Legacy*, a study of leadership based on the experience of the All Blacks rugby team, James Kerr explains that at its core, there is an understanding that being an All Black is much more important than you as an individual. It is about what you inherit and then pass on. The All Blacks jersey doesn't belong to you. You earn the right to wear it with honour and integrity for a while, but then your role as an All Black is to leave the jersey in a better place.[59]

Last year my father died. At his funeral I talked about the powerful impact he had on me and the commitment to others in general and to young people in particular that he had modelled throughout his life. But why do we have to wait until people have died before we reflect on the impact of their lives? Leadership is a scary privilege because it enables us to make so much difference – for good or ill – to the lives of those around us. It is important to consider now what we hope our impact will be on the lives of others when we move on. Looking back, how will what we have done enabled those we have led to be successful and happy? How will they remember us, and what will we have modelled for them that will have a positive impact on their future lives?

It is time for us as learning-centred leaders to renew our relentless pursuit of the goal that every child and young person in our care should be a powerful learner. It is time to renew our commitment to lead our organisations in such a way that our staff feel developed, challenged, empowered and supported. It is time in our own leadership to make sure that we have banished complacency and instead ensure that we are leading with joy, knowing that feeling positive is a skill we can develop and that, as leaders, we can walk into the wind.

It is time to lead the change not just in our own organisation but across the system, to be part of something bigger – an education community committed to access and quality education for all. And it is time to make sure that we are stewards of the future – taking responsibility for passing something worthwhile on to the next generation of teachers and leaders. It is time for inspirational learning-centred leadership.

I spoke really positively about MATs in this speech and, looking back years later, I still think they can be a great model for school-to-school collaboration. There is much to be said for hard-edged and formal collaboration between schools through MATs in England or through charter school groups in the United States, where there is clear governance and where accountability is formalised. However, most systems across the world have not gone down the road of setting up chains of providers of schools, although they do encourage and support school-to-school collaboration.

I now work in different education systems as an international consultant, and I see this as one of the really big challenges. How do we make school-to-school collaboration work when it is voluntary and when at any point a school can choose to walk away? Later, I had the privilege of writing a think piece with Michael Fullan, entitled *Inside-Out and Downside-Up*, which discusses some of these issues and comes to the conclusion that school-to-school collaboration is most effective when it is focused on outcomes, when those outcomes are shared in a transparent way and when, in Michael's words, the collaboration is 'voluntary but inevitable'.[60]

Chapter Ten
Dark Night of the Soul

It's not dark yet, but it's getting there.

Bob Dylan, 'Not Dark Yet'

By the end of the financial year 2013–2014, our turnover was down by £10 million and our net deficit was just as high as the previous year – £4.5 million. I had made no positive impact whatsoever on the bottom line, and I was very worried indeed that my leadership was going to be a spectacular failure – harming both me and the organisation in the process.

I wondered if, indeed, I was up to this. I began to experience serious stomach problems. Worried that I might be getting stomach cancer, I had a series of tests, all of which proved negative. I put it down to the stress that I was under. My diary from August 2014 reads:

> Work is so tough. There is much more bad news than good news and it has been extremely challenging to help to lead our academy trust during a time of great political interference. I have thought about resigning but I am not a quitter. I have a very good team around me now, so I just need to get my head straight and then lead well and we should be OK.

Imperfect leaders don't hide bad news

I asked Vanni Treves, my former chair at the National College, how I would know if the board had begun to lose confidence in me. He said that the early signs would be that the chair would have a quiet word and say something along the lines of, 'Some of the board members are getting a bit restless and could you please change some things in order to calm them down.' Fortunately for me that never happened and the board stayed loyal and supportive even through those dark times.

On reflection, I think there were two reasons for their continued support. First of all, we had developed the strategy together – I had positively encouraged their critique and joint ownership of the overall strategy. Second, throughout the process I was genuinely honest with them. I never hid bad news or tried to present a better picture than was really the case. I was prepared to take brave and courageous decisions if I felt they were necessary and I was always keen to take advice. I think they knew that the issues were complex and that they might not have the most commercially astute CEO, but they did at least have an authentic one.

Apart from the failure to shift the deficit budget, the biggest challenge I had in 2014–2015 was the MAT that we sponsored (CST), which had been set up before I arrived as CEO. MATs are a collection of academies that form a single legal entity with one overall board and CEO. When CST was established, the government's policy, under Lord Hill (the academies minister), was to encourage a dramatic increase in the number of academies and in the number of MATs. The thinking was that a MAT was a good thing in and of itself, and there was little thought at the time about quality assurance or school improvement.

In reality, CST was set up in a way which, in retrospect, was exactly the opposite of how a good MAT should have been organised.

There was no geographical focus. The schools ranged from Doncaster in the north of England, Derby in the Midlands, Cambridgeshire and Lincolnshire in the east of England, Oxford and Reading in the Thames Valley and several schools in London – 21 schools in all. Some of these were free schools, set up from scratch with the support of parents and not necessarily in the areas of greatest need. It has become clearer and clearer over the years that if MATs are to be successful, the academies within the MAT need to be collaborating and helping one another. This becomes extremely difficult if they are scattered all over the country.

There was a lack of clarity on governance. MATs are supposed to be entirely separate from the sponsoring organisation (the 'members'), with their own CEO and board. Sponsoring organisations are forbidden to make a profit from MATs by selling services. In fact, the CEO of CST was on my leadership team and had responsibilities for aspects within CfBT as well as in the MAT. I automatically took over from Neil McIntosh as chair of CST at the same time as I took over from him as CEO of CfBT. Some members of my leadership team were also on the CST board. All of the CST staff were employees of CfBT (they had been seconded to CST) and their office accommodation was in the same building. For several years, CST was treated almost as if it was just part of CfBT, in the same way that our Ofsted work was part of CfBT. This made the finances very difficult to unravel, as CST had been treated more like a contract rather than as a completely separate legal entity.

There was a completely unworkable funding model. If academies join a MAT, they cease to exist as a legal entity and the accounts from each academy in the MAT have to be aggregated and consolidated into a single return. Moreover, the MAT itself has running costs, such as the salaries of the CEO and other central staff, account management and auditing, accommodation and so on. Most MATs nowadays take about 3–5 per cent from school budgets for a membership fee. CST top-sliced school budgets by 0.5 per cent for its membership fee. Clearly this meant that there were insufficient funds for the MAT to operate effectively, especially when things went wrong.

There was no school improvement model or strategy. CST was set up as a family of schools under the overarching concept of 'earned autonomy'. This meant that if you were a good school according to your last Ofsted inspection you could join CST, pay 0.5 per cent of your budget and insist upon being left alone unless you received a negative Ofsted report. Academies which joined CST expected to continue with their own governing body with very little, if any, interference. There was no obvious school improvement strategy at CST, apart from a visit by a school improvement adviser. When some schools began to get into trouble, CST had neither the resources, the capacity nor the strategy in place to do much about it.

In March 2013, I spoke to all the head teachers in CST and, soon after that, to all the chairs of governors of each academy. I set out a broad vision for CST, based on school-to-school collaboration and collective accountability instead of earned autonomy. I also announced that we were going to increase the membership fee from 0.5 per cent to either 3 per cent, 4 per cent or 5 per cent of each school's budget, depending on the needs of the school. Since this would amount to an increase of more than £100,000 for our biggest schools, I said that we would phase this in over two years. I also announced that if schools wanted to leave the trust, because it was not what they signed up for, then we would do what we could to work with them to make that happen. None of the schools asked to leave. However, this still meant that it would be at least two more years before CST would be financially strong enough to have the capacity to lead transformation across the trust.

By July 2014 things were getting very bad indeed. Theodore Agnew, chair of the academies group at the Department for Education, had been (rightly) very challenging about the performance of some of our schools and about our finances. Lord Nash, the new academies minister, also got involved and began to challenge us significantly. The existing CEO of CST left. Six months previously I had appointed Chris Tweedale to be UK director for CfBT, and now I turned to him to step into the CEO role of CST. I was delighted that he agreed to do it.

We were then asked by the Department for Education if we would be open to meeting with David Whittaker, who would provide some challenge and advice. I said that of course we would welcome external challenge and advice. David was a former business associate of Lord Nash. He seemed keen to help, and although we disagreed over certain things, the external perspective was welcome.

Then things took a distinct turn for the worse. We had a large secondary school that was performing badly but which had a big surplus in its budget. We had another school that was improving rapidly but which had a significant deficit in its budget. The minister had issued us with a formal warning notice that unless the school that was performing badly improved, then they would remove the school from CST and allocate it to another, better performing, trust. This would have major financial implications. As all the accounts had to be consolidated, we needed the surplus from the poorly performing school to cancel out the deficit in the rapidly improving school, otherwise CST would be bankrupt and would cease to be a going concern.

In late June we received a rather threatening letter from Lord Nash, stating that if we agreed to a whole list of 13 conditions, he would be prepared to recommend to the education secretary that the school with the surplus budget should not be removed from CST. The conditions included:

- David Whittaker becoming chair of the board of CST.

- David Whittaker and someone approved by Lord Nash to become two of the three members, thus potentially placing CfBT in a minor role.

- Disbanding all local governing bodies.

- Immediately increasing the proposed minimum membership fee for this September (rather than phasing it in over two years as planned).

I was deeply shocked. The minister was threatening to allow CST to become financially unviable unless David Whittaker was put in as chair of the board and unless CfBT were no longer the main sponsor. In my opinion this was an example of a minister abusing his position and going further than he had a right to do.

The board of CfBT discussed the letter from Lord Nash and took things very seriously. After a thorough discussion, they decided to endorse some but not all of the conditions. They refused to hand over two of the three member roles to David Whittaker and to someone else approved by Lord Nash, they refused to have David Whittaker as chair of the board, they refused to increase the membership fee more rapidly than initially proposed and they refused to close down the governing bodies of each school. If they had endorsed all of the conditions in Lord Nash's letter then I would have resigned immediately from my role as CEO of CfBT.

Imperfect leaders
acknowledge their mistakes

Fortunately, the school with the large surplus began to improve and in the end Lord Nash backed down. However, he did insist on me resigning as chair of the board of CST. His letter to Philip Graf, the chair of CfBT, said: 'I would like you to nominate a more independent chair who we are both happy with ... I do not think it appropriate to have the Chief Executive of the Principal Sponsor as the Chair of the Schools Trust.' Provided we did this, he agreed that we could hold on to the school with the surplus budget. Since Theodore Agnew himself was principal sponsor of a MAT and also chair of the board, and since Lord Nash had also been principal sponsor of a MAT and chair of the board, I found this staggering. It was clear that they did not think that an educationalist like me had the nous to chair a board.

In the end I went along with it, which turned out to be a good decision all round. I stayed on the board but not as chair. It definitely took some pressure away from me and, under the chairing of Peter Rawlinson and the leadership of Chris Tweedale, CST very slowly began to improve and to set itself up for the future. Although I questioned his rationale at the time, I now think that Lord Nash had been right to encourage me to stand down as chair. This was a powerful learning experience for me. My context had changed and I had been too slow to spot it myself. Standing down as chair was the right thing to do, but instead of embracing it I had become defensive and had resisted.

Imperfect leaders seek to create
a 'perfect team'

Meanwhile at CfBT, things had slowly begun to take a turn for the better. I think that there were three reasons for this.

First of all, much of the restructure had taken place by then, many staff had left and we were beginning the process of moving on and adapting to the new set-up. We were also working on changing the name and brand of the organisation (the name CfBT was no longer relevant or meaningful) and that helped us to focus again on our collective mission and vision.

Second, the leadership team was now in place and I had great confidence in them. Patrick Brazier was making a very big difference as international director; Tony McAleavy was flourishing in his new role as director of research and development; Maggie Farrar was helping me out as part-time UK director and was weaving her magic; and, perhaps most importantly of all, I finally had a finance director in place, Bob Miles, in whom I had complete confidence. A diary entry from April 2015 reads:

> Work is much better now. Bob is the main person who has made the difference. He is sorting out all the finances and getting us on an even keel ... I sleep much better at night because of him.

Third, we were enhancing our credibility internationally and beginning to see some success. As part of this, I was beginning to gain in confidence as an international consultant. I found it exciting and challenging. It seemed that my experience at the National College and my first two years at CfBT were enabling me to come across to ministers and senior officials as highly credible.

In 2015, I had a fruitful trip to Delhi. The poverty was stark and the corruption obvious, but I felt privileged to be there to try to help, especially on school leadership development issues. We'd had huge success in a very poor part of India, working with a group of schools to improve outcomes. The problem had been that the teachers were not turning up. They were paid whether or not they showed up so many did not bother, and the very basics of what a school should be were often missing. The state government could not afford to pay for inspectors to check what was happening, so we designed a checking process using mothers who took their children to school. There was no internet in the schools but most adults had mobile phones so, using a simple red/amber/green mechanism, the mothers texted the CfBT office to say whether the teacher had arrived in class, whether the textbooks were being used and so on. We then fed this information to the ministry. This dramatically improved teacher attendance. It also showed me that, unlike my time as a civil servant in the Department for Education in England, using a RAG rating can sometimes be highly effective – if it is linked to action!

In partnership with the World Bank, we arranged a study tour in London for senior officials from Bihar state in India. Later that year, I made a trip to Patna in Bihar. I remember that we stayed at the Hotel SS Exotica, which proved to be a misnomer. We met with the permanent secretary but, unlike Delhi, the whole thing felt very chaotic, with people sitting on the floor outside of his office eating meals. The meeting was a little surreal and we did not make any progress, as he was convinced that the answer to raising standards in schools was technology. Nevertheless, all of these things increased our confidence as an organisation that we could lead strategic consultancy and also, personally, it gave me great joy. Of all the things that kept me going during the first two years at CfBT, it was the international work. It inspired me, energised me and reminded me of my moral purpose.

Even though I began to feel that we might be turning a corner towards the end of the 2014–2015 academic year, we also suffered some major blows. We had lost our huge contract with Ofsted because they had decided to in-source future inspection work. We were also told that we were going to lose our very significant contract in Lincolnshire, as the county council had opted to run it for themselves in the future. At around about the same time, the Wales contract for literacy and numeracy was terminated early by the Welsh government. We had also experienced a battering about CST from the Department for Education and things were still precarious there.

Nevertheless, after one of my toughest years ever as a leader, by June 2015 the green shoots of improvement were beginning to show at CfBT. Due mainly to huge efficiency savings and the restructure, for the first time in five years we made a small profit in the 2014–2015 financial year. New opportunities were opening up internationally, the work in Kenya was going well, morale in the organisation was starting to improve and I had a leadership team and senior management group of which I could be proud.

At this time, in England, we had a new secretary of state for education. Michael Gove had become so unpopular with teachers that he was seen as a possible electoral liability and was shifted aside by the prime minister a few months before the general election. There was initially no clear policy change under the new education secretary, Nicky Morgan. Everyone at the time regarded her as a safe pair of hands to calm things down.

In 2015, I was forming some clear views about Ofsted and the need for it to be reformed. The whole high-stakes accountability system – school performance tables and an inspection regime that could make or break people's careers – seemed to me to be getting out of control. As I had said in my speech in 2014, even excellent school leaders who lead brilliant schools think first about the Ofsted implications before they introduce any new initiative. I was concerned that Ofsted and performance tables, including the new English Baccalaureate, were narrowing the curriculum and skewing the behaviour of schools.

There had also been a new announcement by the government on identifying 'coasting schools' and intervening to turn them into academies. I wrote an article in *The Telegraph* in February 2015 arguing that Ofsted should be subject to less political interference, should step back from judging teaching and learning or leadership, should hand over the auditing of safeguarding to local authorities and should only make one overall judgement for schools (adequate or inadequate) and leave it up to the profession itself to make judgements about teaching and learning or what an outstanding school might look like.

> Ofsted should be a regulatory body – ensuring that the Government and parents can have confidence that children are learning and making progress – rather than an agency for school improvement or for implementing government policy. ...
>
> This would release energy and innovation for evidence-based research in schools and for teachers and school leaders to investigate their own practice about what works in teaching and in leadership – not to wait for Ofsted to give a judgement.
>
> Let Ofsted monitor outcomes in a robust and transparent way so that schools are held to account for the progress that pupils make in their learning and let the profession take control of teaching and leadership through a school-led system.[61]

I was becoming increasingly concerned about the negative impact of our accountability system in England, but in my June 2015 speech at the Inspiring Leadership conference, I also wanted to say something really positive about how schools might show leadership under these circumstances. I decided that I wanted my speech to be about invitational leadership at a time of high accountability. Of all the styles of leadership that I have tried to use in my time as a leader, I think that invitational leadership is one of the main ones. I decided that I would try to articulate what I meant by invitational leadership. I was not as happy with this speech as I was with most of my others, but it did contain some important challenges and analysis. Once again, I had great help from Michael Pain, Tony McAleavy and Matt Davis in preparing my speech and, as you can see, I was beginning to become a little more outspoken.

Invitational Leadership at a Time of High Accountability

Inspiring Leadership Conference 2015

When Tim Brighouse became chief education officer in Birmingham more than 20 years ago, it was at a time of flux in schools and local authorities. Morale amongst head teachers was low, schools felt under pressure as a result of the introduction of school performance tables and they were attempting to come to terms with a new school inspection regime called Ofsted. But instead of complaining about the new centralised accountability systems, Tim welcomed the challenge and declared that Birmingham schools would improve by a faster rate than the national average year on year in the core tests.

But he also recognised that these measures – although crucially important – were just one component within the vision of an excellent education for Birmingham's children. In consultation with key partners in the city, Tim developed a much more ambitious approach called the 'Birmingham guarantee'. This provided an opportunity, amongst other things, for every child to have a residential experience and to engage in a public performance.

He invited the education community to join him in tackling two aspects of reform: meeting and exceeding the national standards and accountability agenda, and providing a rich set of experiences specifically for the children of Birmingham. His approach was completely new. Most directors of education were focusing more on the criteria to get a good Ofsted outcome or on developing traded services for schools. However, his approach was very successful. Test results improved by more than the national average every year he was there. Birmingham went from being one of the worst performing local authorities in the country to one of the best. Morale improved. School leaders engaged with the new vision for Birmingham and felt, collectively, part of achieving it. They warmed to the culture of 'cohesive ambition' that Tim invited them to be part of.

The inspection report of the local authority just before he left in 2002 said: 'The leadership provided by the chief education officer is outstanding, and has contributed significantly to the "can do" and aspirational culture demonstrated by headteachers ... without which such a good rate of improvement is unlikely to have been achieved.'[62]

Tim was not a passive victim. He did not focus solely on the targets set for him. He knew these targets were important, but he also knew that a broader and more compelling accountability approach was needed at a local level. He embraced national accountability, but he incorporated that into an aspirational vision that everyone could buy into. In doing so he generated the collaborative capacity necessary for transformation. He was an invitational leader.

Today we find ourselves in a system characterised by even higher levels of accountability, but also, without doubt, higher levels of school autonomy. It is clear that school autonomy and high accountability are here to stay. Over the coming years more free schools and academies will open. In terms of accountability, action is going to be taken on coasting schools, there will be a raised bar for Key Stage 2 tests, new performance tables are being introduced at Key Stage 4 and there will be a new Ofsted framework from September. We will also face further austerity.

The key challenge over the next few years is how we provide positive leadership during this period of autonomy, accountability and austerity. How do we make the most of our autonomy to lead in a way that is efficient and cost-effective, embraces national accountability requirements and creates something compelling and deeply worthwhile?

We are at a turning point in education which means we can work together to create an ambitious and accountable self-improving system. The kind of leadership this calls for is neither isolationist nor reductionist. It is leadership that builds collective capacity and, therefore, at its heart, it needs to be invitational.

That is why the theme of my speech this year is invitational leadership in a high-accountability system.

Invitational leaders have several important qualities:

- Invitational leaders invite you to be part of achieving a compelling vision. They have a story to tell – an exciting journey – and they invite others to be part of it. When we find ourselves led by an invitational leader, we know it is going to be challenging and scary, but we also know it is going to be fulfilling and worthwhile.

- Invitational leaders welcome external and internal challenge. They are strong, self-confident enough to invite scrutiny and open to asking for help from others. The last thing they want is complacency, introspection or isolation. They embrace national accountability, and then enhance it and shape it to meet the needs of their local context.

- Invitational leaders grow capacity, develop trust and create a sense of collective accountability. They engage with others and they value the contribution of others. They build collective capacity and shared ownership.

I would like to explore the concept of invitational leadership in relation to three important aspects of accountability:

1. National accountability – how should we respond to the ways in which the government holds us to account as school leaders?

2. System accountability – how should we hold each other to account for improving the education system and for developing the next generation of leaders and teachers?

3. School and community accountability – at school level, how should the invitational leader work with colleagues, governors, children, parents and the local community?

1. Invitational leadership and national accountability

No government that cares deeply about its education system is going to back off from accountability. Education is one of the biggest costs to the national treasury; robust and transparent accountability is vital. You will hear no call from me to take the foot off the pedal on robust accountability. Politicians and parents are not going to accept a warm and woolly model where challenge is off limits, and nor should they.

But the problem is one of balance – balance between a necessary focus on targets and pressure, and positive support for those the public calls upon to lead our schools. Overly simplistic accountability can create an atmosphere that suffocates trust. We have not always got the balance right. The government wants to remove the leadership from coasting schools, but there are no published criteria on what constitutes a coasting school. I am not decrying the importance of ensuring that every school is a good school, and I will be the first to say that strong school leadership can make a very significant impact on a school and its outcomes. But why are schools in particular being challenged in this way?

Earlier this year I read the headline: 'Cameron to Mobilise Top Heads for "All Out War" on Mediocre Schools'.[63] Can you imagine politicians calling for all out war on underperforming dentists or mediocre civil servants? No, it is schools that tend to bear the brunt.

This type of rhetoric is much less common in many of the countries where we look for inspiration – ironically, where politicians look for inspiration. Singapore, Finland, Japan and Canada (Ontario, Alberta and British Columbia) are all characterised by a fairly positive public perception of educators. There is a general sense of alignment between the governing and the governed. There is a greater focus on capacity building and, as a result, a much better environment for intelligent accountability to develop. You could argue that the politicians in these countries have demonstrated excellent invitational leadership: they have invited everyone working in education to be part of a long-term vision to achieve a collective goal.

So, what must we do as invitational leaders within our national context?

We should be entering into professional dialogue with government, not to denounce accountability, not to call for Ofsted to be abolished, but to point out approaches that might avoid over-simplistic accountability and the perverse incentives it can produce. This means providing ambitious and well-evidenced alternatives that draw on the capacity within the system.

In our Schools Partnership Programme at the CfBT, we invited schools to work together to co-develop an approach to peer review. The programme goes beyond the Ofsted criteria for outstanding and looks at what a truly inspirational school should be. We do this because we believe that Ofsted should have a key role in inspecting and reporting on learning outcomes in a robust and transparent way so that schools can be held to account, but that the profession itself should take control of teaching and leadership through peer review and a school-led system. That would seem to get the balance about right between trust and pressure. But, in the end, it is up to us to lead effectively in whatever accountability system we find ourselves.

Let me give you a powerful example. The official report on the scandal at Mid Staffordshire NHS Trust states that over a number of years a culture was allowed to develop in which the fundamentals of humane care were forgotten. Elderly people weren't fed or bathed, water was left out of reach, privacy and dignity weren't respected. Many people died and many more suffered from deeply inadequate standards of care. In short, professionals seemed to forget their core purpose. The public inquiry made it clear that a management culture that had become obsessed by simple targets was, to a very large part, to blame for this state of affairs.[64]

We can blame a narrow, overly simplistic and high-stakes national accountability system for what happened. But, for me, the main issue is not the accountability system but poor leadership. It is the responsibility of leaders to shape the culture and to ensure that, although we take account of external national accountability requirements, we develop an internal, collective accountability system that leads to the right outcomes. The combination of national accountability systems and poor leadership had a profound effect on the healthcare professionals at Stafford Hospital. Somehow, good people had ended up doing bad things. But where we have great invitational leadership in organisations we see the opposite. In school after school where there is excellent leadership, I see apparently ordinary people doing extraordinary things.

So, our role as invitational leaders is to ensure that the accountability systems at local and school level are intelligent and lead to the right outcomes. That is our responsibility. How do we do this? Invitational leaders manage the existing accountability system proactively and confidently. They use Ofsted positively to improve their school. They welcome the challenge and the professional dialogue. They value the scrutiny and use it as a means to keep themselves and their staff focused on improving outcomes.

As the role of the regional schools commissioners expands, invitational leaders will get on the front foot. If their school is an academy or if their school is currently judged to require improvement, they will invite the regional schools commissioner and those on head teacher boards into their schools to see what they are doing, to tell them the story, to ask for their advice and to build confidence and trust.

When I went to Knowsley as director of education many years ago, we were struggling to raise achievement. Did I try to keep the Department for Education and Skills away and keep us isolated? I did not. I asked them to come and see and to give me advice as to what I should do. I wanted senior department officials to share ownership of the problem, and I wanted the chance to tell them the story of how it was going to be transformed.

2. Invitational leadership and system accountability

How should we hold each other to account for improving the education system and for developing the next generation of leaders and teachers? My fear is that we are not creating sufficient hard-edged collective account-ability to ensure the success of the whole system. In that sense, we are creating an accountability vacuum that Ofsted and the government will fill. We are not yet seeing enough invitational leadership at a system level.

Isolationism is a key problem for many schools. In the most recent annual Ofsted report, Sir Michael Wilshaw argues that schools which work in their own bubble are becoming closed rather than open institutions and are exposing themselves to risk. This is especially true of Ofsted's analysis of converter academies in decline, too many of which are working in isolation: 'most had not made arrangement for external support and challenge until it was too late and serious decline had set in. The academies in question had an overly optimistic view of their current position.'[65] The serious worry is that, during the next few years, we will see more isolationism and too much variability across the system, with schools that already have high capacity to improve getting better but schools with low capacity getting stuck.

At a time of increased austerity, it will be interesting to see how much collaboration develops. Will we see more collaboration to achieve greater efficiencies and cost-effectiveness, or will we see further competition as schools feel more threatened financially and find it more challenging to collaborate with their neighbours?

How should we be proactively addressing the issue of developing system accountability that builds capacity and prevents isolationism?

First, we need to focus on developing leaders at national and local level. Great work has been done over the past decade or so to improve the quality of school leadership. However, we are in real danger of having an uncoordinated and incoherent approach to leadership development that will mean that some schools and localities will have a surplus of great lead-ers and others will struggle to recruit at all.

I welcome the potential that a profession-led college of teaching has to create professional development support and pathways for teachers, and I believe that we now need something similar that is focused on leadership development. If we fail to invest in the development of existing and future school leaders, we will pay the price as a system a few years down the line. Capacity building for school leaders and for potential school leaders is essential for a good education system – it is not optional.

Second, we need to develop our own local collective partnerships that address capacity building and hard-edged accountability in equal measure. Some multi-academy trusts are strong on accountability and hierarchy, but are not always strong enough on capacity building and on learning together; some teaching school alliances and other networks and trusts are strong on learning together and on joint practice development, but are weak on holding each other to account and lack a strong focus on outcomes. We need an approach that addresses capacity building and collective accountability in equal measure.

At last we are starting to see green shoots of voluntary and collective accountability in pockets across the country – in Birmingham, Bradford, Cumbria and many other places. This is invitational leadership at its best. We are seeing strategic partnerships and teaching school alliances going public on the outcomes for students they are aiming to achieve as a result of the collaboration, and placing these on their websites in an open and transparent way for parents and others to see. This mutual accountability embraces national accountability requirements but goes much further. Schools working together in more hard-edged partnerships can look out for the vulnerable or isolated school, broker support where it is most needed and provide a richer, more worthwhile and fit-for-purpose local accountability system.

Let me give you a specific example of this from a teaching school alliance in Lincolnshire. Kyra are accountable to the government to report against a set of criteria – from the number of trainee teachers they recruit to the number of schools they work with to improve their Ofsted judgements. But they have recognised the importance of accountability in creating ownership and achieving results that go well beyond the expectations of government. Each year, leaders across the alliance come together to set targets that reflect their ambitions for their partnership of schools and for their staff.

If it ended there – and these heads 'promised' to keep each other honest without a mechanism for accountability – the approach would be open to criticism of wooliness. Shared and declared moral purpose but low stakes. Kyra has gone beyond this. All the schools have committed to publish their ambitions and to report on them publicly each year, for good or ill. If you visit the Kyra website today you can read about how those involved in the alliance rate each aspect of the alliance's work and what could be done better. They are opening themselves up to be held to account by each other and by those they serve.

The openness, inclusivity and, indeed, invitational aspect of this approach is very powerful. The head of the teaching school has little or no formal managerial responsibility for members from other schools. But the head is an invitational leader and has developed an approach to collective accountability where everyone is invited to play their part and, as a result, they have introduced tangible and specific accountability systems.

Committing yourself publicly to do something in front of your peers — especially when there is funding involved and where there is a published report on outcomes — is a powerful accountability mechanism. We must start from a position of mutual commitment with a shared moral purpose. But from this we need to articulate precisely the nature of the partnership and our roles within it — a partnership contract. We need to commit publicly and on record to the agreed responsibilities, levels of authority and how success will be measured and reported. For it to flourish, we need to make system accountability feel a bit more like contractual accountability.

As invitational leaders, we invite others to work with us to create our own future at local level. Invitational leaders are good at responding to other people's invitations too, which is the essence of making local collaboration work. Provided we also do well at national accountability measures, who is going to stand in our way?

3. Invitational leadership and school and community accountability

At school level, how should invitational leaders work with colleagues, governors, children, parents and the local community?

There is now a faster turnover of head teachers, especially in schools that are judged by Ofsted to be inadequate, and a growth in the number of interim heads who specialise in turnarounds. At their best, these interim heads are talented leaders who can do a brilliant job of turning a school around, injecting pace, focus and high aspirations. Then they leave to address the issues in the next school.

But for all the immediate benefit, I have some concerns about how well this approach tackles entrenched underachievement. Going from awful to good, in Ofsted terms, does not necessarily lead to deeper sustainable success. I was in a school last month where one of the most talented and experienced head teachers in the country is transforming the school, but because some of the key national accountability measures have not yet been achieved, the sponsors are looking elsewhere for a quick fix from another head teacher.

There is a big question in these situations around the long-term ownership of improvement that goes beyond the measures imposed by the government of the day. Leaders who go into very challenging schools need to be given more time to turn things around without facing dismissal, provided there is clear evidence of progress. It is also why we should look beyond short-term improvements in national accountability measures before declaring long-term success. To be blunt, we should be wary of using national accountability systems to judge success – and failure – too early.

It is obvious that a school's staff and, most importantly, its children need to feel there is something sustainable and lasting going on. We need to step away from a focus just on short-term targets and to recognise the capacity and potential of a group committed to sustainable improvement. This is where invitational leadership comes in. Building long-term sustainability is tough but it is the most important part of the role.

So how do we, as leaders, effect long-term sustainable change at school level? What is the role of invitational leadership at school level?

I want to go back to what I said at the start about the characteristics of invitational leaders: invitational leaders invite you to be part of achieving a compelling vision. Invitational leaders develop a compelling vision that is right for their context. No great leader in a school is going to say, 'My vision is for 100 per cent of pupils to get a Level 4 and for 30 per cent to get a Level 5, and for the school to be no longer graded by Ofsted as requires improvement. Will you join me on this exciting adventure?' No, they are going to paint an attractive picture of what the school is going to look like, how it is going to improve the learning and life chances of the children, establish high aspirations for what each one of them can achieve and, of course, as part of that they are going to absolutely make sure that they hit or exceed the national accountability targets and improve their Ofsted grade.

Invitational leaders recognise that many groups – members of staff, children and young people, governors, parents and the community – have a stake in their school and they invite them into the development of the collective vision

There are loads of different ways to run great schools. I am increasingly fascinated by the differences as well as the similarities. But the point is that a school needs an essential set of ideas about how it can best help children to thrive and excel. Getting good exam results or a pleasing Ofsted grade does not constitute an enduring set of core beliefs. What are your school's non-negotiable beliefs about education? How do you invite the school's stakeholders to shape this and then act on these beliefs so that everyone is responsible and accountable?

Invitational leaders welcome external and internal challenge and understand the value of asking for help

A few years ago, the mayor of Oklahoma City announced at a press conference that he had tried everything to lose weight without success, so he was now asking for help publicly. The outcome was that not only did the mayor lose weight but so did many others. The obesity rate declined across the whole city as a result. The overweight residents of Oklahoma were so motivated by the honesty, authenticity and public commitment of the mayor that they lost weight too. Are we prepared to ask for help from our colleagues, our parents and the children in our school? Are we genuine about opening up some of the complex challenges that we face and welcoming advice?

Invitational leaders grow capacity, develop trust and create a sense of collective accountability

What distinguishes high-performing schools from less-effective schools? The first wave of school effectiveness researchers answered this question by talking about teaching and leadership, but they saw these inputs as the work of individuals rather than a collective endeavour. Teaching quality was seen as the aggregate of the work of all the individual teachers, enhanced by the contribution of individual school leaders, particularly the head teacher. More recently, what we might call second-wave school effectiveness researchers have become more interested in shared attitudes and have drawn attention to the extraordinary power of collective teacher efficacy. Schools that punch above their weight, even in the most challenging of circumstances, are likely to have an unusually positive collective mindset. This does not happen by chance. It depends heavily on school leadership.

Ken Leithwood has looked closely across several countries at what effective school leaders do.[66] He compared two styles of leadership: individual leadership and collective leadership. By individual leadership he meant top-down decision-making by a few senior leaders, particularly the school principal. By contrast, collective leadership involves people at every level of the school community in decision-making; I would call that invitational leadership. Based on a substantial statistical analysis he concluded:

- Collective leadership has a stronger influence on student achievement than individual leadership.

- Higher-performing schools award greater influence to teacher teams, parents and students compared to low-performing schools.

- Principals do not lose influence as others gain influence.

So, just as we need to move towards collective accountability for system leadership in groups of schools, so we need to be stronger at developing collective and mutual accountability at school level.

And what about our relationship with our governing bodies? Do we keep them at arm's length rather than having invitational conversations? CfBT undertook some interesting research with the University of Bath a couple of years ago, looking at the functioning of school governing bodies.[67] Often school governance is described in terms such as 'challenging the head teacher' or 'holding the head teacher to account'. That part of good governance is important, but, in reality, we discovered that in the most effective schools this was not the emphasis at all. High-performing governing bodies were places where head teachers and governors jointly attempted to solve the problems the schools were facing. In the most impressive schools studied, the governors and the head teacher spoke of themselves together in the first person plural: how can *we* work together to ensure the success of our school?

In the end, invitational leadership is about a leader's mindset. Jo Owen, the author of a number of books on leadership, argues that as leaders we need to adopt an 'accountable mindset', one where we accept responsibility for our own feelings and our own destiny.[68] We are not passive victims of someone else's accountability system. Instead, we shape things to make a positive impact in whatever context we are in. But being an invitational leader is not something we are born with; we learn it over time and grow into it as leaders.

The one thing we know about school leadership is that it is not just a job – it is a vocation. All over the world, children are walking miles and miles to get to school because they desperately want an education. Some risk terrorist attacks because they want to be able to read and write and to give themselves a better chance in life.

I went to a school in Brunei last year. There were holes in the floorboards, there was no air conditioning and the internet didn't work, except for the one day when they thought the sultan might be coming. There was a library but the children were not allowed to take the books home. You might have thought this to be a sorry state of affairs. Not at all. The children were enthusiastic learners. One of the 10-year-olds hammered me at chess. That would not have happened if one of the teachers had not believed passionately in creating opportunities for learning – including a thriving chess club – and knew what these children could achieve.

It is our privilege to lead schools in England at a time when education is an entitlement for all. But we also know that not all children have the power or the opportunity on their own to make the most of themselves, and it is our role to help them to do so.

We may find ourselves in an accountable system that is overly simplistic and not entirely what we would have chosen, but we understand that it is up to us, as invitational leaders, to develop collective accountability systems within and between schools that are true to our core purpose and mission.

As leaders of schools, you know that much of what you do does not connect directly with the national accountability system. That young person from the tough family who kicked against school throughout their time with you, but because of the patience, kindness and determination shown by you and your colleagues went on to a successful programme at college. That deeply shy child who lacked self-confidence, but because of unflinching support from the school went on to dance in assembly. That residential experience that the children went on that they will never forget. These examples, and countless more, rarely show up on any league table or even in an Ofsted report, but the deep commitment, resilience and patience shown by you and your colleagues continue to make a difference to young lives.

We know it is not either/or. Getting those young people to their Level 4 or grade C at GCSE is important for their future life chances, and we must do all we can to help them do so. Getting a good grade from Ofsted builds confidence in the school and can help to attract high-quality teachers and leaders to come to work with you. So, like Tim Brighouse in Birmingham, we need to be leaders who embrace the national accountability systems but are not dominated or overwhelmed by them. Instead, we invite those we work with to be part of an exciting journey. We build collective accountability to ensure that the schools we lead are focused on doing the right things for the children and young people. We build organisations that have soul and which create energy and collective commitment. We help apparently ordinary people to do extraordinary things.

There are no easy routes to this kind of leadership. It is forged in difficult conversations and scary contexts and, yes, in challenging accountability systems and tough budget environments. Sometimes we may find the challenges almost unbearable, but we know that we are there to lead and we know that leadership in education is hugely fulfilling and worthwhile. Poor leaders ultimately lack the mindset, the courage and the humility to provide leadership in these tough situations. But there are no shortcuts to invitational leadership.

Are we up for this kind of leadership? We take that tough first step along a difficult road because we know it has to be done and we know that it is up to us to take the lead.

In his poem 'Looking for the Castle, Second Time Around', William Ayot says that it is time to put away our self-doubt as leaders and step forward along the path and across the bridge:

> It is time to acknowledge who you really are.
>
> To go in, to the life that's been waiting for you ...
>
> It is time to stop looking upwards at others
>
> What you have is enough
>
> What you are is ready.

It is time, as it has never been before, for us to be confident in our role as leaders. Not to be bowed down but to invite others to be part of an extraordinary journey. To be willing to ask for help and to look out for those who are isolated or struggling. It is time to develop intelligent account-ability that focuses our schools and the system on the things that matter most. It is time for all of us to be invitational leaders.

My views on the accountability system in England were becoming clearer at this time, and this comes across in my speech. Since then, having worked in many different education systems around the world, I am even more concerned about the negative implications of the accountability regime in England. One thing that I highlight here is the danger of declaring failure or success too early as far as schools are concerned. This was reinforced two years later in some research carried out by Ben Laker and Alex Hill for the Centre for High Performance, showing that the head teachers who helped to make the most sustainable long-term improvements in their school (they called them 'architects') often do not get an improvement in examination results until year three of their leadership, whilst schools with head teachers who focus on getting quick wins ('surgeons') see the school's results decline significantly after they leave.[69] I refer to this research in my 2017 speech.

Chapter Eleven
The Long Wait for Sudden Improvement

It's gonna be a bright (bright), bright (bright)

Sun-shiny day

Johnny Nash, 'I Can See Clearly Now'

My diary entry from August 2015 shows that I was starting to feel more optimistic about the future and more confident about the capacity in the organisation to improve outcomes:

> The team around me at CfBT are good and it means that I can relax on holiday, knowing that everything is in safe hands ... Frankly I think we are now doing all the right things but we just need some luck and some clever tactics.

In the summer of 2015 we held our second annual awayday for the senior management group. It took place at our headquarters in Reading, so it wasn't really an awayday for some, but it certainly was for those who travelled from Brunei, Kenya and Abu Dhabi, as well as for those who came from various parts of the UK. We discussed what we are like at our best, we celebrated our successes and we focused on our new priorities. I distinctly remember feeling that day that we were now turning the corner. I felt that we really did know what we were doing much more now and that we had, as Jim Collins says, the 'right people on the bus'.[70]

Even though we had the right people on the bus, I wasn't quite sure that everyone was in the right seats. That autumn, after much discussion within the leadership team and with the board, we decided to create a more distinct consultancy arm of the business and also a separate business unit to set up and run the British international schools (we already had one in Cape Town). We therefore decided to restructure the organisation around three businesses: operations and services (all our contract work) to be led by Patrick Brazier, research and consultancy to be led by Tony McAleavy, and independent schools to be led by someone who would be recruited externally.

In retrospect, this proved to be a great set of strategic decisions – with one exception. The operations and services part of the business began to be more systematised under Patrick's strong leadership, with clear ways of working and effective monitoring, and it went from strength to strength. The consultancy arm was extremely successful, exceeding expectations even in its first year under Tony's effective management. The problem came with the third aspect – independent schools. We appointed someone to lead the work but we struggled to make new schools happen, in spite of the groundwork we had done at the outset.

Overall, 2015–2016 was a year of significant improvement for CfBT. We changed our name to the Education Development Trust, so that people would better understand what we did and who we were. We also moved into a much smaller and more modern headquarters building in Reading. This went down well. People had been rattling around in the old office which had become far too big (and too expensive) for our needs. The new name and new brand gave us impetus and it was clear that morale was on the up.

The Kenya work began to really take off. Thousands of marginalised girls who had not been attending school were starting to do so. This was hugely encouraging and deeply impressive. An added positive was that the Department for International Development began to rate us much more highly as a result.

In November 2015, the Education Development Trust published what was, in my view, one of the most important research reports we had ever produced. It was called *Interesting Cities: Five Approaches to Urban School Reform*.[71] The report was a comparison of the approaches used to improve school standards in five very diverse cities around the world: London, New York, Dubai, Rio de Janeiro and Ho Chi Minh City. All five cities represented hugely different societies in terms of economic development, politics and culture, but each of them seemed to have a promising story to tell about policy leading to improved quality for schools.

Over a 10-year period, student outcomes had risen very significantly in each of these cities. The report showed that although there were very big differences in their educational systems, there were some common aspects to the successful reform agenda, including:

- Using 'big data' to identify and intervene where students are in danger of falling behind (this has had a huge impact on improving literacy in Rio de Janeiro).

- Forging strong coalitions between parents, teachers and professional bodies – taking people with you.

- Making teaching a career of choice – adopting innovative ways of attracting talented people into teaching.

- Increasing both accountability and support for teachers and leaders; not either/or but both.

- Ensuring school-to-school collaboration – pairing strong schools with weaker schools and helping the latter to improve (for example, in London they had national support schools and in Rio de Janeiro they had 'godmother schools').

These findings seemed to me to make a great deal of sense, based on my own experience both in England and internationally. We launched the report in Dubai and Delhi, and I have since spoken about its findings in many different parts of the world. One interesting postscript is that in Rio de Janeiro and in New York the progress was not sustained after the report was published, but it seems to have continued in Dubai, London and Ho Chi Minh City.

My own interpretation of this is that four of the five cities had a charismatic leader of education – Claudia Costin in Rio de Janeiro, Tim Brighouse in London, Joel Klein in New York and Dr Abdulla al Karen in Dubai. Ho Chi Minh City's success had not relied on an individual leader. Joel Klein and Claudia Costin subsequently left their respective jurisdictions and this may partly explain the decline. Dr Abdulla is still leading in Dubai at the time of writing this book, so that helps to explain the reason for the continued progress. But what of London? Sir Tim Brighouse, Sir Mike Tomlinson and David Woods left their roles in London and the whole of the London Challenge was wound up. So why did London continue to improve? Well, there must be a number of social and economic reasons for this, but I would also suggest that it might be because the sense of 'systemness' that had been developed across London during the London Challenge remained even after the charismatic leaders left. The practice of schools helping other schools and working collaboratively in the interests of all children has remained in London, even without centralised leadership. That, surely, is the essence of great leadership – when you can so impact on the culture and ways of working that things carry on even after you have left. I spoke more about these issues in my final Inspiring Leadership speech in 2017.

In 2016, we won a very significant new contract in Brunei. We had worked in Brunei for many years to employ and deploy almost 200 English teachers in government schools, but this contract was completely different – it was to transform the teaching of literacy and numeracy in the country. We had spent a lot of time and effort paving the way for this. I had led a review of their current strategy for school improvement and we had produced a report. We had many meetings with officials, and sometimes with ministers too, to discuss what might be done. They were keen to bring in external coaches to support their teachers – a strategy we had used successfully in Kenya – and, eventually, they asked us to take responsibility for the whole initiative.

It was a real breakthrough moment for us and a great cause for celebration. We knew that if we delivered well on this contract and achieved the (very demanding) outcomes in improved examination results – and, later on, PISA scores – then we would be in a strong position to bid for similar work in other countries. I ended up spending a great deal of time in Brunei. I loved the country and the people, even though everything seemed to shut by 9pm and alcohol was banned.

In February 2016 we held a global dialogue. This was the brainchild of Maggie Farrar. She wanted to connect our schools in the Schools Partnership Programme with schools and thinkers from around the world to create a global dialogue. She arranged for me to write the think piece with Michael Fullan to help to shape the dialogue. At the time I knew Michael pretty well, but the idea of writing something with him blew my mind a little. He was like a guru to me. More than anyone else I had ever read, he had given me the language to describe the kind of leader I was trying to be. I held him in huge regard and now I was being asked to write something with him! I worked hard on the paper and sometimes struggled, but in the end – with important help from Matt Davis and, of course, a huge contribution from Michael Fullan – we ended up with a think piece I was really proud of: *Inside-Out and Downside-Up: How Leading from the Middle Has the Power to Transform Education Systems.*

We involved other education 'big hitters' in the global dialogue: John Hattie, who was in Australia at the time; Viviane Robinson, who was in New Zealand; and Michael Fullan, who was in Toronto. Tony Mackay, my friend and former mentor, chaired and facilitated the whole event from Melbourne. And so it was that at 9.30pm one cold February evening, from our building in Reading, I found myself presenting my views, responding to questions and then debating with some of the greatest education thinkers and writers dispersed across the globe, while hundreds of others watched online from wherever they were in the world. I was increasingly beginning to feel that I had something to say on system reform that had resonance internationally.

Imperfect leaders acknowledge and praise others

Meanwhile, our MAT, CST, was slowly improving. One fantastic development was what happened at Benjamin Adlard Primary School in Gainsborough, Lincolnshire. Benjamin Adlard was a very challenging school on a council estate where there were a very high number of children on free school meals and a great deal of mobility – families moving onto the estate and then off again. I had visited the school in my first year at CfBT and I saw malnourished children, low expectations and a school that was trying to cope rather than a school that was flourishing.

In November 2014, the school was placed in special measures and judged as failing. The head teacher left and we needed a great leader to take responsibility. The extraordinarily talented Marie-Claire Bretherton was already executive head of two of our CST primary schools in Lincolnshire (both of which were judged by Ofsted to be outstanding), so we asked if she would be willing to be executive head of Benjamin Adlard too. To our delight she said yes. She was fired up by the moral purpose and set about the transformation agenda with gusto.

She managed to persuade a young and very talented teacher, Sam Coy, to join her as head of school and together they turned a gloomy, struggling culture into one of pride and high expectation. No teaching staff left the school (except for the previous head teacher); the change was brought about entirely by the existing staff under Sam and Marie-Claire's leadership. In June 2016 (18 months after it was judged to be inadequate), the school was inspected by Ofsted and judged to be good in all aspects. The report stated:

> The executive head teacher and head of school provide an exceptional model of leadership for all staff. Together they have brought about a radical change in the culture of the school. Their combined vision, drive and determination have been key to the rapid improvement the school has made.
>
> The executive head teacher is … an inspiring and visionary leader. …
>
> The appointment of the head of school in May 2015 was a turning point for the school. Since then, leadership, teaching, behaviour and achievement have all rapidly improved. Working with the staff, he has reshaped the school's vision to 'create a haven in which pupils flourish'. This has brought together the whole school in a sense of shared responsibility to ensure high-quality teaching alongside excellent pastoral care. As one teacher put it, 'He made us believe we could do it.'[72]

I visited the school in 2016 and was amazed by the transformation. I could hardly believe that it was the same school. I drove away after the visit in tears – emotionally overcome by how much better the life chances of these children were now compared with 18 months ago. It renewed my sense of wonder about the impact that great leadership can have on an organisation.[73]

Imperfect leaders are self-aware

My first two years at CfBT had been a 'dark night of the soul' period for me and for my leadership, but by 2015–2016 things were beginning to change a great deal. We still had major challenges ahead but by the end of the financial year we had once again made a slight profit. Moreover, the prospects for 2016–2017 were looking much better.

I had not been too happy with my speech at the previous year's Inspiring Leadership conference – both in the tightness of its thinking and in the quality of its presentation – so this year I wanted to talk about something that meant a lot to me, and I also wanted to make sure that it was as good as it could be.

I had been wondering whether I could remain as effective a leader in my sixties as I had been in the previous decade. I knew that, in many ways, the older I got, the better I became as a leader – I could see the bigger picture and I had more experience to go on when interpreting what was happening both within the organisation and outside it. It felt like, over the years, my leadership was becoming less like Flash Gordon – rushing around trying to save the world – and more like Miss Marple – using experience to try to understand motive and behaviours and to work out what to do next.

Of course, I had been an effective leader in my twenties, thirties and forties in many ways. I had been a good communicator, a risk-taker, someone who challenged the status quo and believed in transformation rather than just improvement. I had led with energy, purpose and passion, managing on less sleep but still functioning pretty well. But now I was finding that I had less energy, I needed more downtime and I could not work at quite the same pace as I used to. I was wrestling with the issue of whether it was possible to retain the strengths that I had as a young leader and add these to my strengths as an older leader, whilst avoiding the weaknesses in both. That is how my speech ended up being about grown-up and restless leadership. It was also, I have to confess, because I wanted to weave into my speech one of my very favourite Bob Dylan songs: 'Forever Young'.

In this speech, I also open up about some of the challenges I had experienced at CfBT and the self-doubt I had been through. It is interesting that it was much easier to talk about this publicly after I had started to become more confident again and things were starting to go much better!

Grown-Up and Restless Leadership

Inspiring Leadership Conference 2016

I have spent 38 years working in education in England, including eight fantastic years at the National College for School Leadership. But four years ago, I did something radical.

After the best part of four decades as a teacher and leader in England, I took a new job at the international charity, CfBT, now called the Education Development Trust, and found myself having one of the most intense learning experiences of my career. I was well out of my comfort zone. I had never led an international organisation with colleagues located all over the world, and I had never led an organisation that was entirely dependent upon the commercial market rather than an annual grant from government.

That experience got me thinking a lot about ensuring that we have sufficient challenge in our leadership. How can we remain restless as leaders, constantly seeking to ensure that our organisation is the best it can be?

One of the things that the Education Development Trust invests in is research. Our new report, *Rapid School Improvement*, has identified all the schools in England that have made the move from special measures to good or outstanding in one go. There are about 300 such schools in England and we talked to about a hundred of their head teachers, and to many of their teachers too.[74]

What did these heads do to lead the improvement in their schools? The answer will not surprise you. They were preoccupied with teaching quality and its impact on learning outcomes. They ensured that essential systems were in place. They built coalitions for transformation, inviting teachers, parents and students to support the transformation. They operated at a macro and a micro level – a relentless focus on the school's vision at the macro level and a preoccupation with detail and, as far as possible, personal engagement with specific problems at the micro level. They were good at the analysis of data. They were equally good at spotting talent and using the best to help the rest. They talked a lot about monitoring, but they also talked a lot about morale and motivation and getting the best out of others.

We asked these heads, having taken the school from inadequate to good or better, what their priorities were for the future. For a few the reply was some version of 'more of the same': more monitoring and tracking, more relentless focus on teaching, more robust performance management. We know what works and we are going to keep doing it.

But most took a different view. They knew that sustaining good or achieving outstanding required new thinking. There was a sense that there was a need to inject energy and new ideas into their schools. Where would this energy come from? Our head teachers gave different answers, but collectively they identified a willingness to challenge and a determination to learn:

- The power of challenge above and beyond the challenge of Ofsted; for some, this was a focus on the benefits that can be gained from ensuring a really excellent governing body. For others, it was involvement in serious, robust peer review with head teachers from other schools.

- An outward-looking orientation and a determination to learn from research and the best practice in other schools.

There was a restlessness about the way these heads saw the future – they weren't just sticking to their already proven solution.

This theme of how we can refresh our approach to leadership – how we can be the leader that is required of us now in this new context and how we can maintain a certain restlessness – is central to what I want to say this morning.

I am also passionate about the benefits of mentoring, for all leaders. In my last few jobs I have had a number of mentors, and I still have some now, nearly four years into this job. I also act as a mentor to other leaders. Why would any leader, however experienced, not have a mentor?

We associate mentors with the wisdom of age and experience. However, one of my mentors is younger than me. This got me thinking about the nature of maturity in leadership. Is maturity a fixed thing, earned only through the hard slog of years of experience? Or are there shortcuts to wisdom?

Older leaders can be wise. They tend not to panic in a crisis. They are able to see the big picture. They understand the complexity of situations and know what is needed to lead change in those contexts. They understand team dynamics and culture. They think ahead and can predict what is likely to happen. Experience has enabled them to understand how people work and what motivates them. They also know lots of stuff and have great networks that are sources of intelligence and ideas.

These aren't just the characteristics of the old. Young leaders can have these qualities too. For many of us, our best and most accomplished work may be completed when we are young. By the age of 27, Napoleon had conquered Italy and Brunel was chief engineer at the Great Western Railway. Pitt the Younger became prime minister when he was 24. One of the best school leaders I know, Liz Robinson, became a head at 29.

There is often something great and exciting about young leaders. They tend to be enthusiastic, energetic, restless, driven and pacey. They challenge the status quo – they ask the 'why' question that nobody else asks and they move the thinking forward in a way that stops us stagnating. They have less fear of failure and take risks. And they usually learn fast and hungrily, welcoming feedback and wanting to improve. But these aren't just the characteristics of the young. The best leaders retain these qualities throughout their time as leaders – they don't lose it when they get older.

In their book *Professional Capital*, where they draw on the work of Malcolm Gladwell, Andy Hargreaves and Michael Fullan suggest that teachers go through three stages in their careers.[75] I would suggest that you could also apply the same analysis to leaders:

1.   Early (enthusiasm is great but capability is low).

2.   Mid (enthusiasm and capability are both high and balanced).

3.   Late (enthusiasm is less than capability so they become cynical).

I am challenging this perspective. It implies that there is a brief magic moment when we peak as leaders and then it's pretty much downhill. Have you peaked yet? Do you remember that time when, fleetingly, you were doing rather well as a leader? How about the person sitting next to you – do they look as if they have peaked? Of course this is far too simplistic.

At the age of 14 I went to Ireland and I remember swinging on a rope bridge over a gorge. I wouldn't even go near that bridge now. At 14 I lacked awareness of the risks – it never occurred to me that I would fall; but now I am probably too aware of what might go wrong so I keep away. But I do believe that it is possible for a leader to be both old and bold. An awareness of risk doesn't have to lead to playing it safe. Instead, it can give experienced leaders the ability to read risks and take astute gambles.

What we need are grown-up and restless leaders. And this is categorically not about age. It is a matter of attitude and learning.

Grown-up leaders feel comfortable in their own skin. They don't sulk or have tantrums. Grown-up leaders have adult conversations. They treat people with respect and dignity. They make good calls in difficult situations. They are self-confident but their ego is under control. They are the people you want to be around in a crisis. They see the big picture and they don't overreact when things go wrong. Immature leaders think that they need to prove their own ability to lead; grown-up leaders know that is not what it is about. Instead, they are skilled at drawing on the talents of others.

Restless leaders are enthusiasts. People are delighted to work with them and for them because their excitement about the work and the mission is infectious. They are never satisfied with the status quo. They are 'can do' at their very core and they are determined to make a difference.

I think we need grown-up and restless leadership instead of immature and ground-down leadership. And the question is, how do we develop both those things in ourselves and in others?

Why am I choosing to talk about this subject now? There will soon be a shortage of leaders. If we are to take responsibility for leading the system, then we must develop younger leaders more quickly and be better at maximising the expertise of the not-so-young leaders.

If we treat our young leaders simply as workhorses they will go elsewhere. As many older leaders stay in work longer, we will need to find ways to engage them meaningfully and to help them continue to be restless and enthusiastic – to make better use of their skills and expertise. There are barely enough good leaders to go round, so it makes sense to value and cherish the leaders we have. When we think about diversity in teams, let's look at creating teams with diverse ages too so that we can make the most of the different skills and expertise that younger and older leaders can bring.

I want to consider the following three key challenges:

1. How can we learn wisdom quickly?

2. What kind of leadership does the current context need from us – how grown-up and how restless?

3.   How do we make the most of our wisdom and retain our restlessness as we get older?

1. How can we learn wisdom quickly?

Alan Hansen famously said on *Match of the Day*, 'You can't win anything with kids,' referring to the young Manchester United side in the mid-1990s. That team went on to win the football Premier League in England. Sir Alex Ferguson, the manager of the team, understood that if you're good enough, you're old enough. He also understood, crucially, the need to provide controlled exposure to testing and challenging situations. He didn't play the so-called 'kids' in every game. He phased them in until they were ready to cope with the really big matches, and he protected them when they needed protecting.

Sports psychology has led the way in developing people's ability to cope with pressure. The Royal Air Force College now uses sports psychology techniques with its trainee pilots. They realised that pressure and the resulting failure to think straight was one of the biggest problems young pilots faced in the air, and that lowering their stress levels led directly to better performance. More flying time isn't an option – it's too expensive. And, as one of their trainers observed, you can't just shout 'relax' when the situation becomes stressful. Instead, they identified one-to-one coaching during a high-stress situation as the key to improvement. It worked. In a trial, those trainees who were given this type of support outperformed a control group at every stage of their training.

I can see really interesting parallels with leadership development in education. One of the problems that we found with the National Professional Qualification for Headship is that the theory meant nothing unless you found yourself in the real situation. Even role plays don't do it. As one head said to a colleague, 'We practised 20 scenarios on NPQH, and on day one of my headship scenario number 21 walked through the door.'

If we are serious about developing our young leaders, we should deliberately and proactively give them the opportunity to try out the most significant things we do as leaders and provide focused coaching to help them – for example, leading on setting the school budget, acting as the lead professional at a full governing body meeting, handling a very difficult staffing issue or chairing a really problematic meeting with unhappy parents. Sometimes we don't do this because of our preference for control as leaders and the need to manage risk, and sometimes we don't do this because of our desire to protect our colleagues from some of the worst aspects of our jobs as leaders. We need to reflect on this.

As part of our research into leadership, we spoke with a head of a large secondary school in outer London. For the next stage of the school's journey, he had deliberately changed his style of leadership from a directive one to one that was all about building the leadership capacity of others. This had taken time. Although his style was increasingly towards greater delegation, one area where he had not delegated at all was his personal responsibility for dealing with difficult staffing issues. He had a very clear rationale:

> … that's the bit I haven't given to anyone else because I think, ultimately, it isn't pleasant. I am very aware that that's someone's husband or wife, son or daughter, mum or dad, so I think these issues need to be handled with dignity and delicacy, but, equally, firmly and consistently. So I haven't delegated this role. They know what I'm doing and they know how I do it. I've never actually asked them to do it.[76]

This represents an important challenge for us in growing other leaders. I understand why this head did what he did, but there is a fine line between protecting our staff and disempowering them. If we are serious about developing leaders, they should get a chance to lead in the really difficult moments too.

We should learn from our successes in developing teachers. Over the years, we have become better and better at coaching teachers and improving pedagogy. We observe them and give them feedback. We plan lessons together, deliver them together and review learning together. But we don't have anything like that sophistication when it comes to leadership. If I say that I am going to watch you lead, what will I be watching? A speech you make? A multitude of conversations you have? A meeting you chair? A card you write? It is much harder to capture what we are watching when we are coaching leaders than when we are coaching teachers. What is the equivalent of joint practice development for leaders?

Teachers improve their teaching by targeting a skill to improve and then working on it over time with regular feedback and modelling. Does each leader – young and old (including yourself) – have an aspect of leadership that they are working on in an open and transparent way, and is each one expecting regular and constructive feedback on that aspect of their leadership? Are we treating improvement in leadership as seriously as we now treat improvement in teaching?

There are new and exciting ways to grow and develop leaders that didn't exist before. Multi-academy trusts and other hard-edged collaborations can give greater responsibility to the most talented leaders. They can enable young leaders to lead on a curriculum area across the trust or alliance. They can enable a head of school to receive support in the role from a chief executive before perhaps becoming a CEO themselves. We can create new roles that have never existed before and build in challenge and learning in powerful new ways.

Many CEOs of trusts and executive principals are finding their new roles hugely challenging, requiring skills that they have not had to use before. Being in charge of five schools is a different role from being in charge of one. Providing leadership across a MAT for schools with heads who have been used to running their own show is not without its challenges! So, how can those with experience of doing these roles in other trusts provide mentoring and support? Are we in danger of moving from autonomous and isolated schools to autonomous and isolated MATs? Where is the cross-MAT support for CEOs?

Here are two challenges to take away on the issue of helping leaders to grow up quickly:

- Reflect on the most challenging aspect of your current leadership role. How could you safely hand this over to another leader in your school as part of their development?

- Consider how you might ensure that every leader in your school – including yourself – is working on a specific improvement in an aspect of leadership.

2. What kind of leadership does the current context need from us?

Perhaps the best example I can give you of the transformation of a school system is the story of a truly inspirational leader I met this year: Claudia Costin. For five years she led the transformation of schools and student outcomes in Rio de Janeiro. What is most striking about her leadership is that she was precisely the leader that the Rio de Janeiro context needed her to be. She moved things on at pace and she challenged the status quo. And she took the teachers with her, with 70,000 following her on Twitter. She went over the heads of the vested interests directly to the teachers themselves to keep them on board, she introduced 'godmother schools' (like our national support schools) to support other schools and she increased accountability, but she also increased support and professional development for teachers and leaders. This wasn't a system in which change was easy. At one point, the military – with tanks – had to go into the favelas to take control of schools that were run by drug gangs. In comparison, Sir Michael Wilshaw looks like a pussycat.

The case I'm interested in, however, is a bit more subtle. She introduced grade retention. If children failed to meet a certain standard, they didn't move up to the next grade with their peers. Now, all the evidence and all the orthodoxy suggests that grade retention is a bad thing – it demotivates the children held back and puts off their younger peers. Claudia ignored this, but she did so in a very deliberate way. She identified children without the foundation skills to progress, extracted them, supported them intensively and then, when they were ready, reintegrated them back into their chronological peer group. As a result, in three years the illiteracy rate fell from 13 per cent to 3 per cent. Claudia valued the international evidence, but she did not let herself be ruled by it. She was impassioned and restless in her approach but she innovated wisely. She learned from older systems but injected her own way of doing things too. She challenged the accepted way of doing things and achieved remarkable success. This is grown-up and restless leadership.

I want to give you another example – this time about a programme led by the Education Development Trust in Kenya. There are still millions of children worldwide who don't go to school, and a disproportionate number of them are girls. We are leading an initiative to get over 81,000 'out of school' girls into education and, crucially, once they are in school, to make sure that they make good progress.

The reasons why girls don't go to school are complex. They include topics as diverse as parental attitudes, the prevalence of sexual violence and the quality of sanitation in schools. It's also determined by school quality. There is not much point going to school if you don't learn much and the staff don't seem to care about you. So we have been trying to bring about change at several levels.

The early findings from our project are really positive. We are enrolling lots of 'out of school' girls and they are sticking around and doing well in their tests. So how come? If you ask the remarkable Mark Rotich, who led this work, what had the most impact, he identifies four things:

1. The power of data. If we understand the performance of schools and can benchmark them in terms of girls' enrolment and learning, then we can target our improvement support and challenge underperformance.

2. The importance of great multi-agency working and the hard slog of knocking on doors. The schools have teamed up with health workers

– people who live and work in these communities – and health visitors are proving to be great at knocking on the doors of houses and asking why the girls are not in school.

3. The effectiveness of classroom coaching as a way of improving teaching. We have put in place a team of teaching and learning coaches who visit teachers in their classrooms and help them to develop their skills. This is making a big difference.

4. The centrality of school leadership. Some of the schools are well led, others are not. There is a clear relationship between leadership quality and the way the schools are breaking down barriers to girls' participation.

Sound familiar? Data. Hands-on collaboration beyond the school. Coaching and leadership. Yes, one of the things I've learned over the past four years is that whether it's the UK or Kenya, there are some universal ingredients to the business of transforming young lives.

Those who lead in education systems, as well as those who lead in schools, need to welcome new ideas from other systems, but then be wise in applying the learning to their own context. They should value evidence but not be so controlled by the evidence that they don't trust their own judgements within their context.

Age still seems to be a prerequisite for many of the top jobs in public life. Hillary Clinton and Donald Trump, the candidates for president of the United States, are in their late sixties, as is Jeremy Corbyn. Compare this to some of the world's best-known revolutionary leaders and the age at which they started to rule: Fidel Castro (33) and Napoleon (30). The same is true of the private sector. Interestingly, whereas most CEOs of Fortune 500 companies are between 50 and 59 years old, entrepreneurial leaders tend to be considerably younger.

It would seem that when the leadership task requires knowledge, values and connection to the community, there is a tendency to choose an older leader; but when we are looking for entrepreneurialism or radical change, we tend to go for younger leaders.

For me, this prompts a genuinely important question: what kind of leadership do we need *now* in our schools, given the significant change that is taking place in England at the moment? If our approach is negative – without constructive ideas for moving things forward – we have to question our place as leaders. If we are resisting change because we just don't want to change, then we have a real leadership issue. Is our current leadership style in this changing context part of the problem or part of the solution? Is now the time for more radical restless leadership?

We also need to apply our wisdom and a big picture perspective to the current change agenda in England. The most obvious illustration of the challenges for leaders in schools at the moment is in the decisions around academisation. Laura McInerney, the editor of *Schools Week*, hit the nail on the head when she tweeted that the advice to heads and governors about becoming an academy or joining a MAT should be: 'Same advice you would give kids about sex. Be safe, be sure, be legal & don't do it hurriedly just because everyone else is.' To which Penny Rabiger added: 'and choose the right partner that will still respect you in the morning'.

What is the response of the grown-up and restless leader in this situation? 'Should my school become an academy or join a MAT?' is the wrong question. The right question is, 'How can my school best collaborate with others to ensure that each of the children in our schools is a powerful learner and that the adults are given opportunities to learn and develop as teachers and leaders?' If that is through a multi-academy trust then fine. If it is through some other kind of outcomes-focused collaboration for the moment (which may turn into a MAT later) then that is also fine. Who knows what things will look like in 2020? Rather than ask ourselves the wrong questions reluctantly, we need to ask ourselves the right questions enthusiastically. It is leaders who make the weather proactively in their schools and it is grown-up and restless school leaders who, together, can 'create the climate' across the system.

Moving from individual autonomous schools to MATs and other system partnerships will require high-quality grown-up leadership – putting the ego to one side, holding adult conversations, asking what is best for the children and not necessarily what is best for me.

So, my challenge is, what kind of leadership is needed from us now? Does it need to be wise and measured, or does it need something more risky and radical? Like those heads in our research report who said that now that their school was good or outstanding it needed a different leadership approach from them, do we know what is now needed from us? Have we got the balance right between maturity and restlessness in our own leadership?

Here are two challenges to take away on the issue of leading for context:

- Create a forum in which young leaders can challenge organisational assumptions. Ask them to identify the areas of leadership which are too slow or too inflexible and come up with suggestions for how to do these things better.

- Ask someone you trust to work with you to reflect on your own leadership approach over the past few years. In the context you are now in, discuss with them what might need to change about your leadership.

3. How do we make the most of the wisdom we have learned as leaders and retain our restlessness as we get older?

If you watched *War and Peace* on TV – or, better still, read the book – you will remember that it was the old Russian General, Prince Kutuzov, who, against the advice of his more headstrong younger officers, decided to retreat and let Napoleon march into Moscow unchallenged. It was a decision that won Russia the war: Napoleon's supply line dried up, winter set in and he had to retreat. Kutuzov had used his wisdom to be a grown-up leader.

In some cultures, the notion of the importance of elders is at the heart of how the society operates. Late in his life, Nelson Mandela founded The Elders, a group of older leaders who are committed to working together to support peace-making and social justice around the world. Shouldn't we have more of this concept of using elders in the world of education too?

As I mentioned at the start of this speech, I'm living proof that even older leaders can throw themselves into new and scary challenges. The decision to change your role can be a really difficult one to make and you often have to force yourself to change. You tell yourself that you are still needed here. But, of course, 'the job' is never finished. Instead we should be asking: am I still growing as a leader? Am I still as impassioned, as driven and as restless? Does this organisation need a shake-up and, if so, am I the person to do it?

At points in the last few years in my role at the Education Development Trust, I have felt completely out of my depth. I have not known what to do. Some of my friends have been seriously worried about me as I struggled to make sense of my new environment. I found myself trying to use leadership 'toolkits' that have worked elsewhere, but just didn't apply to my new context. I had to learn new skills and develop different approaches. But what I have always tried to do is to be a learner, so I knew how to ask for help. And I also knew that I needed to show leadership. As Michael Hyatt says, 'More often than not, being brave means doing it scared.'

Sometimes gradual change is called for; at other times some radical change is just what you need to take you to the next level. If you are sitting here now wondering what to do, then maybe it is time to jump in and go for that new challenge. That may well not mean leaving your present role; the challenge could be a new development for you in your existing role.

And such reflections/efforts don't just apply to ourselves. If we want leaders to retain their restlessness, what more can we do to re-energise the older leaders in our schools? Are we doing enough to seek out and capitalise on their wisdom and proactively develop their restlessness, either through a job share or through the opportunity to lead beyond their school or through coaching and mentoring others in different contexts? Perhaps that older leader on your team who you currently perceive as a problem might – with the right new challenge – become part of the solution.

One of the heads we interviewed in our post-Ofsted school improvement research was determined not to rest on her laurels. Having moved the school from inadequate to good, she put in place a comprehensive programme of benchmarking provision against the best. She asked important questions such as, 'How well are we spending the pupil premium?', 'How effectively do we deploy our teaching assistants?', 'How well are we supporting our students with SEN?' She found a school in her county with a reputation for excellence and expertise in each area and persuaded it to lead the review of provision in her school. This type of tough peer review is a serious antidote to complacent leadership and a great way of ensuring mature and restless leadership.

The Education Development Trust has also been doing some interesting work on peer review. Our approach is called the Schools Partnership Programme, and I was very struck by this comment from one of our participant heads from the north-east of England. She contrasted the transformative potential of peer review with the weaker impact of traditional external review via inspection: 'The difference with peer reviews is you show your reviewers the things that worry you most, whereas you would probably want to hide these from inspectors! This results in much deeper impact and therefore real school improvement.'

Colleagues, traditional inspection is about proving how good you are; robust peer review is not about proving, it is about improving. And as grown-up and restless leaders, we know that leadership is about improving rather than proving too.

Here are two challenges to take away about staying restless in our leadership:

1. Take on a new personal challenge. Look for a way to extend yourself and move out of your comfort zone.

2. Invite peer review. Ask for the critical eye of leaders from other institutions, young and old. Specifically seek challenge on your own leadership.

Conclusion

In Kenya, you sometimes don't say hello when you meet someone. Instead, you say 'Kasserian Ingera', which means 'How goes it with our children?' The hoped for reply is, 'All the children are well' – not 'my children' or 'your children' but 'all the children'. For the Maasai, the society can't be well unless all the children are well. It is about the future. It is about our young people.

The good news in Kenya is that there are now thousands of girls for whom it is starting to go better and whose life chances are being enhanced. But what about here in England? How goes it with our children? Well, the answer is mixed. As a result of your leadership, children overall in England are getting a better deal. Our schools are better led and are improved places for learning. But there is so much more to do ensure that all children – not just the children in your school but all our children – do well and make the most of their lives. Some of the challenges I have described in Kenya and in Rio de Janeiro are experienced by children here in England. There are still the marginalised, the oppressed and the vulnerable. There are mental health issues, illiteracy and sexual exploitation. That is why it is so important that we never lose that restlessness and moral purpose in our leadership.

Leadership is a great privilege because through leadership we can make a huge and positive impact on the lives of hundreds and thousands of people. We are not leading for ourselves. We lead in order for the world to be in a better place for those who will follow on after us. There is an old saying: 'We have not inherited this world from our ancestors. We have been loaned it by our children.' It is our moral responsibility to leave things in a better shape than we found them. Our overwhelming mission is to ensure that the organisation and the people in it are in a better place than when we started, and then we pass the torch on for those younger than us to pick up.

As grown-up and restless leaders, we commit personally to developing our future leaders in a more meaningful and focused way than ever before. To invest in them and to encourage them to challenge us. We commit to considering new ways to re-energise our experienced leaders. We agree, metaphorically, to step out onto the rope bridge, even if it makes our stomach churn, and to embrace new challenges because our organisations need us to be bold and restless as well as wise and grown-up. We don't just keep our heads down. We look outward and see the big picture, and we understand that the context in which we are working is changing.

Like Claudia Costin in Rio de Janeiro and Mark Rotich in Kenya, we use our knowledge and expertise wisely to think through what is needed now in our context and then to take decisive action. We understand, because we are grown-up, that leadership isn't about being ambitious for ourselves. It is not about proving ourselves or about ego. It is about being ambitious for the children and young people we serve. We have a strong foundation based on wisdom and we retain that youthful restlessness deep in our beings.

In one of his greatest ever songs, Bob Dylan summarised wise and restless leadership with these powerful words:

> May your hands always be busy
>
> May your feet always be swift
>
> May you have a strong foundation when the wind of changes shift.
>
> May your heart always be joyful
>
> May your song always be sung
>
> And may you stay forever young.

Looking back at this speech years later, I think the issues are just as relevant now as they were then. Study after study is showing that work-load amongst teachers and leaders in England is very high compared to other education systems. We face increasing difficulties in attracting and retaining high-quality school leaders, especially in our more challenging schools. We need to be more proactive in helping young leaders to develop wisdom – with support and coaching – and in finding new ways to retain and refresh older leaders. Also, without good school leadership, we will have an even bigger retention challenge with teachers because it is the quality of leadership that makes such a big difference to retention rates and to teachers' job satisfaction.[77]

Chapter Twelve
Ethical Leadership

There are heroes in the seaweed.

Leonard Cohen, 'Suzanne'

My diary entry in August 2017 summed up how I felt at the end of my time as CEO at CfBT/Education Development Trust:

> I think that in the end I did pretty well at CfBT/Education Development Trust, though at one point I believed that we were never going to turn it round ... This year we are predicting growth of £10 million in the company and we are investing £2 million in new initiatives. So, I leave with my head held high and I think I leave a transformed (for the better) organisation ... but it was close. I have enjoyed it but it has been the toughest job I have ever had. I will not miss the stress of being a CEO, the agendas, the board meetings, the reports, the admin, the worry about something going wrong ... but I will miss the teamwork, making a difference and, most of all, the international work in Kenya, Rwanda, India, Brunei, UAE and Jordan.

In 2016, I met up with my long-time friend Andy Hargreaves (we started writing a book together in 1987). Andy went on to become an internationally renowned speaker and author and a very big name in education worldwide, but he has always been supportive and kind to me, which I have hugely appreciated. He told me that he was hoping to form a collaboration between eight education systems from around the world that were committed to advancing equity, excellence, well-being, democracy and human rights for all students within high-quality and inclusive school systems. It sounded like a great idea, and it sounded even more exciting when he asked me if I would consider facilitating the first annual summit in Reykjavik. I knew that I was good at chairing meetings and summarising outcomes but I had never thought of myself as a facilitator. Nevertheless, this seemed too good an opportunity to miss, and I was delighted that Philip Graf (who was chair of the board) gave me his approval to get involved.

The event took place in September 2016 and there were eight education systems represented: Iceland, Finland, Ontario, California, Vermont, Aruba, Ireland and Scotland. Most were there with their minister, along with senior officials and a representative from a union or professional association. Some great thought leaders were present at the event including Vicky Colbert (whose work in Colombia has been so transformational), as well as Sir Ken Robinson, Pasi Sahlberg, Pak Tee Ng, Jeannie Oakes and, of course, Andy Hargreaves. The summit was hard work to facilitate but it was also a huge privilege.

We built into the summit a process of reciprocal system-to-system consultancy. What impressed me most was the way that the systems were prepared to open up with each other about the challenges and problems they faced, as well as to share their successes. It was also pretty stark that – with its focus on inclusion, equity and well-being – this was a collaboration that England under its current regime would not choose to join. The other strong conclusion that I came to (and this has been reinforced more recently) was that in many ways England is out of step with the education systems in other countries. Some of these systems (for example, Finland, Ontario and Ireland) are much higher-performing than England but they have very different accountability systems.

To be honest, many leaders in other systems look at what is happening in England with bewilderment; school performance tables, even for primary schools, result in massive pressures on schools to avoid being labelled as failing, leading to harsh interventions, with people's jobs and careers on the line. It is no surprise to me that, at the time of writing, Ireland, Finland and Ontario have no problems with recruiting teachers or school leaders, yet it is a major issue in England.

Imperfect leaders hold on to their moral purpose

I made some important international visits in 2016–2017. One was to speak at a conference in Jordan. The Education Development Trust was running an initiative in Jordan to support teachers in schools that were struggling to cope with the huge numbers of Syrian refugees that had come into their country. Many schools had to open for two sittings to cope with the massive influx of Syrian children who needed an education. As I say in my speech, I found my visit to Jordan to be profoundly moving. The country was reeling under the pressure of taking in so many refugees (who made up more than a quarter of the population), but it continued to do so because it believed that this was the right thing to do – to help their neighbours who were in the middle of such a terrible war. I couldn't help but notice the stark contrast with the anti-immigration feeling in some parts of the UK. As far as I was concerned, the Jordanians were unsung heroes.

I also made a trip to Rwanda in 2017. We were on the point of securing a new contract to improve literacy and numeracy in primary schools across the country, based on our successful experience in Kenya and Brunei, and we needed to meet with senior officials from the ministry and also with representatives from the Department for International Development. I was struck by how the country seemed to be much more organised and ordered than Kenya was. I found the people of Rwanda to be friendly and warm, and it was a strange feeling to know that within living memory there had been civil war and genocide.

I was particularly interested to find out that in Rwanda the tribal chiefs and leaders used to make a public *Imihigo* or 'vow to deliver'. They would publicly state in front of their tribe what their goals were and declare that they were determined to overcome any possible challenges that arose in achieving those goals. In order to attack corruption and promote transparency and public accountability, President Paul Kagame has introduced the notion of a public *Imihigo* for all senior leaders in the public sector.

I like the idea of promising publicly in front of your peers. It can make it more likely that you will do what you are committed to doing, especially when things get tough, and it also helps to develop collective accountability. I refer to this in my speech when I talk about the fact that promising my friends and colleagues that I was going to run a half marathon helped me to be committed to putting in the time and effort to do the training. But this was also true of my public pledge in 2005 to make 500 phone calls to school leaders when I started at the National College – if I hadn't made a public pledge, I suspect that I wouldn't have seen this one through.

Perhaps the most memorable of my international visits that year was to Kenya. There had been an independent evaluation of our work in helping 81,000 girls go to school. The success indicators were not just about attendance at school but about the girls continuing at school and doing well in national tests. During my visit, I attended a conference where the independent evaluator reported that we had mainly achieved one of the success criteria and fully achieved all the others. It is difficult for me to think of any other initiative that I have been involved in throughout my whole career that has had such a positive impact on so many needy children. It was a very moving moment, and one that gave me a great sense of pride in the organisation I was leading. These colleagues of mine, mainly Kenyans, were real heroes.

Later that day, at the same event, we announced the early findings of our NLE pilot in Kenya. We had identified school principals who were doing well and having some success and linked them with other school principals who needed help. We didn't copy the whole initiative from England – we 'nuanced' it. Nevertheless, it was great to see an idea that I had helped to get off the ground in England in 2005 now beginning to make an impact in Kenya in 2017.

In my view, the education system in England at this time was struggling. The amount of top-down change was continuing unabated, leading to exhaustion amongst some and fear amongst others. I was beginning to see five different and worrying behaviours from some school leaders:

1. Ground down. Worn out by the accountability system – they know what they have to do but are just too tired of pushing and pushing without the support or capacity needed.

2. Victim behaviour. They just do whatever the government says they should do. They feel powerless. They become overly dependent. They choose to abrogate their power as leaders.

3. Copying the top-down approach. Leaders experiencing top-down and high-stress approaches from government start to demonstrate the same approaches with their own staff. Instead of encouraging creativity and empowering others, some school leaders were creating stress and fear within their own school by mimicking the overly controlling top-down approach from government.

4. Isolationism. Even highly effective leaders keep their heads down. Instead of looking outwards, helping to support other schools and leading the system, they conclude that this is too risky and that they have enough problems in their own school to worry about.

5. Competition. Leaders competing for the more able students and seeking to avoid the more demanding or disadvantaged students.

By 2016–2017, I was becoming increasingly concerned about the government's reform agenda. I was very worried about what I perceived to be far too much emphasis on structures and accountability and not enough emphasis on learning and capacity building. It seemed to me that the system was not so much losing its way but, even more worrying, proactively creating greater division and inequity. The focus on market forces and on high-stakes accountability pushed comparison between schools to new limits. As a result, some schools were competing for the brighter students and some were beginning to think of ways to push out those who would otherwise bring their school's results down.

At the same time, too many young people were being disempowered and disenfranchised as a result of a narrow curriculum, assessment that was strong on reliability but not on validity, and a system that downplayed vocational qualifications – and, indeed, the arts and music – rather than enabling young people to take the next step that was right for them.

Some schools were also setting themselves up as 'no excuses' schools that combined a knowledge-based curriculum with very high behaviour standards (no talking in the corridors, etc.). This was working very well in those schools, and the children were rising to these high expectations, but, in my view, too many children who lived nearby were not attending those schools – either because they had been excluded or quietly asked to go elsewhere, or because their parents felt they could not cope with the pressure of sending them there. Schools can be very successful if they set standards high and refuse to include any student or parent who can't embrace or cope with those standards. But what about the vulnerable children and the parents who are struggling to cope? Too many children were now falling between the cracks, being lost to the system and either receiving no education or a very limited one.

Under the National Health Service all children have the same entitlements even if they are obese or have mental health challenges, or their parents are drug addicts. Could the same be said for our education system? I had not been a universal fan of the Every Child Matters agenda under Ed Balls, but this seemed to be taking things to the other extreme. Of course, there was some fantastic ethical, inclusive practice going on in many schools and in some MATs and teaching school alliances, but this was increasingly hard to maintain and to some extent was going against the grain of the existing accountability system.

I began to think very seriously about the importance of ethical leadership and of staying true to your values: doing what is right, rather than doing what will get you the highest accolade in the accountability system. I had attended a workshop earlier that year led by Carolyn Roberts (chair of the Association of School and College Leaders' Ethical Leadership Commission) which had got me thinking more about this. What should our ethical standards be as school leaders? Does every child matter, or do those who might get better results require more of our time and attention? Is our first priority to our own school, or should we be equally concerned about all children in the locality?

Throughout my career as a leader I had wrestled with ethical issues, and I am not sure that in every case I made the right decisions. It is often tough to decide whether to take disciplinary or competency action against a member of staff, whether to introduce a restructure that will lead to redundancies, or whether to close down or sell-off part of the organisation. I know that in some cases I have upset people deeply as a result of the decisions I have taken as a leader.

There are other ethical issues too: do I keep quiet about a new policy from the elected government if I am uncomfortable about it? Do I travel business class on a long flight if I have high-level meetings at the other end when the organisation is short of funds? Do I support improvements in education in countries where human rights is an issue? What I was most keen to do was to encourage leaders to 'flex their ethical muscle,' to think for themselves and to work out issues and actions after careful consideration, rather than just following the crowd.

Imperfect leaders are aware of their strengths as well as their weaknesses

By August 2016, I had decided that I would retire in a year's time. I had discussed it at length with Philip Graf and also, of course, with my wife, Jacqui. She had been semi-retired for a couple of years and it felt like the right time for me, after almost five years as CEO of CfBT/Education Development Trust, to step down – at the age of 61 – and to hand over to the next leader.

I had taken the organisation forward on a range of fronts, but I was also aware that there was much more to do. I had played to my strengths. The organisation now had a much higher profile in the UK. The Schools Partnership Programme (schools collaborating together, including conducting peer review) had started with a pilot of 30 schools in 2013 and now comprised 1,000 schools. The Inspiring Leadership conferences had created a much greater awareness of our organisation amongst school leaders. The focus on system reform meant that our international work moved strongly in this direction, to great effect. Our research on whole-system reform was highly credible and was enhancing our reputation. We now had an organisation that was fit for purpose – one that was making a decent margin, able to invest in the future and making an even more positive difference to children's lives.

But there were other aspects of the organisation that needed a lot more work – aspects that I had neglected, such as the use of technology. I was too close to the organisation. Like the analogy I had used in my 2007 speech regarding the new house, I had stopped noticing things that weren't good enough. It now needed fresh eyes and a different perspective. A new leader needed to come in and tackle the areas of weakness that I had not addressed, which is exactly how these things should work.

By the time of my speech in June 2017, the board had announced my successor. Patrick Brazier, who had done such great work as the director of operational services, would be the new CEO. I was delighted for him and I knew that the senior team were also delighted. The message was continuity with some change. Given all the radical change we had been through during the previous five years, I think it was the right message and the right decision.

I walked onto the platform in Birmingham on 8 June in front of 1,000 school leaders and made my final speech as the leader of an organisation. It was a year after the Brexit vote and the same day as the snap general election in the UK. Prime Minister Theresa May had gone to the country to ask the electorate to support 'strong and stable leadership'. She lost her majority and, at the time of writing, there is still a great deal of turmoil in the country and in both main political parties. It made sense, perhaps even more powerfully in retrospect, that the theme of my speech that morning was principled leadership in challenging times.

Principled Leadership in Challenging Times

Inspiring Leadership Conference 2017

On Sunday 9 April three security guards boarded a United Airlines plane. They forcibly hauled a 69-year-old passenger from his seat and dragged him off. The passenger, Dr David Dao, suffered a broken nose, concussion and lost two front teeth. Dr Dao had done nothing wrong but he was treated like a criminal. As a service business, the success of United Airlines should have been driven by their customers' needs. Instead, their operating systems overrode everything else. Getting most of the passengers to their desired destination and getting the crew to their next flight superseded the concept of care for the individual customer.

Guess what United Airlines' official slogan is. Fly the Friendly Skies. It is difficult to imagine a greater gap between the rhetoric and the reality.

I started to ask myself, what does the rhetoric–reality gap look like in my own organisation? How much do we live the values? Call to mind your organisation's mission statement. Does it truly describe how you operate or is it just warm words? One of my themes in this speech will be that, as leaders, it is up to us to model the behaviours we expect from others. If there is a disconnect between our rhetoric and our behaviours, then trust is lost and the organisation is in trouble.

Let me take this idea of leaders modelling and influencing behaviour further. It has been a remarkable and turbulent 12 months since our last conference. A year ago, few of us expected a Brexit vote, a Trump presidency or Theresa May as prime minister. But it's not just the events themselves that are so striking. For me, it is the kind of political leadership we have seen: the viciousness of the personal attacks during the recent presidential elections in the United States and in France. An American president who mocks a disabled reporter and claims that reports of things he said that he now regrets are 'fake news'. In India, over a fifth of MPs have been charged with serious criminal offences. It gives a whole new meaning to the term 'conviction politics'.

Niccolò Machiavelli wrote pretty much the world's first leadership manual, *The Prince*, which was published in the early 16th century. Somebody recently had the bright idea of producing a new version and promoting it as a guide for today's corporate leaders. Let me read you some of the blurb: 'It deals with many of the subjects which confront the modern manager and executive every day: managing hatred, contempt, and opposition, eliminating your enemies, successful deceit, cruelty, compassion, corporate independence, opportunism ... and the careful use of brutality.'[78]

Machiavelli's big and radical idea was that leadership sometimes required proactively immoral action. He asked the question: can a good person be a great leader? His answer was emphatically no, because the great leader must at times do bad things. Soft, kind leaders, he argued, get eaten alive.

Certainly, some of our world leaders seem to be modelling Machiavelli's approach to leadership. There are many highly principled politicians out there, but public trust in them is at an all-time low. Unlike politics, school leadership is seen as one of the bastions of ethical, moral and trustworthy leadership. Yet even in schools we have witnessed, in a small number of cases, behaviours that are not great examples to children or their parents.

In the *TES* a few months ago, there was an article with this heading: 'Charting the Downfall of the "Famous Five" Superheads'.[79] Some of the head teachers lost their jobs following financial misdemeanours and one was jailed. I don't want to go into the specific cases – I am making a more general point – but what this exemplifies is that some heads and CEOs are blurring the lines between what is good for themselves and what is good for the children. There are leaders who achieve some success and then seem to forget what it is all about.

The pressure on school and multi-academy trust leaders to cross an ethical line is greater in England now than it has ever been. The combination of high accountability and high autonomy, with the lack of a 'middle tier', makes England's education system more extreme than almost any other in the world. This is what creates many of the moral dilemmas for school leaders, especially at times of austerity and when many schools are struggling to recruit quality staff.

Our high-stakes accountability system places pressure on school leaders to behave in a way that maximises their performance as a school or MAT, but may not always be in the best interests of the individual child or, indeed, the wider community of schools. When you are fighting for the reputation of your school and every inch of progress in learning is hard won, and when you are in a system where falling below a floor target can cost you your job, it can be tempting to drift away from the ethical line you would ideally want to take.

At a time of reduced funding and teacher shortages, real tensions exist between what is right for *my* school and what is right for *our* schools in the local area. There are very real and complex dilemmas for school leaders. Do I permanently exclude a child when he or she is having such a negative impact on the other children, but I am not sure what will happen to that child once excluded? Do I accept a big pay rise when I am making staff redundant due to budget cuts? Do I go out of my way to covertly steal talented staff from another school when I know it will have a negative impact on the school they are leaving? Do I either make a member of staff who desperately needs a job redundant, or do I (amongst other things) write off the CPD budget? A school nearby needs help; do I keep my head down and focus on the many challenges in my own school or do I offer support? I genuinely want my school to be inclusive but I know that by taking in challenging children from other schools we will probably do less well in terms of accountability measures – should I refuse to take any more children?

It is dilemmas like these, and many more like them, which make it so important that at times we step back from the day-to-day challenges, take some time to reflect and ask ourselves the big questions about our ethics and our values.

The theme of my final speech to this conference will be principled leadership in challenging times. Many writers have tried to pin down the key elements of principled leadership. In the UK, the seven principles of public life – known as the 'Nolan principles' – were established in 1995 and apply to anyone holding public office. They are:

1. Selflessness.

2. Integrity.

3. Objectivity (impartial and fair).

4. Accountability.

5. Openness (transparency).

6. Honesty.

7. Leadership (demonstrate these behaviours in their leadership).

Are there some principles that apply particularly to schools and school leaders? Professions such as law and medicine have their own codes of conduct that are regulated by the profession. Should we have a similar code specifically for educators?

I believe that the teaching profession should take responsibility, as other professions do, for setting out guidance on matters of conduct. But for us as individual leaders, will a list of principles, however well-defined, be enough to guide our behaviour? Maybe not. They are a basis for reflection but we need to grapple with the issues ourselves.

Unexamined principles are not enough. For me, there are three pitfalls.

1. It is possible to be principled but prejudiced

Many of the most appalling leaders of the last 100 years were highly principled. Think Hitler in Germany, Pol Pot in Cambodia and one of the world's current monsters, Abu Bakr al-Baghdadi – the self-styled caliph of the so-called Islamic State. In a much milder way we can probably all think about leaders we know today who combine principle with prejudice.

2. Principles are fluid and are affected by culture and context

Surely, certain principles are set in stone – timeless. For example, isn't it always right to respect others and treat all individuals equally? At a general level these principles may well be timeless, but in terms of their application they change over time: 250 years ago many purportedly principled people found the slave trade acceptable; 100 years ago being sent to prison for practising homosexuality was generally accepted by the British public; 60 years ago children with some special educational needs were described as uneducable and 'retarded'.

When I started teaching in the seventies, corporal punishment was legal and widely seen as acceptable and, indeed, expected in schools. Now it is unthinkable that schools should beat children. And – as has been shown so starkly in court cases in Rotherham, Rochdale and elsewhere – not that long ago, 14- and 15-year-old girls who had sex with much older men were seen to have made a lifestyle choice. Now, quite rightly, we think of them as children and as victims of abuse.

Looking back in 20 years' time, what will we see as the ethical shortcomings of current educators? What do we presently tolerate or see as acceptable that will be seen as abhorrent, just as we now see corporal punishment as abhorrent? I don't know. Will we be ashamed and embarrassed in 2037 that in 2017 we didn't take children's mental health and well-being as seriously as we took their physical health?

3. A clear set of principles and values is not enough – we need to be both principled and effective

Ethical behaviour is an essential precondition for winning trust, but leaders must also be competent at doing the job. Some of the weakest school leaders I have ever come across have been principled; they were acting ethically but letting the staff and children down by failing in their core responsibility to make things better for those they served.

Researchers at the Centre for High Performance tracked the leadership styles and educational outcomes in 160 secondary academies in England.[80] They asked two questions: what do head teachers do to bring about rapid school improvement? And what happens in an improving school after the departure of the head teacher?

They called one group of head teachers the 'Philosophers'. The Philosophers were strong on values. The staff were told how important their work was and how much value they added to society. Teachers were encouraged to go on trips to observe other teachers and to share ideas and approaches. But fundamentally, nothing changed. Students carried on misbehaving, parents were still not engaged and performance – both financial and examination results – stayed the same. This is principled but ineffective leadership.

The researchers were also unimpressed by the work of specialist 'super-heads' – they called them the 'Surgeons'. The Surgeons typically took tough action but did not stick around. They could be ruthless in the way they dealt with staff and were keen on excluding students to maximise exam results. They were skilled at the quick fix. They focused not so much on the children and their learning, but on what was needed to do well in the accountability system – whatever it took. While they usually brought about an immediate improvement, these results were not sustained after they left. Here we have leadership that is not principled and, in the long run, isn't even effective.

The most successful approach was the work of a group the researchers called 'Architects'. They had a more holistic view of what it took to move a school in the right direction. They focused on teaching and leadership by introducing coaching, mentoring and development programmes. But they did other things too: bringing in systems to improve student behaviour and collaborating with other organisations to open up opportunities and build sustainable solutions.

Interestingly, the Surgeons (the superheads) were typically paid much more than the Architects. They were also more likely to have received a government honour, such as a knighthood or damehood. Shortly after the Surgeons left, the schools' results dropped by an average of 6 per cent. By contrast, the improvement continued in the schools led by the Architects in the three years after their departure. This is ethical and effective leadership, and it is sustainable. You are just not likely to get a knighthood or damehood!

So, leading with principles is desirable but not as straightforward as it first seems. Not all principles are 'good', principles are relative and change over time and being principled on its own is not enough. We need to combine principles with the ability to lead and manage effectively.

We each have to make our own personal choices about values and princi-ples in our leadership. I want to go a little further than the Nolan principles and share a few of the overriding principles that I have tried to use to guide my decisions and behaviour over the years:

1. Keep the focus on moral purpose and social justice.

2. Be constantly aware of the power of leadership, for good or ill.

3. Foster trust as the basis for successful leadership.

4. Be open and welcome challenge.

5. Once you have listened to others carefully, listen to your inner voice and exercise your ethical muscle.

1. Keep the focus on moral purpose and social justice

One of the recurrent themes in my speeches to this conference and the predecessor conference over the past 12 years has been the centrality of moral purpose to great school leadership.

Perhaps the greatest moral imperative for educators is the need to fight against the corrosive impact of poverty. It is not just about economic poverty. It is also a question of helping children to escape from a poverty of ambition, and to escape from a poverty of experience in terms of life enhancing opportunities in areas such as the arts, sport and travel. All my experience – nationally and internationally – tells me that this is fundamental to what we are trying to do.

There is a lot of talk in England just now about social mobility, particularly in the context of grammar schools. I have no problem with social mobility, but in terms of moral purpose the focus is too narrow for me. Social mobility means increasing the extent to which clever poor children can get top jobs. That is a good thing, but the bigger prize is not just social mobility – it is social justice. In a socially just society all children – whether or not they are poor or rich, whether or not they are gifted, whether or not their parents push them forward – get a fair chance to learn and thrive.

In spite of much progress over the years, this is now under threat. The more that we give school leaders responsibility for leading the whole system, for sorting out admissions and for supporting school improvement in other schools as well as their own, and then judge their whole career success on how their own individual school performs, the bigger the social equity challenge becomes.

Who, under a school-led system, picks up responsibility for every child across that system? Who has the lead role for social equity?

England does not have a high-equity education system. The problem is not the attainment of the more able children – they do pretty well against international comparators; it is the long tail of low attainment, mainly from those who are from deprived backgrounds. The moral and principled imperative is to focus our efforts and our best talent on those children. We have come a long way, with the pupil premium, national leaders of education and multi-academy trusts, but neither the current funding arrangements nor the accountability incentives do enough to shift the school-led system towards that focus and that priority. As a result, too many children and young people are still falling through the cracks.

If we are to address this issue properly in a school-led system, it will require a huge amount of selflessness, generosity and collective moral purpose across a group of schools. It will require principled leadership in challenging times.

Of course, the other side of this coin is the fantastic job that many schools do already. We all know that the data suggests that schools in London seem to do a particularly impressive job in terms of equity. What is less well known is that schools in some other places seem to be doing equally well. In the Key Stage 2 tests last year, schools in Warrington, Redcar and Cleveland, Sunderland and Gateshead all outperformed the average for London schools.

2. Be constantly aware of the power of leadership, for good or ill

In the 1970s there were two leaders of resistance against unjust apartheid in their countries: Nelson Mandela and Robert Mugabe. Both were lauded by some as honourable men fighting for justice and dismissed by others as terrorists. Both became leaders of their free, independent countries. Both made decisions on how they were going to lead – one in a selfless, principled way to unite the country, heal wounds and break down barriers, and the other encouraging corruption, violence and hate, leading to economic disaster. Their stories demonstrate the power of leadership for good or for ill.

As a leader, I know that I have wrestled with many ethical issues. Sometimes, perhaps, I have not wrestled hard enough. I am clear that there have been occasions when I have made mistakes, that my judgement, in retrospect, was too narrow and that I have not, in every case, navigated my way through the grey areas well – or, indeed, even identified what they were. I am not setting myself up as a paragon of virtue. What I am saying is that we need to reflect upon and review our own personal principles. And we need to be very aware about how our behaviour as leaders can have unintended consequences and a negative impact on the culture of the organisation.

I remember many years ago when I worked in a local authority. One of my senior team was a very likeable man – always enthusiastic and professional. He seemed to be pretty good at his job. When one of my finance team said that he had some concerns about his budget, I was convinced that it would be nothing more than a minor glitch. It turned out that this polite, professional member of my senior team had been paying his own mortgage from public funds. I was shocked. He was eventually jailed, but I had to ask myself, as a leader, how come the operating systems under my leadership weren't strong enough to prevent this happening, or to spot it more quickly? And, second, what was it about my style of leadership that made him think that he could get away with it? I was so focused on the outward-facing aspect of the role – school improvement – that I had neglected to do enough to incentivise good internal financial management. My behaviours had unintended consequences.

When colleagues in our organisations behave in undesirable ways, it is a good idea to ask ourselves, as leaders, whether our own behaviours or systems are encouraging them to do so.

Over the past 12 years or so, I have visited many schools in England – and later internationally – to see how different leaders and education systems operate. I have seen the difference that good, effective and principled leadership makes and the impact of weak or poor leadership. I have had my own assumptions challenged by those experiences and have had to ask myself some hard questions about morality and principles. I have been shocked by what I have seen internationally in terms of corruption, abuse and complacency, but I have also been moved to tears by the moral courage of some leaders. We should never underestimate the power we have as leaders either to do good or to do damage, and we should always be sensitive to unintended consequences as a result of our leadership.

3. Foster trust as the basis for successful leadership

Unless we actively demonstrate that we are principled professionals, we will fail to win and retain the trust of parents, teachers and young people.

Parental trust is gold dust. Think about a parent who, for whatever reason, does not trust you or does not trust the school. How much of your professional time is spent on this parent? How much harder is it to educate their child well?

It is also important to win trust from teachers through principled leadership. People don't expect leaders to be their friends or to take their side in an unconditional way when things go wrong. But they will choose to follow your lead because you have earned their respect through your demonstrable competence and integrity.

The children and young people in our care need to trust us and trust their teachers. It is vital that we role model the values we promote and create an environment where young people can grow up to develop their own set of principles and become good citizens and humane adults. This is at the heart of what schools should be about. Not just the curriculum taught but the curriculum lived. This is ultimately down to the culture that leaders create in their schools and is influenced by their own behaviour as leaders.

A particular challenge we face just now is how to establish trust between schools when accountability and resourcing pressures are conspiring to make us look inwards. I believe there is a simple way for principled leaders to catalyse a change here. Trust and reciprocity are integrally linked, so I would challenge any of you who are struggling to establish better partnerships to make the first move. Commit an act of kindness.

I was told recently by a head about how the parents of an 11-year-old boy were desperate to get their son into the school next door to hers, but they lost their appeal and the boy came to her school instead. The pupil was extremely bright and had strong parental support, so the chances of a whole string of A*s at GCSE was very high. However, the boy had a stunning singing voice and her school's music department didn't cater for choral singing, although the school next door did.

What did the head do? It was better for her school if the boy remained, but probably better for the child if he went to the neighbouring school. She wrote to the appeals panel and asked to get the boy admitted to the school next door. The head was modelling principled decision-making in the interests of the child, not putting her school first. And the knock-on effect? The other heads she worked with began to behave in a more principled way themselves – towards student exchange, managed moves and admissions. Acts of kindness and principled leadership are not only good in themselves, they can have positive consequences for the system too.

4. Be open and welcome challenge

We increasingly live and work in atomised and divided groupings where we choose whose views we listen to and can, more easily than ever, cut ourselves off from those who disagree with us: we simply 'unfriend' them on Facebook or block them on Twitter. This is more and more the case in education too. The often vitriolic debate on social media between affirmed traditionalists and progressives provides a striking example. The drawing of battle lines and accusations of lying just cannot be right. Not because I shy away from robust discussion of the evidence, but because the polarisation and forming of cliques inevitably makes us less likely to consider all the available evidence rationally and objectively.

Agatha Christie said that the secret of solving a crime is keeping an open mind as long as possible. The moment you make up your mind as to who committed the crime, you only see the evidence that fits your thinking – or, even worse, you make it fit your assumptions.

In the ever more fragmented system of education in England, we also should be slightly wary of groupthink within multi-academy trusts or individual schools – those who operate a single closed mindset, believing that only certain beliefs are acceptable.

However, if MATs can be the problem, then they can also be the solution. They encourage collaboration between schools and challenge schools within their trusts to think differently. What we need to do now is to make sure that we have peer review and challenge, not just between schools but also between MATs, and it is encouraging to see this happening. It is important to welcome different perspectives within our own organisations too. Are our colleagues encouraged to 'speak truth to power' or do they just say whatever they think it is we want to hear? Are we prepared to change our minds and openly admit it when we get things wrong?

Today, lots of organisations build into their culture an 'obligation to dissent'. This term comes from the management consulting firm McKinsey, but it is common across business and the public services. When there is complete agreement on an important decision, for example, this could be seen as a sign that more time is needed for debate. In any given meeting, the most senior manager should actively invite contrary opinions from others. To do this well, leaders must show humility and real trust in their colleagues.

But, of course, when we do ask for feedback and open ourselves up to challenge, sometimes the response can be a little bit over the top. Here is a child's response to a request for feedback about her teacher:

Things my teacher can do better: not use collective punishment, as it is not fair on the many people who did nothing wrong and under the Geneva Convention it is a war crime.

5. Once you have listened to others carefully, listen to your inner voice and exercise your ethical muscle

There is a real danger that the more successful we are, the more likely we are to not ask others for advice, to fail to exercise our ethical muscle and to fail to listen to our own conscience.

A clinical study by Daniel Sankowsky illustrates that when charisma overlaps with narcissism, leaders tend to abuse their power and take advantage of their followers.[81] Leaders who have a lot of success can start to believe in themselves too much, and that the rules don't apply to them. They believe so much in their own judgement that they flout the procurement process, they give a job to a relative without due process, they take additional money for themselves that should go to their school, they exclude lots of children from their school but refuse to take any in from other schools because their school needs to be the best.

Two things that can help to prevent this are good, robust governance and a wise mentor. Instead, charismatic leaders too often get an echo chamber of their own views coming back at them.

Even if we are not charismatic leaders, many of us can start off full of moral purpose and determination to change the world, but can get ground down, become overly pragmatic and lose that idealistic perspective and passion. We may not even realise that we are not the people we once were.

In the final analysis, most of us possess a pretty good internal moral compass as a guide to our actions. But we must listen to it rather than ignore it. I like the way that Marc Le Menestrel suggests some quick tests to see if we are possibly stepping over that line:[82]

- The sleeping test. If I do this, can I sleep at night?

- The newspaper test. Would I still do this if it was published in a newspaper?

- The mirror test. If I do this, can I feel comfortable looking at myself in the mirror?

- The teenager test. Would I mind my children knowing about this?

Going back to the Dr Dao and United Airlines example, and the potential gap between rhetoric and reality, it is worth exercising our ethical muscle by revisiting our organisation's statement of values. Not necessarily with an eye to changing them, but really challenging ourselves to consider how we apply these values and how we live them day to day. We should ask ourselves:

- What is the best recent example we have seen of our values in action?

- Is there anything we have seen or done recently which contradicts our values?

- What more could we do to use our values to promote better outcomes for all children?

I retire in August. After 17 years of being in charge, in three different organisations, I am taking off the mantle of leadership. It has been a huge privilege. It has been tough and extremely challenging, but also exhilarating and fulfilling.

Leadership is fascinating. You go into an organisation and try your best to address the weaknesses left by the previous leadership, and you work hard to turn those weaknesses into strengths and to maintain the good things you found there. Then you leave and the new leader goes through the same process you did – working to address the weaknesses that you have left behind. And so it goes on.

I think that the four questions for any leader leaving a role to reflect upon are these:

1. Did I leave the organisation in better shape than when I started?

2. Having experienced my leadership, were colleagues more likely to want to be leaders themselves and more equipped to do so?

3. Did I make more of a positive than a negative difference to the lives of those I came into contact with? Are they better or worse people for having worked with me?

4. Have I shown authenticity and integrity in my leadership? Have I led with moral purpose?

A few months ago, I was in Jordan where the Education Development Trust is working in schools. Most of the children are Syrian refugees – 2.7 million of Jordan's total population of 9.5 million are refugees. Queen Rania, who I met during my visit, is a passionate advocate for refugees. She said: 'Does my husband order his soldiers to close the borders? How is he going to sleep at night? It was never a question of yes or no; it was always a question of how are we going to make it work.' But the same view came from all the Jordanians with whom I spoke. They said to me: 'These are our neighbours – how can we turn them away ... These are children – how can we not try to give them an education.' Principled leadership in challenging times.

You don't have to be an extraordinary person like Mother Teresa or Martin Luther King to show principled leadership or to be a hero. Every person can be a hero – by choosing the right thing over the wrong thing. Day after day and hour after hour, school leaders are demonstrating principled leadership and moral courage – all over the country and, indeed, all over the world. They may not be famous. They may not appear in the national media. They may never make it onto a list on a minister's desk. They may not have multitudes of followers on Twitter. But they are heroes. Ordinary people doing extraordinary things. Hidden heroes. They are givers of love to the adults and children in their care throughout their careers. Leonard Cohen, who died in 2016, wrote:

There are heroes in the seaweed.

There are children in the morning.

They are leaning out for love

And they will lean that way forever.

We need to see things from other points of view and open up our beliefs to challenge. We need to exercise our ethical muscle through reflection and dialogue. And then we need to remind ourselves of our power as leaders to do good, to connect with our best selves, to renew our sense of moral purpose and to do the right things to the best of our ability.

Nelson Mandela was imprisoned for 27 years. His favourite poem, the one that gave him solace during all those years of captivity was William Ernest Henley's 'Invictus':

Out of the night that covers me,

Black as the pit from pole to pole,

I thank whatever gods may be

For my unconquerable soul. ...

It matters not how strait the gate,

How charged with punishments the scroll,

I am the master of my fate,

I am the captain of my soul.

Now, more than ever, it is time for us, as leaders, to be captains of our souls.

Since I made this speech there have been further examples of school leaders being banned from teaching as a result of unethical behaviour, and important concerns have been raised by Ofsted about children being 'off-rolled' by some schools, meaning they are sent to be educated at home in order for them not to appear on the school's books during examinations. These issues have certainly not diminished in importance. However, I am greatly encouraged that the Association of School and College Leaders' Ethical Leadership Commission published a powerful and timely framework for ethical leadership in education in January 2019, stating that leaders should be truthful, open and selfless, and arguing for the importance of trust, wisdom, kindness, justice and courage.[83]

Conclusion

Let us not talk falsely now,

The hour is getting late.

Bob Dylan, 'All Along the Watchtower'

In the final chapter, I want to bring together some of the themes of this book – from the speeches and from my leadership experiences. Each of my speeches made reference to the education landscape that year, so I am going to start with some reflections on the education system in England.

The current education landscape in England

Education in England has changed very significantly over the past 14 years. The top-down National Strategies approach introduced by New Labour from 1997–2004 gave way to a new relationship with schools that was more empowering and gave leaders more autonomy to make decisions within a very strong accountability system. The Every Child Matters agenda, which gathered pace from about 2005 – and, in particular, the focus on integrated children's services – pushed the whole system down a broad 'whole child/whole community' road. And then the radical transformation under Michael Gove from 2010–2014 pushed the whole system down a completely different 'academic rigour and free market' road. But even that doesn't tell the whole story. New Labour introduced the London Challenge, and later the Black Country and Greater Manchester Challenge, with a focus on school-to-school collaboration, but they also pushed the National Challenge with its added top-down pressure as well as its extra support.

The coalition government began by talking about freedom, autonomy, empowerment and a self-improving system. They introduced teaching school alliances and expanded the NLE programme. They enabled parents to open up new free schools. They incentivised schools that were already quite autonomous to become even more autonomous by converting to academies. For a while 'a hundred flowers bloomed', as schools did their own thing and the system changed irrevocably. But after a couple of years, the government realised that more autonomy did not necessarily mean better schools, so they began to try to manage the market and to inject greater controls and quality assurance through the expansion of MATs – with the ones that were viewed as most effective being given lots more schools to lead and manage.

Meanwhile, the Department for Education introduced huge top-down change through a new phonics test, new tests at the end of Key Stage 2 (for 11-year-olds), a more academic curriculum and a new examination system at GCSE (for 16-year-olds). They also introduced new school performance tables which focused on progress, attainment and the English Baccalaureate. These tables helped to prevent an unhealthy focus on moving students from a D grade to a C grade; however, they also narrowed the curriculum and, overall, led to disadvantaged children struggling even more to demonstrate success.

At the time of writing, the turmoil has halted for a while and there has been a slight row back on the accountability system, but what we are left with is mainly unsatisfactory. We now have a mishmash of local authority maintained schools, individual academies and MATs – a piecemeal system with too many different players operating in that middle space between government and schools. Sir David Carter (the impressive and talented national schools commissioner from 2016 to 2018) has tried to keep people focused on the moral purpose of it all, on collaboration within and between MATs and on school improvement. However, he was pushing against a largely closed door at the Department for Education. The government now seems to veer between hard-edged intervention and control (as it moves schools to different MATs without much transparency) and a hands-off, 'let the market decide' stance ('leadership development is not our responsibility – you get on with it').

The recent announcement that Ofsted will now look more at the quality of the curriculum and place less emphasis on examination results is to be welcomed, but unless Ofsted gets rid of grades and unless inspections can no longer make or break careers, it is likely to achieve little. The announcement in November 2018 that there will be a move away from requiring struggling (but not inadequate) schools to become academies and, instead, for support to be provided by NLEs, is also to be welcomed as a positive move back to the more supportive approaches used effectively towards the end of the New Labour government and in the early years of the coalition. There are some small but limited grounds for optimism.

Since I left the Education Development Trust, I have had the opportunity to work with a wide number of different systems internationally. I have worked with several Scandinavian countries, some Canadian provinces, various states in the United States and in Australia, as well as with Ireland, Scotland and Wales, and it is interesting to reflect on the similarities and differences between the various systems. There is much that is still great about the education system in England. I believe that the quality of school leadership is at least as good, and possibly better, than in any other system in the world. I also believe that, at their best, MATs and teaching school alliances are moving school-to-school collaboration to a new level that is hardly seen in any other system globally. It is refreshing to see at first hand the way in which the best MATs are addressing collaborative, invitational and lateral leadership and developing approaches to collective accountability that do well for the diverse range of children and communities they serve.

But I know of no other system in the world where the whole career of a school leader is so precarious. I am not aware of anywhere else where it is so easy for principals to lose their jobs as a result of the performance of the school, as measured by test results and/or by a school inspection. What is worse, these judgements by Ofsted about the performance of school leaders are dependent not only on how good and talented the leaders are, but also on the kind of school they happen to be leading. I read with some horror in 2018 that 58 per cent of secondary schools that are predominantly made up of white privileged young people have been judged as outstanding, but only 4 per cent of schools predominantly made up of young people from the most deprived groups have been judged as outstanding.[84] This is completely unacceptable.

As it stands in England, an Ofsted judgement of good or outstanding can help to make a school principal's career. It can enable him or her to become an NLE and their school a national teaching school. It can lead to the opportunity to train as an Ofsted inspector and provides a great chance for promotion to an even bigger school or to lead a MAT. In contrast, if the principal has been in post for more than two years, an Ofsted judgement of inadequate is more likely than not to lead to the principal resigning or being dismissed. Ofsted judgements are incredibly high stakes and, at the same time, the odds are hugely stacked against a leader of a challenging or very deprived school being judged as successful.

How can this possibly incentivise teachers and leaders to work in the most challenging schools – where they are most needed? How does it attract teachers and leaders into the profession and encourage them to stay there? What is it doing for the mental health and well-being of those who teach and lead in challenging schools? When the balance tips so far away from capacity building/support and development and so heavily towards accountability, then we are in serious trouble as an education system. No wonder many other systems around the world are bewildered by our approach.

Whenever you set targets or lay down criteria for success, and make the consequences of success or failure very significant, then people will focus on those things to the detriment of other things. They may look for ways to 'game' the system or, in more extreme cases, there will be incidents of cheating. In England, the combination of school performance tables and the expectation that every school should be average or above creates perverse incentives. The pupils that will help the school to perform well will be welcomed and cherished, but there is no inducement to be an inclusive school or to welcome children from families with high levels of mobility. Since academies in England manage their own admissions and exclusions policies, this makes vulnerable children even more vulnerable. The most needy become the least wanted. The pupil premium helpfully provides more funding to schools for those children from more deprived backgrounds, but the incentive not to have these children on the school register at examination time is still a huge factor. In these circumstances, school leaders need to show principled and ethical leadership that treats every child equally. That the vast majority do so is fabulous, but the fact that a small number do not is a worry for the system itself.

The challenge for many systems around the world now is how to develop large-scale assessment and accountability strategies that disturb complacency, command public confidence and ensure the good use of public money, whilst avoiding negative consequences for children, teachers and schools. Can we have a system that promotes accountability and equity, that raises expectations and incentivises inclusion, that ensures rigour but supports the rights of the child, that seeks academic excellence but also celebrates the arts and vocational skills? There will never be a perfect solution and, of course, context matters, but there are some possible ways forward.

In some countries and states, we are seeing an increasing emphasis on a balanced scorecard approach to accountability, where schools are judged not just on attainment outcomes but on student well-being and other aspects, with some national indicators and some local ones. We need to have a more balanced approach – one where a principal's career and future livelihood is not dependent upon the type of school they end up leading. We need a system where the emphasis is on improving rather than proving. I am not against national testing or school inspection. The problem is neither testing nor inspection per se; it is the high-stakes nature of the accountability system which leads to negative consequences, especially for more vulnerable schools and more vulnerable children.

There is hope for a better way in England, but it would require exceptionally courageous political leadership, a deep understanding of change management processes and a commitment to invitational leadership so that schools themselves help to shape the strategy (see the section beginning on page 260 on power and love).

The role of government in school leadership development

The National College for School Leadership opened in 2000 and closed, finally, in 2018. Between 2005 and 2012, I was the CEO. It is hard for me to be objective about the work and the legacy of the National College. On a personal level, I don't feel bitter. I think I always understood that when you work in the public sector in a democracy some things may flourish for a time but most don't flourish for ever. The National College was great while it lasted and it was a real privilege to be part of it. But what of its impact?

Clearly, the education community in England has coped pretty well in recent years in the absence of a strong and influential National College. Schools continue to be led well and, in many cases, led brilliantly. The NPQH (now voluntary) continues to be a qualification which is valued by many aspirant principals and by many governing bodies. A new qualification called the National Professional Qualification for Executive Leadership has also been introduced. The two not-for-profit, high-quality school leadership development organisations, Future Leaders and Teaching Leaders, have recently amalgamated to form Ambition School Leadership, which has thrived under James Toop's strong leadership as CEO. Teaching school alliances have stepped up to take a bigger role in leadership development. So, in a sense you could argue that the demise of the National College was right: it did its job, it built capacity, and then disappeared, which is what ought to happen if you are trying to build a self-improving system.

However, I think it would also be fair to say that the demise of the National College has left a big gap. For a number of years, the National College helped to build morale amongst school leaders in England. There was a sense that the government valued school leadership enough to invest in it through a national body; that school leadership and its development was at the cutting edge internationally; that there was a national publicly funded organisation out there that gave school leaders not only support but also some leadership and inspiration. That time is no more.

I do not believe that morale is currently high amongst school leaders or, indeed, that they feel as valued as they once did when the National

College was around. The significant shift towards academisation (at the time of writing, more than 50 per cent of school-age students in England are educated in academies) and the creation of hundreds of MATs has meant that it is hard for school leaders to have a sense of any local or national body outside their own school showing an interest in them, except for professional associations and, perhaps, the brand-new Chartered College of Teaching. Some MATs perform this role well, as do some teaching school alliances, but, overall, I believe that the hard-edged and high-stakes accountability system, the reduction in support from local authorities and the lack of national support and development from organisations such as the National College has meant that school leaders feel more vulnerable and isolated than before.

Withdrawing funding for leadership development inevitably has consequences. Schools are struggling with reduced budgets. At times like this, many schools will reduce their budget for professional development in order to pay for staff salaries. Moreover, it is inevitable that during times of hardship many schools will not be prepared to invest some of their budget in the development of the deputy head teacher to prepare him or her for headship, since that person may well end up leaving the school for a headship elsewhere.

This is why, in my view, preparation for headship has to be the role of the state. The licensed provision set up by the National College is now patchy in its quality; it depends where you are geographically. There will be a whole generation of potential and aspirant school leaders who will miss out on the kind of succession planning and talent management strategies that the National College provided at a local level. The research pamphlets and reports generated by the National College which helped to ensure that school leaders in England were some of the most informed and reflective in the world have ceased. In 2012, the OECD stated that school leaders in the UK were more likely than those in any other country to be doing the things that made the biggest difference to improving teaching.[85] I believe that part of the reason for that was the work of the National College.

It is fascinating that so many other systems later developed their own leadership institute, including the Scottish College of Educational Leadership, the Bastow Institute of Educational Leadership in Victoria, Australia, and, more recently, the National Academy for Educational

Leadership in Wales. I am not aware of any high-performing school system, or one that is rapidly improving, that leaves leadership development to chance. It is too big a risk for the future. England is now in danger of doing just that. There will continue to be exceptional school leadership, but my worry is that, over time, we will see a gradual erosion in the quality of school leadership in England.

Leading change with the right balance between power and love

Power and love was the theme of my 2012 speech and since then the importance of a good balance between power and love in leadership has become clearer and clearer to me. If we want to make change happen, then we need to lead with power, pace, determination and absolute resolution. At times we may have to take tough decisions, hold courageous conversations and, for a while, this may feel very lonely. I certainly experienced this feeling of loneliness when I led the restructuring of senior roles at the National College and when I did something similar at CfBT.

Once we have made up our mind that a particular course of action is absolutely necessary for the organisation, after careful reflection and taking advice, then this may need to be pushed through in spite of opposition, anger and hurt from some within the organisation. This is the extreme version of the power side of leadership. It is sometimes unavoidable during the first 18 months in your role as CEO/principal if the organisation is in great difficulty. But this kind of leadership should be used rarely. On its own it does not lead to sustainable success. Unless we also demonstrate love, kindness and empathy we will end up not taking people with us; we will find ourselves leading with pace but nobody will be following. Leaders who create long-term success, rather than just quick wins, demonstrate love in their leadership.

I have always tried to have a good balance of power and love in my leadership, but there have clearly been times when I have over-focused on the power aspect and times when, perhaps to compensate, I have over-focused on the love aspect; times when I have been too tough and times when I have been too tender. Much of this is about the context in which we find ourselves. We need to ask ourselves, what kind of leadership is required from me now – in this context?

One thing I am absolutely sure about is that the need for a balance between power and love in leadership is important for governments as well as for leaders of organisations. I was struck by a comment made by Claudia Costin, who was then the inspirational leader of education in Rio de Janeiro, that 'you can only transform education together with the teachers': 'The speed was given by the capacity of having teachers on board. We challenged them to the limit, but not more than the limit.'[86] Claudia knew that she had to move with pace and that children only get one chance at an education, but she also knew that she could only push so far without losing the teaching profession – and without their support the change wouldn't be successful. She led with power but also with love.

Looking back on Michael Gove's time as secretary of state for education in England, it is clear to me that he was much stronger on the power side than the love side. He seemed to spend far more time driving radical change than he spent being inclusive and invitational. In the end, he appeared to be moving in smaller and smaller circles and talking predominantly to people who agreed with him. This was leadership with drive but without empathy and without taking people with you. As Michael Fullan and I wrote in 2016:

> Many of us have worked for years in systems which are caught in a struggle between state- and country-level policy on the one hand and the action or inaction of individual schools on the other. Policy pushes in one direction, the profession pulls in another. The result is a type of friction which produces heat but not light: plenty of activity but not enough systematic change or improvement in outcomes.[87]

This was certainly true during Michael Gove's time as education minister.

However, it is easy for me to comment from the sidelines on what political leaders should or should not do. As President Theodore Roosevelt famously said, it is not the critic who counts but those who actually strive to do the deeds; the individual who fails 'at least fails while daring greatly'.[88] Those who lead huge reform agendas in education are daring greatly and often do more (or, conversely, do more harm) for children and schools than those who settle for low-risk strategies and who accept the status quo.

In some ways I feel sorry for ministers in charge of education. If they are in a democracy there will be whole groups of people whose sole function is to oppose whatever they say or do. Meanwhile, the media, and often the general public, are looking for quick wins and instant improvements. Most education ministers understand (rightly) that the best thing to do is to develop a long-term sustainable strategy, implemented over 10 or 20 years, with a clear rationale to go with it. The problem is that in the meantime – long before any change has had a chance to embed – there may well be a general election to fight and a party machine pushing for evidence of short-term impact and looking for encouraging feedback from focus groups. We may well find that the next education minister also has a commitment to a 10- or 20-year long-term strategy, but with a completely different set of policies and priorities, especially if the government has changed. The result is often turmoil, with children, young people and teachers on the receiving end of yet more change.

Of course, the content of the proposed change matters, and those advising government are often very bright people with great ideas and initiatives. But what matters just as much as the policy itself is how the change is managed. Education has its own ecosystem and tampering with one aspect of it can have a significant impact on the rest of it, even if that consequence was not planned for or expected. There may be good reasons for a particular initiative or new approach, but those who lead change don't always think through the implications. Even great ideas can backfire if the culture isn't right or if there isn't sufficient time or resource to implement it properly.

I have worked with several education systems which have had great policies but they have not known how to implement them. The focus has been more on developing the right policy than on how to make it owned by the profession and how to make it stick. I have never been an education minister but the lesson from my own limited leadership experience is that culture, listening, engagement and motivation matter just as much as strategy and policy. The stories in this book about the 500 phone calls, the handwritten cards to school leaders, the misty vision, the invitational approach, the public acknowledgement of mistakes, the visioning conferences, the importance of effective programme management, the need for consistent and aligned systems, and the open focus on authenticity and moral purpose all have resonance here.

If we are going to lead change effectively in a school, or across a whole education system, we need the following eight aspects:

1. A perceived need (or burning platform).

2. A clear analysis of the ecosystem and of what needs to change.

3. A compelling narrative (something that excites, engages and enthuses colleagues).

4. An invitation to participate and to help to shape the change. This is about far more than consultation. It is about giving some flexibility, within certain parameters, for those who will be responsible for implementing the change to help to shape it. This can be messy and time-consuming, but it is worth it in the long run as it builds in ownership and collective accountability.

5. A clear strategy for implementation – focusing on impact.

6. Peer support and pressure. In a school, this will be teachers supporting and challenging other teachers, and in an education system this will be schools/MATs supporting and challenging other schools/MATs.

7. Resource and capacity building (time, professional development, mentoring).

8. Integrating the change into systems and having procedures to incentivise it.

Too often I find that governments are good at points 1 and, possibly, 5 – and even 4 – but less good at the rest. They sometimes start out with a focus on the love side of leadership but when they get kickback on their ideas and proposals and they meet with resistance (which is almost inevitable), they either revert to the power side and give up on the love or they give up altogether and try another initiative. What is required from leaders – in schools, in organisations and in whole countries or states – is both power and love in leadership. Driving change forward but showing empathy and taking the time to make sure that you are taking a critical mass with you. Political leaders who are serious about implementing change would benefit from being slightly less certain that they are always right and, instead, embrace the concept of invitational and imperfect leadership.

Deciding on your next job

On a more personal level, one of the themes of this book has been deciding if a leadership role is the right one for you. Whenever you step up into a new leadership role, you are usually stopping doing something you know you are pretty good at and embarking on something you are not sure you are really good at. So, how much competence of the technical aspect of the role do you need to possess in order to be confident that you can do it, and how much can you learn on the job?

One of the themes running through several of my speeches was the extent to which the leader needs to be an expert in the core business of the organisation. Does a school principal need to be an expert in teaching and learning? Does the CEO of the National College for School Leadership need to be an expert in school leadership? Does the CEO of an international commercial organisation need to be an expert in international development and commerce? Does the CEO of a hospital need to be a medic? For me, the answer is that it can help a great deal. It would have been much easier for me to build my credibility as CEO of the National College if I had been a head teacher, and it would have been much easier for me as CEO of CfBT/Education Development Trust if I had gone there with a better grounding in commerce and international development. A leader who has a deep understanding of teaching and learning is potentially a great asset to a school, and if you happen to appoint a CEO who is also a medic to lead a hospital then that is likely to help enormously too.

But there are three reasons why I believe that this is not absolutely essential. The first is that, over time, the basics can be learned – not to become an expert but to know enough to be able to ask the right questions and to form a view on the appropriateness and usefulness of the response. The second is that the key skill is not being an expert yourself, but in knowing how to help and support others to become expert. Sometimes being an expert can actually get in the way of helping others. If a leader is highly skilled at something that a more junior colleague is meant to be good at, then it can sometimes be intimidating and disempowering. Some of the best teachers are poor at helping others to improve their teaching, just as some of the best footballers turn out to be poor managers of football teams. As I said in my speech on learning-centred leadership (Chapter

9), the school leader doesn't have to be the best teacher, but he or she has to be passionate about teaching and learning. The third reason is that, as I say in a number of my speeches, it is not about being the perfect leader, it is about creating a great team. Most organisations, including schools, are too complex for the person in charge to be an expert in all of the key aspects, which is why a great team that, collectively, has the range of expertise needed for the organisation is so important.

So, when is a role right for you? I was fortunate to be appointed to the CEO roles at the National College and CfBT in spite of my lack of school leadership or commercial experience. But I do think that I met three important criteria for leadership: I was absolutely passionate about the work at the National College and CfBT, and my passion came across in my behaviour and in my leadership; I knew how to ask for help, listen to advice and be a learner; and I understood that I was an imperfect leader and (with one or two notable exceptions) I didn't feel that I had to control everything. I focused on building and empowering powerful teams.

These are the four questions people might usefully ask themselves to help them decide whether they are suited for a new leadership role:

1. Am I genuinely passionate about the work, mission and values of the organisation?

2. Do I have the generic skills needed for the role?

3. Where I lack technical expertise, am I committed to learning and asking for help/taking advice/listening?

4. Does this role give me the potential to create a high-performing and balanced team?

Imperfect leadership

This book is called *Imperfect Leadership*. I believe it is the term that best describes my leadership, so, in conclusion, I would like to draw together some themes around imperfect leadership.

Imperfect leaders are self-aware – they know their own strengths and weaknesses

When we introduced revised entry criteria for the NPQH in 2008, we included self-awareness as a key success criteria. Those prospective school principals who were not aware of their own weaknesses or areas for development did not meet the entry criteria. We were of the view at the time, and I am even more convinced of this now, that the chances of someone who lacks self-awareness becoming an effective leader are very small. In contrast, imperfect leaders are very aware of their weaknesses and areas for development. They see themselves as learners and never as the finished article.

Imperfect leaders know their weaknesses so they try to appoint people who are noticeably better at things than they are. They try to ensure that the team has the balance of skills and expertise that no single person can possibly have

It is pretty clear that we only started to fly at the National College and at CfBT/Education Development Trust when we got the right senior team together. I have taken delight in having people in my leadership team and senior management group with strong views, self-confidence and talent. I can remember several occasions when my views were challenged at team meetings, but I cannot remember ever feeling intimidated or wishing that I had appointed someone less talented.

However, there have been times in my leadership when the team has been neither effective nor balanced, and then I have struggled. This is about getting the right people on the bus and in the right seats. But even when you do have a great team in place, a key member can leave and you might upset the balance of the team by appointing a replacement that you later regret. Furthermore, high-performing teams can easily become mediocre if the culture is not continuously addressed. For me, finance and systems are not my strong points, and I have not coped well without a very able chief operating officer or finance director. However, when you get a team with a balanced set of expertise and when there is genuine trust between all members of the team – which was the case during most of my time at the National College and most of my time at CfBT/Education Development Trust – leadership can be truly joyous, even though it might also be tough.

I believe there are a number of reasons why leadership teams may not work effectively, many of which I have struggled with at some point in my career as a leader:

1. The team is not sufficiently clear about their mission, values and overall strategy. Priorities therefore can conflict rather than align. After some early mistakes on this one, I tended to prioritise a focus on mission, values and overall strategy with every team I led.

2. People are there because of their role rather than their expertise on the issues being addressed. At any given time, the person in the organisation with the most expertise on the issue being discussed may not even be in the room! This is a real weakness with executive teams – and I am not sure that I addressed this as well as I should have done over the years. On reflection, I did not listen sufficiently well to the voices of younger leaders and of experts who weren't senior.

3. People can think it is the CEO or principal's meeting and his or her responsibility to make it work, not theirs. Therefore, they tend to do scant preparation and give the agenda little prior thought (but see point 4 below). I have found this easy to slip into. The key is very strong delegation to others (to each member of the team, not just to some) so that increasingly there is collective accountability. It requires constant vigilance, since the default position for any executive team is to rely on the CEO/principal to make things work.

4. People tend to compete for favours/promotion/a bonus and can thus see their colleagues as competitors. This is made worse when there is a competitive performance management system with bonuses attached, as there was at the Department for Education in 2012. This problem occurred on numerous occasions throughout my leadership (for example, during organisation restructures), but

it happened less and less once we had appointed really good people on to the team and had some stability.

5. Trust between team members can be lacking. An absence of reciprocity and generosity within and outside meetings can lead to tensions. This is always something to be mindful of, but sometimes I took this for granted and was caught out. It was fine when everything was going well, but during times of restructuring, downsizing and uncertainty it was problematic. When the context changes, behaviours often change too.

6. Poor behaviour (for example, turning up late, being rude to/about a colleague) is not confronted and challenged, so it continues. I usually made it a priority to have a quiet word if I saw any examples of bad behaviour.

7. If agendas are too crowded and meetings meander then there can be a lack of clear, strategic decisions, with no specific actions or allocation of responsibility. Meetings then become not only a waste of time but also frustrating and counterproductive. Avoiding this was one of my strengths. It was tested to the full when I chaired the advisory group that developed the NLE initiative. I find it interesting that the ability to listen carefully and to summarise the key points and outcomes in meetings turned out to be such an important part of my leadership.

8. After a while, many teams can develop groupthink – they all start to see things the same way (and those who don't have been ground down, become isolated and have left). This leads to a lack of challenge and to complacency. I know this happened for a couple of years at the National College. Most of the time we liked each other too much and I did not do enough to bring in challenge to the leadership team from the outside.

9. After a few years in the role, the CEO/principal can start to feel too comfortable in the meetings of the executive team and thus doesn't do enough preparation and pre-thinking to make them work. I think this began to happen for me in 2008–2009 at the National College. Complacency is a terrible thing – it creeps up on you without you realising it.

10. In busy, fast-moving and time-poor organisations, the urgent and operational can too easily dominate the important and strategic. Operational issues usually require less preparation and less thought in advance, so they are easier to discuss than strategic issues. I found this to be a constant battle, especially during very busy times.

Imperfect leaders are more likely to show empathy. They know that they are imperfect, so they understand that everybody else is likely to be imperfect too and that few people live simple, uncomplicated lives

To be honest, I think that I have been reasonable at empathy but sometimes I have failed to recognise upset and trauma (even amongst members of my leadership team), and I have had to rely on people like Maggie Farrar, Geoff Southworth or my executive assistants to spot it and let me know. I tend to be good at empathy when I know there is an issue to be dealt with, but really great leaders notice the relevant body language and respond accordingly in a much more sophisticated way than I do. The lesson here is that if you are not great at empathy, surround yourself with people who are and take their advice.

Imperfect leaders understand that it is not all about them (why should it be?), and that it is better to be right at the end of a process than to be seen to be right at the beginning

Sometimes my ego has led me to seek acknowledgement and external recognition. This was definitely true of me as a younger leader. I occasionally liked scoring points off people and being seen to be a successful leader. But in my later years, I have, on the whole, been relaxed about this. No leader is going to be effective if they don't take real joy in members of their team getting the glory and the praise for a successful outcome.

Imperfect leaders make public promises because they are acutely aware of their own weaknesses and they know that, without making public promises, they might fail to deliver on something that is really important

As I have argued throughout this book, making public promises helps to make sure that you do the right thing. It is why Weight Watchers (now WW) works. It is why the president of Rwanda reintroduced the *Imihigo*. If used rarely and appropriately, it is a powerful strategy for the imperfect leader. In the same way, speaking to others about what good leadership looks like helps to make sure that you are more likely to practise good leadership yourself.

Imperfect leaders are learners. If they mess up – and they often do – imperfect leaders learn from their mistakes and try to do it better next time. They worry about having got it wrong today (sometimes they worry too much), but they are even more concerned about getting it right tomorrow

There are numerous examples in this book of me messing up: my unnecessary aloofness during the first restructure at the National College and how I dealt with some individuals; my linking of the Ofsted outstanding grade to the criteria for NLEs; my handling of the second restructure at the National College; my interview for the CfBT role; and my reluctance to resign as chair of CST. There are also plenty of other instances of mistakes I've made that didn't make it into this book. But after each one, I reflected and came back determined to learn from the experience. As I said in my 2014 speech: 'Detached involvement is the essence of leadership. Reflecting on how we approach particular situations, being mindful of what we are doing (in the moment) and then reflecting later on what went well and what we could have done differently is how we learn to lead.'

Good leaders embrace the old Japanese proverb: 'Fall down seven times, get up eight.' It is just that imperfect leaders may well need support to help them to get back up again. Fortunately, imperfect leaders are good at asking for help.

Imperfect leaders have self-doubt (sometimes too much) but they also have confidence in their areas of strength as leaders

In my 2009 speech, I talked about the importance of wearing the mantle of leadership with confidence and humility. I have struggled with this one over the years. There have been a few times in my leadership when things have been going particularly well – for example, in 2008–2009 when I was at the National College. At these times, I have become overconfident and complacent, not welcoming challenge enough. There have also been a few times in my leadership when I have been too fearful and have lacked the confidence to know in which direction to lead the organisation. This happened to me in 2012 at the National College and in 2014 at CfBT. My colleagues have told me that I am at my best when I am scared but not so scared that I become frozen and debilitated; neither overwhelmed nor overbearing. I agree. Some fear of failure has been crucial in my effectiveness as a leader. As Ben Laker has written: 'success requires a moderate fear of failure because it is the balance of such fear with the desire to excel' that leads to great leadership.[89]

When I am at my best, I lead with clarity and decisiveness, but I am constantly thinking about what might go wrong and managing risk. I am keen to welcome challenge and to take advice.

Imperfect leaders are not afraid of being seen to be imperfect. They ask for help and are prepared to admit that they need it

There are very few political leaders who can be described as authentic – asking for help and admitting that they need it, and being honest about their weaknesses as well as their strengths. Estelle Morris is one of those, as is Nelson Mandela, but it is hard to think of many. Even in schools, especially in England, there is a sense that you can only succeed by being bloody-minded, strong and confident; if you show weakness, especially in front of your staff, it is a real problem. This is the Margaret Thatcher (or even the Donald Trump) style of leadership.

I believe that there is something deeply wrong about the kind of culture that requires leaders to behave in this way. As I said in my 2014 speech, nobody admires a quivering wreck of a leader, but asking for help and admitting it when you get something wrong is at the heart of effective leadership. Without doubt, asking for help, seeking advice and listening to it has been the main reason why my leadership has had some success over the years. Imperfect leaders, and this is true of me, believe that they need mentors at least as much when they are highly experienced as they did when they embarked on the role. They welcome external challenge. They know that after a year or two they can grow too close to the organisation and be unable to see it clearly, so they look for outside perspectives to help them see it better.

Imperfect leaders are authentic

Imperfect leaders are comfortable in their own skin. They lead with authenticity and honesty because they know who they are and who they are not. Their context may change and their leadership style may change with that context, but they are always authentic. They don't talk falsely. As an imperfect leader, I have to admit that I haven't always led with authenticity at the forefront, but on the whole I think it has been a hallmark of my leadership. In all my 360° feedback processes – over many years and in different organisations – the strongest and most consistent finding has always been that I have led with integrity, moral purpose and authenticity.

My twelve speeches have been about moral purpose, values, authenticity, toughness, tenderness, resonance, resilience, courage, restlessness and service. They have had many themes but, in the end, leadership is about trying to do the right thing for the organisation within the context that you find yourself, and doing it in the right way. Naturally, there are days when we get it wrong, but if we are learners then we can try to get it right tomorrow.

Being a leader in the world of education has been the greatest privilege of my life. Of course, it has brought me many hours of anxiety and concern, but also a deep sense of joy and fulfilment. In my 2017 speech, I suggested four questions for any leader leaving the role to reflect upon:

1. Did I leave the organisation in better shape than when I started?

2. Having experienced my leadership, were colleagues more likely to want to be leaders themselves and more equipped to do so?

3. Did I make more of a positive than a negative difference to the lives of those I came into contact with? Are they better or worse people for having worked with me?

4. Have I shown authenticity and integrity in my leadership? Have I led with moral purpose?

Ultimately, leadership is about making a positive difference, not just to organisations (although that is essential) but also to people – and, in education, to the lives of children and young people. My hope for those of you who have read this book is that it will remind you how important leadership is and the impact it can have. I hope that it will encourage you to renew your commitment to leadership and, if you are not yet a leader, to take the next step. If we want sustainable, well-led schools, if we want long-term and effective education systems, if we want to attract the next generation into leadership, then we should ditch all the striving towards perfection, focus on doing what is right for the students, genuinely ask for help from others and celebrate the fact that we are imperfect leaders.

End notes

Foreword

1   M. Fullan, *Nuance: Why Some Leaders Succeed and Others Fail* (Thousand Oaks, CA: Corwin, 2019), p. 12.

Introduction

2   D. Wiliam, Assessment for Learning: Why, What and How (2006). Available at: https://www.dylanwiliam.org/Dylan_Wiliams_website/Papers.html, p. 11.

3   M. Fullan, *Nuance: Why Some Leaders Succeed and Others Fail* (Thousand Oaks, CA: Corwin, 2019).

Chapter One

4   Department for Education and Skills and National College for School Leadership, *School Leadership: End to End Review of School Leadership Policy and Delivery* (London: DfES/NCSL, 2004).

5   Department for Education and Skills, *14–19 Curriculum and Qualifications Reform. Final Report of the Working Group on 14–19 Reform* [Tomlinson Report] (Nottingham: DfES, 2004). Available at: http://www.educationengland.org.uk/documents/pdfs/2004-tomlinson-report.pdf.

6   Department for Education and Skills and Ofsted, *A New Relationship with Schools* (London: HMSO, 2004).

7   M. Barber, *Instruction to Deliver: Fighting to Transform Britain's Public Services* (London: Methuen, 2008), pp. 235–239.

8   M. Fullan, The Role of the Principal in School Reform. Speech delivered at the Principal's Institute, Bank Street College, New York, 9 November 2000. Available at: https://michaelfullan.ca/wp-content/uploads/2016/06/13396042460.pdf; citing P. B. Sebring and A. S. Bryk, School Leadership and the Bottom Line in Chicago. *Phi Delta Kappan*, 81(6) (2000), 440–443 at 441–442.

9   R. Putnam, *Bowling Alone: The Collapse and Revival of American Community* (New York: Simon & Schuster, 2011).

10   C. Desforges, with A. Abouchaar, T*he Impact of Parental Involvement, Parental Support and Family Education on Pupil Achievements and Adjustment: A Literature Review.* Research Report RR433 (Nottingham: Department for Education and Skills, 2003).

11   R. Heifetz and M. Linsky, *Leadership on the Line: Staying Alive Through the Dangers of Leading* (Boston, MA: Harvard Business School Press, 2002).

Chapter Two

12   Quoted in M. Morrell and S. Capparell, *Shackleton's Way: Leadership Lessons from the Great Antarctic Explorer* (New York: Penguin, 2001), p. 209.

13   J. Collins, *Good to Great* (London: Random House, 2001).

14   A. Hargreaves and D. Fink, *Sustainable Leadership* (San Francisco, CA: Jossey-Bass, 2006), p. 251.

15   J. Stevens, J. Brown, S. Knibbs and J. Smith, *Follow-up Research into the State of School Leadership in England.* Research Report no. 633 (Nottingham: MORI/Department for Education and Skills, 2005).

Chapter Three

16   S. Terkel, *Working: People Talk About What They Do All Day and How They Feel About What They Do* (New York: New Press, 1972), p. xi.

17   D. Ancona, T. W. Malone, W. J. Orlikowski and P. M. Senge, In Praise of the Incomplete Leader. *Harvard Business Review* (February 2007). Available at: https://hbr.org/2007/02/in-praise-of-the-incomplete-leader.

18   Ofsted, Evelyn Community Primary School: Inspection Report (23–24 November 2005). Available at: https://files.api.ofsted.gov.uk/v1/file/806993.

19   R. Goffee and G. Jones, *Why Should Anyone Be Led By You? What It Takes to Be an Authentic Leader* (Boston, MA: Harvard Business Review Press, 2006), p. 26.

20   P. Matthews, *Attributes of the First National Leaders of Education: What Do They Bring to the Role?* (Nottingham: National College for School Leadership, 2007).

21   For more information on the Mont Fleur Scenario Exercise, visit:
      https://reospartners.com/learning-from-experience-the-mont-fleur-scenario-
      exercise/.
22   Department for Education and Skills, *2020 Vision: Report of the Teaching and
      Learning in 2020 Review Group* (Nottingham: DfES, 2006). Available at: http://
      www.educationengland.org.uk/documents/pdfs/2006-2020-vision.pdf.

Chapter Four

23   M. Fullan, *Nuance: Why Some Leaders Succeed and Others Fail* (Thousand Oaks,
      CA: Corwin, 2019).
24   Audit Commission, *National School Survey Results 2008: The School Survey,
      England* (London: Audit Commission, 2008).
25   Organisation for Economic Co-operation and Development, *Education at a
      Glance: OECD Indicators* (Paris: OECD, 2007).
26   M. Barber and M. Mourshed, *How the World's Best-Performing School Systems
      Come Out On Top* (London: McKinsey, 2007).
27   D. Hirsch, *Experiences of Poverty and Educational Disadvantage. Round-up:
      Reviewing the Evidence* (September) (York: Joseph Rowntree Foundation,
      2007).
28   A. Harris, *Distributed Leadership in Schools: Developing the Leaders of
      Tomorrow* (Abingdon and New York: Routledge, 2008), p. 51.
29   D. Reynolds, *Schools Learning From Their Best: The Within School Variation
      (WSV) Project* (Nottingham: National College for School Leadership, 2007).
30   They are now called millennials.
31   Association of Graduate Recruiters, *The AGR Graduate Recruitment Survey
      2007: Summer Review* (London: AGR/Trendence, 2007).

Chapter Five

32   D. Mongon and C. Chapman, *Successful Leadership for Promoting the
      Achievement of White Working Class Pupils* (Nottingham: National College for
      School Leadership, 2008).
33   Lord Laming, *The Protection of Children in England: A Progress Report* (London:
      TSO, 2009). Available at: https://www.gov.uk/government/publications/
      the-protection-of-children-in-england-a-progress-report.
34   The white paper was published in June: Department for Children, Schools and
      Families, *Your Child, Your Schools, Our Future: Building a 21st Century Schools
      System* (Norwich: TSO, 2009).
35   See A. Hargreaves and D. Fink, *Sustainable Leadership* (San Francisco, CA:
      Jossey-Bass, 2006), p. 251.

Chapter Six

36   Address by Nelson Mandela announcing the ANC election victory, Johannesburg, 2 May 1994. Available at: http://www.mandela.gov.za/mandela_speeches/1994/940502_anc.htm.

Chapter Seven

37   Department for Education, *The Importance of Teaching: The Schools White Paper 2010*. Cm 7980 (London: TSO, 2010). Available at: https://www.gov.uk/government/publications/the-importance-of-teaching-the-schools-white-paper-2010.

38   M. Gove, Public Bodies Reform [letter to Vanni Treves], 10 November 2010.

39   A. Harris and A. Hargreaves, *Performance Beyond Expectations* (Nottingham: National College for School Leadership, 2011).

40   C. S. Dweck, *Mindset: The New Psychology of Success* (New York: Random House, 2006).

41   M. Barber, F. Whelan and M. Clark, *Capturing the Leadership Premium: How the World's Top School Systems Are Building Leadership Capacity for the Future* (London: McKinsey, 2010). Available at: https://www.mckinsey.com/industries/social-sector/our-insights/capturing-the-leadership-premium.

42   V. Robinson, *Student-Centered Leadership* (San Francisco, CA: Jossey-Bass, 2011), p. 9.

43   D. E. Tutu, *No Future Without Forgiveness* (London: Ebury, 1999), p. 35.

Chapter Eight

44   M. Fullan, Learning is the Work [unpublished paper] (2011). Available at: http://michaelfullan.ca/wp-content/uploads/2016/06/13396087260.pdf.

45   A. Kahane, *Power and Love: A Theory and Practice of Social Change* (San Francisco, CA: Berrett-Koehler Publishers, 2010).

46   D. Goleman, Leadership That Gets Results. *Harvard Business Review* (March/April 2000). Available at: https://hbr.org/2000/03/leadership-that-gets-results.

47   Dr Edward Miller quoted in A. Deutschman, Change or Die. *Fast Company* (1 May 2005). Available at: https://www.fastcompany.com/52717/change-or-die.

48   R. Hill, J. Dunford, N. Parish, S. Rea and L. Sandals, *The Growth of Academy Chains: Implications for Leaders and Leadership* (Nottingham: National College for School Leadership, 2012).

49   The Paradoxical Commandments were originally written by Kent M. Keith in 1968 – see www.paradoxicalcommandments.com. Numerous adaptations have since emerged, including this version which Mother Teresa reportedly hung on the wall of her children's home in Calcutta.

Chapter Nine

50 Others left too: Michael Pain to set up a successful consultancy business; Dominic Judge to join the Youth Sport Trust; Jonathan Dale, our international expert, joined Toby Greany at the London Institute of Education; Melvin Kenyon and Paul Bennet took early retirement; Matt Varley went to Nottingham Trent University; Sue Egersdorff went on to trail blaze early years education elsewhere; and Aidan Melling – the last person standing from the senior management group as it was when I was there – was seconded to the College of Policing and later left to become a successful consultant.

51 J. Hattie, *Visible Learning: A Synthesis of Over 800 Meta-Analyses Relating to Achievement* (Abingdon and New York: Routledge, 2009).

52 P. Sammons, A. Kington, A. Lindorff-Vijayendran and L. Ortega, *Inspiring Teachers: Perspectives and Practices* (Reading: CfBT Education Trust, 2014).

53 D. Goleman, Focus: *The Hidden Driver of Excellence* (New York: HarperCollins, 2013), p. 163.

54 D. Hargreaves, *A Self-Improving School System: Towards Maturity* (Nottingham: National College for School Leadership, 2012).

55 See https://educationendowmentfoundation.org.uk/evidence-summaries/teaching-learning-toolkit.

56 J. Haidt, *The Righteous Mind: Why Good People are Divided by Politics and Religion* (New York: Penguin, 2013).

57 B. Brown, The Power of Vulnerability. *TED.com* [video] (June 2010). Available at: https://www.ted.com/talks/brene_brown_on_vulnerability?language=en.

58 National College for Teaching and Leadership, *Lessons from Tim Brighouse* (Nottingham: NCTL, 2015).

59 J. Kerr, *Legacy: What the All Blacks Can Teach Us About the Business of Life* (London: Constable & Robinson, 2013).

60 S. Munby and M. Fullan, *Inside-Out and Downside-Up: How Leading from the Middle Has the Power to Transform Education Systems* (Reading: Education Development Trust, 2016), p. 10.

Chapter Ten

61 S. Munby, We Must End Political Interference in Ofsted. *The Telegraph* (10 February 2015). Available at: https://www.telegraph.co.uk/education/educationopinion/11400751/We-must-end-political-interference-in-Ofsted.html. Interestingly, research by Toby Greany and Rob Higham at the UCL Institute of Education has showed how the association between a school's Ofsted result and its likely level of deprivation increased between 2010 and 2015. Essentially, schools that performed higher in Ofsted inspections became less deprived overall, and schools that performed lower became more deprived: T. Greany and R. Higham, *Hierarchy, Markets and Networks: Analysing the 'Self-Improving School-Led System' Agenda in England and the Implications for Schools* (London: UCL Institute of Education Press, 2018).

62   Ofsted and Audit Commission, Inspection of Birmingham Local Education
      Authority (April 2002) (London: Ofsted). Available at: http://www.
      educationengland.org.uk/documents/pdfs/2002-ofsted-birmingham.pdf, p. 6.

63   M. Savage, Cameron to Mobilise Top Heads for 'All Out War' on Mediocre
      Schools. *The Times* (2 February 2015).

64   House of Commons, *Report of the Mid Staffordshire NHS Foundation
      Trust Public Inquiry. Executive Summary*. HC 947 (London: TSO,
      2013). Available at: https://www.gov.uk/government/publications/
      report-of-the-mid-staffordshire-nhs-foundation-trust-public-inquiry.

65   Ofsted, *The Report of Her Majesty's Chief Inspector of Education, Children's
      Services and Skills 2013/14: Schools* (London: Ofsted, 2014). Available at:
      https://www.gov.uk/government/collections/ofsted-annual-report-
      201314, p. 34

66   K. Leithwood and B. Mascall, Collective Leadership Effects on Student
      Achievement. *Educational Administration Quarterly*, 44(4) (2008), 529–561.

67   C. James, S. Brammer, M. Connolly, M. Fertig, J. James and J. Jones, T*he
      'Hidden Givers': A Study of School Governing Bodies in England* (Reading: CfBT
      Education Trust, 2010).

68   J. Owen, *The Mindset of Success: Accelerate Your Career from Good Manager to
      Great Leader* (London and New York: Kogan Page, 2017).

69   A. Hill, L. Mellon, B. Laker and J. Goddard, How the Best School Leaders Create
      Enduring Change. *Harvard Business Review* (14 September 2017).
      Available at: https://hbr.org/2017/09/research-how-the-best-school-leaders-
      create-enduring-change.

Chapter Eleven

70   J. Collins, *Good to Great* (London: Random House, 2001), p. 13.

71   A. Elwick and T. McAleavy, *Interesting Cities: Five Approaches to Urban School
      Reform* (Reading: Education Development Trust, 2015).

72   Ofsted, Benjamin Adlard Primary School: School Report (7–8 June 2016).
      Available at: https://files.api.ofsted.gov.uk/v1/file/2580865, p. 3.

73   In 2018, Benjamin Adlard School received the award for School of the Year –
      Making a Difference at the Pearson National Teaching Awards.

74   T. McAleavy, A. Riggall and R. Fitzpatrick, *Rapid School Improvement* (Reading:
      Education Development Trust, 2016).

75   A. Hargreaves and M. Fullan, *Professional Capital: Transforming Teaching in
      Every School* (Abingdon and New York: Routledge, 2012).

76   McAleavy et al., *Rapid School Improvement*, p. 100.

77   S. Sims, TALIS 2013: Working Conditions, Teacher Job Satisfaction and
      Retention Education. Statistical Working Paper (London: Department for
      Education, 2017).

Chapter Twelve

78   See https://www.amazon.co.uk/Machiavellian-Management-Chief-Executives-Guide/dp/849408531X.

79   R. Vaughan, Charting the Downfall of the 'Famous Five' Superheads. *TES* (14 October 2016). Available at: https://www.tes.com/news/charting-downfall-famous-five-superheads.

80   A. Hill, L. Mellon, B. Laker and J. Goddard, The One Type of Leader Who Can Turn Around a Failing School. *Harvard Business Review* (20 October 2016). Available at: https://hbr.org/2016/10/the-one-type-of-leader-who-can-turn-around-a-failing-school.

81   D. Sankowsky, The Charismatic Leader As Narcissist: Understanding the Abuse of Power. *Organizational Dynamics*, 23(4) (1995), 57–71.

82   See http://marc-lemenestrel.net/IMG/pdf/corruption.pdf.

83   Ethical Leadership Commission, *Navigating the Educational Moral Maze: The Final Report of the Ethical Leadership Commission* (Leicester: Association of School and College Leaders, 2019).

Conclusion

84   S. Tierney, Graphically Exposing Ofsted Bias. *@LeadingLearner* [blog] (12 June 2018). Available at: https://leadinglearner.me/2018/06/12/graphically-exposing-ofsted-bias/.

85   Organisation for Economic Co-operation and Development, *Preparing Teachers and Developing School Leaders for the 21st Century: Lessons from Around the World*, ed. A. Schleicher (Paris: OECD Publishing, 2012).

86   Quoted in A. Elwick and T. McAleavy, *Interesting Cities: Five Approaches to Urban School Reform* (Reading: Education Development Trust, 2015), p. 99, 100.

87   S. Munby and M. Fullan, *Inside-Out and Downside-Up: How Leading from the Middle Has the Power to Transform Education Systems* (Reading: Education Development Trust, 2016), p. 3.

88   Quoted in P. O'Toole (ed.), *In the Words of Theodore Roosevelt: Quotations from the Man in the Arena* (London and Ithaca, NY: Cornell University Press, 2012), p. 27.

89   B. Laker, A Lesson in Success from the Hubris of Hollywood. *Dialogue Review* (19 January 2018). Available at: http://dialoguereview.com/lesson-success-hubris-hollywood/.

Bibliography

Ancona, D., Malone, T. W., Orlikowski, W. J. and Senge, P. M. (2007). In Praise of the Incomplete Leader. *Harvard Business Review* (February). Available at: https://hbr.org/2007/02/in-praise-of-the-incomplete-leader.

Association of Graduate Recruiters (2007). *The AGR Graduate Recruitment Survey 2007: Summer Review* (London: AGR/Trendence).

Audit Commission (2008). *National School Survey Results 2008: The School Survey, England* (London: Audit Commission).

Ayot, W. (2012). *E-Mail from the Soul: New and Selected Leadership Poems* (Glastonbury: PS Avalon).

Barber, M. (2007). *Three Paradigms of Public Sector Reform* (London: McKinsey).

Barber, M. (2008). *Instruction to Deliver: Fighting to Transform Britain's Public Services* (London: Methuen).

Barber, M. and Mourshed, M. (2007). *How the World's Best-Performing School Systems Come Out On Top* (London: McKinsey).

Barber, M., Whelan, F. and Clark, M. (2010). *Capturing the Leadership Premium: How the World's Top School Systems Are Building Leadership Capacity for the Future* (London: McKinsey). Available at: https://www.mckinsey.com/industries/social-sector/our-insights/capturing-the-leadership-premium.

Brown, B. (2010). The Power of Vulnerability. *TED.com* [video] (June). Available at: https://www.ted.com/talks/brene_brown_on_vulnerability?language=en.

Collins, J. (2001). *Good to Great* (London: Random House).

Department for Children, Schools and Families (2009). *Your Child, Your Schools, Our Future: Building a 21st Century Schools System* (Norwich: TSO).

Department for Education (2010). *The Importance of Teaching: The Schools White Paper* 2010. Cm 7980 (London: TSO). Available at: https://www.gov.uk/government/publications/the-importance-of-teaching-the-schools-white-paper-2010.

Department for Education and Skills (2004). *14–19 Curriculum and Qualifications Reform. Final Report of the Working Group on 14–19 Reform* [Tomlinson Report] (Nottingham: DfES). Available at: http://www.educationengland.org.uk/documents/pdfs/2004-tomlinson-report.pdf.

Department for Education and Skills (2005). *14–19 Education and Skills*. Cm 6476 (Nottingham: DfES).

Department for Education and Skills (2006). *2020 Vision: Report of the Teaching and Learning in 2020 Review Group* (Nottingham: DfES). Available at: http://www.educationengland.org.uk/documents/pdfs/2006-2020-vision.pdf.

Department for Education and Skills and National College for School Leadership (2004). *School Leadership: End to End Review of School Leadership Policy and Delivery* (London: DfES/NCSL).

Department for Education and Skills and Ofsted (2004). *A New Relationship with Schools* (London: HMSO).

Desforges, C. with Abouchaar, A. (2003). *The Impact of Parental Involvement, Parental Support and Family Education on Pupil Achievements and Adjustment: A Literature Review*. Research Report RR433 (Nottingham: Department for Education and Skills).

Deutschman, A. (2005). Change or Die. *Fast Company* (1 May). Available at: https://www.fastcompany.com/52717/change-or-die.

Dweck, C. S. (2006). *Mindset: The New Psychology of Success* (New York: Random House).

Elwick, A. and McAleavy, T. (2015). *Interesting Cities: Five Approaches to Urban School Reform* (Reading: Education Development Trust).

Ethical Leadership Commission (2019). *Navigating the Educational Moral Maze: The Final Report of the Ethical Leadership Commission* (Leicester: Association of School and College Leaders).

Fullan, M. (2000). The Role of the Principal in School Reform. Speech delivered at the Principal's Institute, Bank Street College, New York, 9 November. Available at: https://michaelfullan.ca/wp-content/uploads/2016/06/13396042460.pdf.

Fullan, M. (2011). Learning is the Work [unpublished paper]. Available at: http://michaelfullan.ca/wp-content/uploads/2016/06/13396087260.pdf.

Fullan, M. (2019). *Nuance: Why Some Leaders Succeed and Others Fail* (Thousand Oaks, CA: Corwin).

Goffee, R. and Jones, G. (2006). *Why Should Anyone Be Led By You? What It Takes to Be an Authentic Leader* (Boston, MA: Harvard Business Review Press).

Goleman, D. (2000). Leadership That Gets Results. *Harvard Business Review* (March/April). Available at: https://hbr.org/2000/03/leadership-that-gets-results.

Goleman, D. (2013). *Focus: The Hidden Driver of Excellence* (New York: HarperCollins).

Gove, M. (2010) Public Bodies Reform [letter to Vanni Treves], 10 November.

Gove, M. (2013). I Refuse to Surrender to the Marxist Teachers Hell-Bent on Destroying our Schools. *Daily Mail* (23 March). Available at: https://www.dailymail.co.uk/debate/article-2298146/I-refuse-surrender-Marxist-teachers-hell-bent-destroying-schools-Education-Secretary-berates-new-enemies-promise-opposing-plans.html.

Greany, T. and Higham, R. (2018). *Hierarchy, Markets and Networks: Analysing the 'Self-Improving School-Led System' Agenda in England and the Implications for Schools* (London: UCL Institute of Education Press).

Haidt, J. (2013). *The Righteous Mind: Why Good People are Divided by Politics and Religion* (New York: Penguin).

Hargreaves, A. and Fink, D. (2006). *Sustainable Leadership* (San Francisco, CA: Jossey-Bass).

Hargreaves, A. and Fullan, M. (2012). *Professional Capital: Transforming Teaching in Every School* (Abingdon and New York: Routledge).

Hargreaves, D. (2012). *A Self-Improving School System: Towards Maturity* (Nottingham: National College for School Leadership).

Harris, A. (2008). *Distributed Leadership in Schools: Developing the Leaders of Tomorrow* (Abingdon and New York: Routledge).

Harris, A. and Allen, T. (2009). Ensuring Every Child Matters: Issues and Implications for School Leadership. *School Leadership & Management*, 29(4), 337–352.

Harris, A. and Hargreaves, A. (2011). *Performance Beyond Expectations* (Nottingham: National College for School Leadership).

Hattie, J. (2009). *Visible Learning: A Synthesis of Over 800 Meta-Analyses Relating to Achievement* (Abingdon and New York: Routledge).

Heifetz, R. and Linsky, M. (2002). *Leadership on the Line: Staying Alive Through the Dangers of Leading* (Boston, MA: Harvard Business School Press).

Hill, A., Mellon, L., Laker, B. and Goddard, J. (2016). The One Type of Leader Who Can Turn Around a Failing School. *Harvard Business Review* (20 October). Available at: https://hbr.org/2016/10/the-one-type-of-leader-who-can-turn-around-a-failing-school.

Hill, A., Mellon, L., Laker, B. and Goddard, J. (2017). How the Best School Leaders Create Enduring Change. *Harvard Business Review* (14 September). Available at: https://hbr.org/2017/09/research-how-the-best-school-leaders-create-enduring-change.

Hill, R., Dunford, J., Parish, N., Rea, S. and Sandals, L. (2012). *The Growth of Academy Chains: Implications for Leaders and Leadership* (Nottingham: National College for School Leadership).

Hirsch, D. (2007). *Experiences of Poverty and Educational Disadvantage. Round-up: Reviewing the Evidence* (September) (York: Joseph Rowntree Foundation).

House of Commons (2013). *Report of the Mid Staffordshire NHS Foundation Trust Public Inquiry. Executive Summary.* HC 947 (London: TSO). Available at: https://www.gov.uk/government/publications/report-of-the-mid-staffordshire-nhs-foundation-trust-public-inquiry.

James, C., Brammer, S., Connolly, M., Fertig, M., James, J. and Jones, J. (2010). *The 'Hidden Givers': A Study of School Governing Bodies in England* (Reading: CfBT Education Trust).

Kahane, A. (2010). *Power and Love: A Theory and Practice of Social Change* (San Francisco, CA: Berrett-Koehler Publishers).

Kerr, J. (2013). *Legacy: What the All Blacks Can Teach Us About the Business of Life* (London: Constable & Robinson).

King, M. L., Jr (1967). Where Do We Go From Here? Annual report delivered at the 11th Convention of the Southern Christian Leadership Conference, Atlanta, 16 August. Available at: https://kinginstitute.stanford.edu/king-papers/documents/where-do-we-go-here-address-delivered-eleventh-annual-sclc-convention.

Laker, B. (2018). A Lesson in Success from the Hubris of Hollywood. *Dialogue Review* (19 January). Available at: http://dialoguereview.com/lesson-success-hubris-hollywood/.

Laming, Lord (2009). *The Protection of Children in England: A Progress Report* (London: TSO). Available at: https://www.gov.uk/government/publications/the-protection-of-children-in-england-a-progress-report.

Leithwood, K. and Mascall, B. (2008). Collective Leadership Effects on Student Achievement. *Educational Administration Quarterly*, 44(4), 529–561.

McAleavy, T., Riggall, A. and Fitzpatrick, R. (2016). *Rapid School Improvement* (Reading: Education Development Trust).

Matthews, P. (2007). *Attributes of the First National Leaders of Education: What Do They Bring to the Role?* (Nottingham: National College for School Leadership).

Mongon, D. and Chapman, C. (2008). *Successful Leadership for Promoting the Achievement of White Working Class Pupils* (Nottingham: National College for School Leadership).

Morrell, M. and Capparell, S. (2001). *Shackleton's Way: Leadership Lessons from the Great Antarctic Explorer* (New York: Penguin).

Munby, S. (2015). We Must End Political Interference in Ofsted. *The Telegraph* (10 February). Available at: https://www.telegraph.co.uk/education/educationopinion/11400751/We-must-end-political-interference-in-Ofsted.html.

Munby, S. and Fullan, M. (2016). *Inside-Out and Downside-Up: How Leading from the Middle Has the Power to Transform Education Systems* (Reading: Education Development Trust).

National College for Teaching and Leadership (2015). *Lessons from Tim Brighouse* (Nottingham: NCTL).

Ofsted (2005). Evelyn Community Primary School: Inspection Report (23–24 November). Available at: https://files.api.ofsted.gov.uk/v1/file/806993.

Ofsted (2014). *The Report of Her Majesty's Chief Inspector of Education, Children's Services and Skills 2013/14: Schools* (London: Ofsted). Available at: https://www.gov.uk/government/collections/ofsted-annual-report-201314.

Ofsted (2016). Benjamin Adlard Primary School: School Report (7–8 June). Available at: https://files.api.ofsted.gov.uk/v1/file/2580865.

Ofsted and Audit Commission (2002). *Inspection of Birmingham Local Education Authority* (April) (London: Ofsted). Available at: http://www.educationengland.org.uk/documents/pdfs/2002-ofsted-birmingham.pdf.

Organisation for Economic Co-operation and Development (2007). *Education at a Glance: OECD Indicators* (Paris: OECD).

Organisation for Economic Co-operation and Development (2012). *Preparing Teachers and Developing School Leaders for the 21st Century: Lessons from Around the World*, ed. A. Schleicher (Paris: OECD Publishing).

O'Toole, P. (ed.) (2012). *In the Words of Theodore Roosevelt: Quotations from the Man in the Arena* (London and Ithaca, NY: Cornell University Press).

Owen, J. (2017). *The Mindset of Success: Accelerate Your Career from Good Manager to Great Leader* (London and New York: Kogan Page).

Putnam, R. (2011). *Bowling Alone: The Collapse and Revival of American Community* (New York: Simon & Schuster).

Reynolds, D. (2007). *Schools Learning From Their Best: The Within School Variation (WSV) Project* (Nottingham: National College for School Leadership).

Robinson, V. (2011). *Student-Centered Leadership* (San Francisco, CA: Jossey-Bass).

Sammons, P., Kington, A., Lindorff-Vijayendran, A. and Ortega, L. (2014). *Inspiring Teachers: Perspectives and Practices* (Reading: CfBT Education Trust).

Sankowsky, D. (1995). The Charismatic Leader As Narcissist: Understanding the Abuse of Power. *Organizational Dynamics*, 23(4), 57–71.

Savage, M. (2015). Cameron to Mobilise Top Heads for 'All Out War' on Mediocre Schools. *The Times* (2 February).

Sebring, P. B. and Bryk, A. S. (2000). School Leadership and the Bottom Line in Chicago. *Phi Delta Kappan*, 81(6), 440–443.

Sims, S. (2017). TALIS 2013: *Working Conditions, Teacher Job Satisfaction and Retention Education. Statistical Working Paper* (London: Department for Education).

Stevens, J., Brown, J., Knibbs, S. and Smith, J. (2005). *Follow-up Research into the State of School Leadership in England*. Research Report no. 633 (Nottingham: MORI/Department for Education and Skills).

Terkel, S. (1972). *Working: People Talk About What They Do All Day and How They Feel About What They Do* (New York: New Press).

Tierney, S. (2018). Graphically Exposing Ofsted Bias. @LeadingLearner [blog] (12 June). Available at: https://leadinglearner.me/2018/06/12/graphically-exposing-ofsted-bias/.

Tutu, D. E. (1999). *No Future without Forgiveness* (London: Ebury).

Vaughan, R. (2016). Charting the Downfall of the 'Famous Five' Superheads. *TES* (14 October). Available at: https://www.tes.com/news/charting-downfall-famous-five-superheads.

Wiliam, D. (2006). Assessment for Learning: Why, What and How. Available at: https://www.dylanwiliam.org/Dylan_Wiliams_website/Papers.html.

Index

About the Author

Steve Munby has spent his whole career in education, first as a teacher and then as an adviser and inspector before moving into leadership.

Steve was director of education in Knowsley, near Merseyside, for five years before serving as CEO of the National College for School Leadership between 2005 and 2012. As CEO, he had overall responsibility for the training and development of school principals in all state-maintained schools in England and directors of children's services in local authorities. In August 2017 he retired as CEO of Education Development Trust, an international education charity working in Asia, Africa, Europe and the Middle East.

Steve is now a self-employed consultant and speaker on leadership and on system reform, and is also a visiting professor at University College London Institute of Education and the facilitator for the ARC summits, which bring together education systems from across the world. He was awarded a CBE in the New Year honours list in 2010.

email: steve@munbyeducation.co.uk

Twitter: @steve_munby